Dare B&B

MARY HADOW

Other Titles by Mary Hadow:

Surviving Solo

Back on the Shelf

Moving on by Staying Still

Snow Way

To Suz

without whom none of this would have been possible

CONTENTS

1 BABY STEPS

B&B and me – a match?
14/12/2012

The computer on my Harrods green Range Rover, with its ironic EKO number plate, says there's enough fuel to last 65 more miles.

Lying again. Dammit. The stupid car has ground to a halt just inside my daughter's school gates, blocking the drive, and preventing 100+ other Yummy Mummies from getting their little darlings to assembly on time.

Bugger. One after the other, their 4x4s wind a path around me, digging a six inch deep muddy rut into the once billiard-table-smooth school cricket pitch which runs alongside the tarmac. Ten-year-old Faye tries to hide in her seat beside me, red-faced with shame and humiliation in front of her peer group, the other mothers glancing over with expressions of annoyance and derision as they pass us by.

"Hey ho morning Mrs Hadow – will you be wanting our red diesel again?" wanders over Jake, the groundsman, in front of the poshest Mum of all, who is scowling over at me, above her Hermes scarf and Barbour jacket, from her twin naff posh car, only her one's silver.

This is just so not what I needed to happen today. I am already shaking with nerves at the thought of what lies ahead.

A film crew comprising a BAFTA award-winning director, three cameramen and a sexy actress, are coming to film in my house, and to test out whether it's going to work as a luxurious and expensive B&B. They're due to arrive at 4.30pm, when I'm not actually going to be there.

My friend Malcolm is at home right this moment, attempting to fit a new loo into what was once Faye's room. It will create an 'en-suite' of the main bedroom, which will be needed for two of the crew to sleep in. When I left for school, all Faye's furniture, including a huge chest of drawers, was piled right up til it reached the ceiling, on their bed.

Kathy, who cleans for me twice a week, and Sashka, who is my right arm, left arm and both legs, are due to arrive at my home of nearly twenty years - Wydemeet - at 9am, ready to sort everything out for my glamorous guests, while I enjoy a little relaxation at the health club, and a spot of shopping.

I think I shall swim a few lengths of the pool, and then sink into the Jacuzzi.

A couple of hours later, refreshed and relaxed, with nice clean hair, and a full tank of legal diesel, I leave the club, en route for Ashburton.

I need to get in some 'local quality produce'. Nothing but the best for my discerning and sophisticated visitors!

What? Two pounds for a loaf of bread?? My tummy hurts just hearing this! How do people afford proper food? I am reliably informed that this artisan baker is usually sold out by lunchtime! Personally I prefer sliced brown wholemeal at 45p a loaf - no crumbs, and no washing up as you can eat it straight from the packet.

The organic tomatoes on the vine and a few mushrooms at the farmshop cost over £4. Agh!

During the twenty minute drive home I am overcome with terror as to what on earth I am going to find when I get there.

Well goodness gracious me! The place is immaculate!

Malcolm, Kathy, Sashka – I could kiss them all! Except they would hate that. And also except that the new bathroom still has an unattached loo, and Faye's pile of bed and wardrobe has now found a new home in the recently purchased plastic B&Q bath.

I'm just sitting down, ready to decide what to do next, when Sashka rushes in, wild eyed, long blonde hair flying.

"Mary – I've got to be at my next job half-an-hour ago, and you've gone and blocked us all in, and there's a massive great hole in your front tyre!" she yells.

It's clearly time for a coffee and a fag. Because I've got more things to worry about.

Christmas is nearly here, and I've organised mulled wine for the Form 4 Mums at Brown's Hotel in Tavistock this evening, before we all pick our babes up from their Hogwarts-like 'Christmas Feast'. How on earth am I going to get there now?

And assuming I manage it, the film crew is due to arrive while I'm away. Malcolm has volunteered to greet them, and cook them their supper somehow or other.

I've had two 'Wild Mushroom Lasagnes' delivered from that magic hopeless-hostess-saviour-company 'Cook', which look home-made, and should taste miles better than anything I could do. My angst is, will they defrost and bake properly in my much-loathed Aga?

The beef joint I recently bought from Neighbour, that I put out to defrost this morning for tomorrow's dinner, is still solid. I haven't cooked a full English breakfast for nearly fifteen years, and I can't remember (if I ever knew) how to fry an egg.

I think it's unnatural to get up when it's still dark outside, and I don't know what hospital corners are.

But earning some money via B&B is the only way I can think of to hang on to the home that represents stability and continuity for my children, Faye, and fourteen-year-old Will, since their Dad went off with 'Her' three years

9

ago. That and/or renting the thing out in its entirety. The financial settlement now on the table will result in my having no cash to speak of, and I don't have much opportunity of getting a proper job, what with the school run and living in the middle of absolutely nowhere and everything. Clearly, the house itself must now become my cash cow.

Ring ring! It's the AA calling from Neighbour's Cold Comfort Farm.

It would seem that the bossy sat-nav woman has got her way yet again, and sent them to the wrong destination.

Thirty minutes later, spare tyre in place, and Sashka and I are finally free to escape on our individual now possible missions.

Poached vs Fried
15/12/2012

'Dartmoor Killings' is the working title of Peter's film. He is an old friend who recently won the use of a camera worth millions, to film a 'promo' which will be used to help source finance for his planned feature film.

The small problem is that the camera is so complicated that it takes three people to use it, which is why he's got such a large crew coming. I hope nobody drops it.

Their two night sojourn represents a golden opportunity to try out my potentially non-existent B&B skills.

Ultimately I would like to charge the maximum possible rate for a Dartmoor B&B (about £100 a room for a night) which means that whatever I offer is going to have to be good.

I've spent the last fortnight on the internet, tracking down diddy kettles, diddy thermoses for fresh milk, and diddy cafetieres for each room. Then there are the individual tea bags (Earl Grey, Camomile etc) and filter coffees; the titchy toiletries and even the baskets to put everything in – I've got to find them all on eBay or somewhere.

But the Christmas rush has meant that the only things to have arrived in time for the film crew are the kettles. Which turn out to be fitted with continental plugs, and have had to be despatched straight to my present drawer.

I race back from my School Mums' mulled wine evening - which nobody came to after all that - to discover that the crew still hasn't arrived!

Finally they appear two hours later than anticipated, and, having requested drinks at 8.30pm followed by dinner at 9.00pm, instead film without stopping until 11pm. One shot is of my kettle on the Aga, and another is of the sexy actress, nude, in the sunroom. Faye's eyes are on stalks!

The lasagne miraculously remains delicious, and I fall into bed at 1.30am. Up again at 6.30am to prepare Mary's Special Organic Breakfast.

God - what order do you cook everything in? Croissants, muesli, Golden Nuggets, fancy bread... how many sausages? Bacon in the oven, or fried? Eeek! Two people request poached eggs, and two want fried. My poached eggs are likely to turn out looking like embryos covered in afterbirth.

Help! Two massive great frying pans (one rusty); a baking dish in the oven with sausages, bacon, tomatoes and mushrooms in it. Baked beans in the microwave. Artisan toast. Plates heating in the lower oven.

Nowhere to hide - we are all in the kitchen together - my mistakes on full display. How much of each thing for whom? I can't let them know that I am a walking zombie and I have never done anything like this before.

Somehow not an egg broken, and my poached ones look bright yellow and white and fairly symmetrical, and not full of mucus. But how do you serve them? Genius! I grab a couple of pieces of thinly sliced brown toast and pop them on that. Then I stick the whole lot onto a large platter so everyone can help themselves, which means that I don't have to wonder how much of what to serve to whom.

Pheeeeew! All done.

It's been fun!

I am a pale ghost of my former self after 48 hours of this. Peter's first 'Dartmoor Killing' perhaps.

But I have done it. And what's more, I can do it again.

Owners Direct
31/12/2012

You already know all about Amazon, eBay and Google. But are you aware of another monopolistic internet company out there, which is surreptitiously taking over the world? It's called 'Owners Direct'.

Innocently looking for the perfect agent through which to market my house, I've recently discovered that I'm not alone in opting for Owners Direct.

It turns out that, of around 100 families paying the fees for my children's posh, expensive school, five are renting out their homes to help make ends meet. And all are signed up with Owners Direct.

I learn that both my friends who rent out their houses abroad also use the company - whether it's called 'Owners Direct', or 'HomeAway' it's the same headquarters based in Bressenden Place in London, representing nearly 200,000 properties around the world.

I chose Owners Direct to market my house because you just have to pay them up front, to include your blurb for a year on their website, and that's that.

Nobody demanding that all your cupboards are clean and empty, that you must get rid of your stained carpets and buy guaranteed fire-retardant beds and sofas, or that the jolly pictures and messages pinned to your kitchen notice board and stuck to your fridge door have to go, etc. Nor is there any commission (typically 20-30%) payable.

Well. Fancy that! I've signed up, and now I have just received my first enquiry. From a nice-sounding man called Jim, who is looking for three nights, for three families comprising six adults and five children altogether. Perfect. I immediately confirm I have availability.

I then spend nearly £2,000 in a morning, on 100% Egyptian cotton sheets, duvets, duvet covers, mattress protectors; twenty pillows, twenty pillow protectors, and thirty towels.

Jim gets back to me the following day, to say he has found somewhere else, cheaper.

Phew! That was a narrow escape! I was beginning to panic!

But hey! It works! This could really happen! I could actually find myself renting out my home in its entirety, and for a substantial sum!

Yikes!

Plenty of Room for Willies
17/01/2013

I've had another enquiry! A bloke called Ben Hardon has contacted me via Owners Direct about renting my house! Hurray!

This is my third enquiry, even though my entry on the Owners Direct website has only been up for a month or two. Clearly I am going to make my fortune by renting out my house!

Mr Hardon has completed the form and says he wants to stay with his five children for two nights, January 31st and Feb 1st, 2013.

"I'm single too! love to stay with my children. FYI i have a big willy!" (sic) he writes. I note with increasing dismay that the email address he gives is bigwillywam@hotmail.co.uk

Oooer. What do I do? Should I call Owners Direct or what? I ring up my great mate Susannah, who rents out two of her properties through the company.

"Oh my God! I've never been contacted by a weirdo in all the years I've been using the site!" she cries. "Maybe you should tone down the 'single Mum' bit in your copy?"

The next day, driving Will back to his school for the beginning of term, when he asks me how the new rental business is going, I hesitantly tell him about my little problem.

"Ha ha ha ha!" he chortles. "That was me! I was typing it up, in the kitchen, while you were cooking the sausages last night!"

And I suddenly realise what has set him off on the whole willy-thing. This is how Owners Direct's predictive text has interpreted my entry: Property Ref E7392: "Plenty of room for willies, macs and outside toys in the cloakroom."

The Work/Life Balance
21/01/2013

Oh dear.

I lost it with the garage man yesterday. He didn't phone to tell me that the compressor for my Range Rover hadn't turned up, so he couldn't mend my car after all, and now I had taken the trouble to drive the 35 minutes to his garage for our agreed appointment, all for nothing.

"Don't you realise that I've only got twenty hours a week during which I can earn enough to support my family?" I ranted when I turned up to find that I'd wasted half my afternoon. "I've bust a gut to get here an hour earlier than I need have for the school run, and for what?!"

I suppose to fill that hour, I should have gone to Costa's for a Skinny Cappuccino, and given myself a great big slap for being an over-demanding posh twat.

Instead I went searching for half-price offers in the Co-op, even though

14

there'd been a Tesco delivery earlier in the day, and, as usual ended up late for school pick-up.

So why is it that I'm always so stressed, and in such a rush? Could it be that during the few hours each week Faye is at school, I try to squeeze in the health club, muck out and ride our two horses, watch either child playing in a sports match or concert, and be a Lady who Lunches, Teas, Breakfasts and Elevenses?

Obviously the minute I get the poor girl home I morph into pushy mother - homework, music practice (two instruments), supper, bath, reading, bed.

By 'support the family', do I actually mean 'earn enough to pay my half of the children's school fees'?

If the nice garage man knew the real reasons why every hour is so precious to me, I don't imagine that he'd be hugely sympathetic.

I know. I'd better visit a Life Coach to help sort out my work/life balance.

But of course I don't have the time.

eBay Addict
23/01/2013

My darling daughter Faye is jumping up and down squeaking.

My underarms are sweating and my heart is pounding. We watch the clock - five, four, three..

"It's ours!" We leap about the kitchen in joy, clapping our hands and grinning at each other.

I have just won a 1999 Ford Focus, 50,000 miles, off eBay. I've only paid £831 for it! It's in Southampton, and it's blue. Does it work? Who cares? It's ours!

I'm now properly broke and I've got to downsize.

The Range Rover has to go. It's haemorrhaging money. £130 a week on diesel for the twice-daily 26 mile return school run across stunning central Dartmoor.

£750 for four new tyres (not much different from buying the whole of this Focus). £500 for a belt. £500 for an air bag and now another £500 for the compressor which turned up in the end.

And that's since December.

So I am going 'reverse chic' with my new old Ford. I can't wait to show it off in the school carpark. It'll be the only one, whereas there are five other Range Rovers.

This new car of mine will be the straightforward simple proof to one and all, if any were wanted or needed, of the havoc my Nemesis has caused in all of our lives. I am going to park it next to Her BMW Sports, and grin at Her.

But hey - what am I doing now? I seem to be at it again. This is all such fun! I've just pressed the button twice and discovered that I'm about to become the proud new owner of a Land Rover (£1,500) and also of a Mitsubishi Shogun (£2,450). Help! What if I get both?

I lose the Land Rover (phew!) but eBay emails to inform me that I am the lucky owner of an old Shogun (silver) based in Swindon.

Oh dear. Now I've got three cars, they're scattered all over the country, and I'm marooned all by myself, snowed in, in the middle of Dartmoor. I am a bit alarmed at what I might find myself doing next.

Stupid Idea
24/01/2013

I think Ex and I have finally agreed our financial settlement, and hopefully now we can get divorced, at last. Tra la!

It's been 3 1/2 years since he left, and I am proud of us both, because I don't think a single cross word about the 'Agreement' has been exchanged between the two of us over the past twelve months. Not since a memorable morning when Ex rolled down his car window, shouting "This is War!" And it never was.

A wise solicitor recently advised me that in divorce you will always lose out financially unless you marry someone richer than you are, whatever the rights and wrongs of the marital breakdown. So you need to cut your losses, bury the resentment, and move on.

I am lucky enough to have a 'charm' (collective noun for goldfinches) of grown-up men (yes there are such a things), who, throughout these years have guided me with great tact, gently, kindly, and wisely through the divorce, allowing me to rant and rage, and by the tenth "and another thing" they've heard a million times before, they patiently suggest how I might learn to communicate more pleasantly.

For instance, rather than yelling "That's a bloody stupid idea!" it might be better to calmly describe how a particular course of action somebody is suggesting could affect me, or make me feel.

I tried it out the other day, during a phone call with Ex, and damn me, it worked.

Perhaps I should have given this approach a bit more of a go during our marriage - I wonder where we would be now if I had?

Anyhow, so it's looking as though, after everything that's happened, Ex and I might soon be properly free to live our separate lives, and on speaking terms too!

Snowed Under
24/01/2013

My part of Dartmoor has been under snow for a week now.

As it's become icier and icier I have left my daughter to board at her school for a couple of nights.

I am marooned, in the middle of nowhere, in a five bedroom house, all on my own, like Robinson Crusoe was, only surrounded by snow and ice instead of sea.

It's wonderful!

It did cross my mind that if I slipped and broke my leg getting the horses in, I would die alone in the dark in a blizzard. So I have trod gingerly.

But otherwise there is suddenly all the time in the world to get on with things. Such as sorting out a picture for next year's personalised Christmas card. I've got real snow available outside the door, and still haven't put away our Christmas decorations, so there are some suitable props lying around.

Our 2012 Christmas card was a struggle because the winter had been snowless, so I didn't have any suitable seasonal happy snaps available to send to Vista Print.

Instead I used one very kindly set up by the film crew's cameraman, of our house glowing in the dark under stars, looking a like a pumpkin on Hallowe'en.

As for Owner's Direct – I haven't got any recent sunny pictures of the house to illustrate my slot on their website either. All it did was rain last year.

Midas
25/01/2013

Well blow me down and who would have thought it.

I'm sitting here looking at two cheques made out to me. One is for £2,500 for a week's rental this Easter holidays; and the other is a £350 deposit for July. They both arrived today - the first time the postman has made it to our house in five days, thanks to the snow.

So it's worked.

I really am going to rent out my home in its entirety. Twice. Each time for a whole week. We're going to be rich!!

Now all I've got to do is to buy a high chair and a cot, and, in order to be really smart, find two blobs to go on the end of the strings that pull the lights on in the bathrooms.

I'm feeling a bit wobbly and spaced out about all of this. It has been a vision for so long. And now it is a reality.

So much less stressful than doing a proper job, with a boss and targets and clients and deadlines and statutory working hours and daily commutes and sandwich lunches and whatnot.

While these strangers are enjoying my house, I think I might go skiing!

And when the second lot come, I have already accepted an invitation from my sister to go and stay with her, in one of the most luxurious country estates there is, just outside Siena, in Italy.

How hard can life be?

They always said my middle name was Midas.

Bye-bye Website Provider
07/02/2013

Hmmmm. I am severely struggling with trying to create a website to promote my B&B side of the business. I've signed up to some hoster-thingy, called 'Go Daddy' for some reason, and I absolutely can't work it. The whole process is driving me completely and thoroughly nuts.

Call me old, and technically incompetent. I've spent so many hours, not to mention quite a lot of money - nearly a hundred pounds - trying to get to grips with the thing, and I have had to give up.

It's all been an A1 total disaster and waste of time. I just can't work it. And I have finally lost my rag.

And now, for £36, I've just signed up to another jolly little website-builder called 'justhost.com', which turns out to be potsie-pie to play with. After all that! Oooh I'm having so much fun. I would almost rather be doing this than watching X-Factor!

Why is it so important that I should have my own website? Well I'll tell you.

Because I've finally discovered, after what feels like months of unreturned emails, impossible-to-find-phone numbers etc, that TripAdvisor won't list Wydemeet as a B&B and a holiday rental at the same time.

It seems that they run two separate businesses, one for rentals, which you have to pay for, and which goes through some company called "Holiday Lettings" and the other is the TripAdvisor B&B/hotel listings service that we're all so much more familiar with. And in order to get a listing on this one, they have finally informed me that I will have to have my own proper, independent website describing my B&B. Eeek! How do I make one?

The Ashburton Cookery School, to whom I initially sent a sales-flyer, is hardly swamping me with enquiries. They did warn me not to rely on their customers to see me through. So I really do have to start marketing my B&B a little harder.

I think I am the only B&B on Dartmoor with a hot tub, and for £45 you can also enjoy a relaxing massage, on-site, from Malcolm. He specialises in something called 'trigger points' and if you suffer from a bad back - well your cure lies at my door. Are those my USP's?

It's up to me I suppose, to make sure that people hear about me. Here goes!

Bevan Trumpington
10/02/2013

Yes - that's his name - Bevan Trumpington. How funny. He's a real person. Not just some fictional idiot in a PG Wodehouse comedy. What do you know? He's probably reading this right now!

I have just heard that he is Her new squeeze, now that She's predictably dumped Ex.

Apparently She introduced him to everybody at the local hunt meet yesterday, and he is to be Her partner at the hunt's annual smart dinner, in front of about 100 people whose average age is 152, in a couple of weeks' time.

What will the Great and the Good of the county think of Her flaunting yet another new chap so soon?

Before She got married She was affectionately referred to by Her friends as 'The Ferry' - apparently because She 'went from Peer to Peer'. Old habits die hard.

I am surprised by the impact this news has had on me. When I heard of his existence, I found myself reaching for a Cava and a fag.

For some reason I'm not feeling quite so gung-ho about parking Marv, the Ford Focus, next to Her BMW in the school carpark tomorrow. Perhaps it's because I'm oddly a bit indignant on Ex's behalf, that he could be replaced so soon, after all that our little family has been put through.

2 FEELING GLOOMY

Angry of Dartmoor
11/02/2013

Today finds me wondering whether to sue my electric gate company.

The gate was bought for £3000+ by Ex's mum, a decade ago. Since then, the longest spell it has ever worked for is two years. The minute it gets stuck open, entire flocks and herds of sheep, cattle and ponies rampage across my 'lawn' and over into the fields beyond. They're on automatic pilot, I promise you. Guided missiles aimed at my garden.

The gate is a heavy 5-bar wooden thing. Underneath it is mud mixed with fresh poo.

Just perfect to wade through in my favoured high heeled back suede boots. And I look like Esther Rantzen if my hair gets wet.

Whenever the gate breaks down, I have to step out of my car, plough through the horizontal rain and mud, to push the heavy mildewed reluctant centrepiece of all my nightmares open and shut, climbing, dripping brown water, back into my prestige vehicle with slime all over my feet, chest and hands.

The total sum paid by the film crew of five staying half-board for two nights failed even to cover the cost of the gate's broken control panel. And I had only just paid £150 to the same stupid company to supposedly finally put everything right, after they'd fitted no less than five faulty open/close switches, causing an invasion of animals every time.

And on top of all that, just two weeks later, they now want £645 + VAT because the motor has just broken. 'Unfit for Purpose' I believe might be the legal jargon.

Neighbour next door doesn't appreciate my problem. She suggests I try going back to a latch.

Maybe I should just go back to London.

I Wouldn't Credit It
25/02/2013

Now that we're poor (relatively speaking), I thought we should bid adieu to Lesley, our efficient, effective, expensive private dentist, and test out the NHS's effort down the road instead.

The building was silent and empty, its enormous waiting room resplendent with sofas and magazines remaining unused, as we were ushered straight through to the charming pretty dentist - no queue.

"Very nice clean teeth," she said to Faye.

Phew! Perhaps I am not such a Bad Mother.

And it appears that I have also got away without the need for any further treatment.

We went to pay on reception, where the lady courteously informed me: "If you're on child tax credits, it's free."

I'm allowed tax credits because they don't count spousal maintenance as income. Whyever not? In effect doesn't that mean the taxpayer is subsidising philandering?

I subsequently discover that a blue-blooded friend from an even more privileged background than mine, has just had his tooth capped for nothing (normal cost around £400), because he is on something called 'working tax credits'. Eh? It seems to me that working tax credits mean you don't actually have to work at all!

Another well heeled mate says she spends her child benefit on Cava, as her children's private school fees are already covered.

No wonder the country's going bust. This whole free handouts thing is completely loony!

But if they're giving it away - well. Thank you very much!

Oh bother. It turns out that my income is, in fact, too high after all for me to qualify for the child tax credit 'white card' allowing free dental treatment, and I have had to stump up £17.50 for my examination after all.

Yours Anonymously
03/03/2013

The other day one of the few people I'd told about my diary said, "If you name me in your blog I will never speak to you again!"

He happens to be one of my favourite friends, and his comment made me think. Other people are considerably more protective of their privacy than I am, and my not remaining alert to this fact has got me into trouble in the past!

I have checked the issue with another close mate, who was actually the biggest motivator and inspiration behind my starting this in the first place. Let's call her Miriam. She used to be a policewoman, and she was optimistic about all the confidentiality issues that I might find myself facing. She pointed out how much information on anyone you can get simply by googling them, and she then sent me a list of over 30 sites which can, apparently, be used to track down all your most private moments.

Then I thought about one of my favourite columnists and authors - Lucy Pinney - who wrote "A Country Wife". Apparently she had to stop writing because, as a result of her column, she's got no friends left.

Well my friends mean far more to me than anything else does. I'd better tread carefully.

Three and a Half Years
07/03/2013

Three and a half years since Ex exited.

The sense of disruption is still here. I wonder how long it will take to go away.

I have just been visited by Olga - I bid at a pledges evening for her to come and help me with my garden. She's a widow. Over a cup of Earl Grey and a fig roll, she mused that of course I still feel unsettled. The sense of not really knowing where you are, nor where you want to be, remains for a long time, following on from a couple of years of shock, bewilderment and disbelief, she said.

I'm feeling like this because I've been wondering why I find myself living alone with two children, in a five-bedroomed house, twenty minutes from a pint of milk, with so many bedrooms that I have to rent most of them out to make ends meet.

Especially when my fifteen year old son, Will, would much prefer to live on a main road with buses and a railway station, near friends, cinemas and coffee shops. Maybe even in London, but being a Dartmoor hillbilly, he is still slightly apprehensive about crossing roads, asking for things in shops, the underground, and muggers. When the children were little and we played I Spy, they would regularly say, "I spy something beginning with 'H'. The answer was 'House'. They didn't see many of those.

My sense of disruption is caused by considering whether I should move. But no. I think I belong here now. I've promoted myself, after 17 years, from 'Blow In' to 'Incomer', and know most of the people I drive past. My son Will will just have to learn to enjoy walks, while Faye's riding skills must continue their rapid upward trajectory.

Meanwhile Olga says I have a very nice woodland garden. She is going to come back and plant some 'drought pots' to give it some colour after its initial 'Spring flourish'. And I must ask my friend, Patrick, who does everything, to come over and pick up sticks, and rake up leaves.

We are 'all systems go' before my first rental guests arrive at the end of the month!

Homeless
17/03/2013

In two weeks' time I'm going to be homeless.

Kathy, Sashka and I have a 'working elevenses' of coffee and fags twice a week now, sometimes we even sit and smoke inside, in the kitchen, because it is so much more comfortable than squatting outside in the wind and horizontal rain, and nobody's going to know.

We are all armed with lists, and thanks to this powerhouse of a team, I'm not panicking. Quite.

Sashka's got an additional new job overseeing the rental on another Dartmoor house, and the stories she comes back with make me quake in my willies I mean wellies. She says it takes twenty minutes to make each of the house's beds because they all have six pillows, and cushions as well! What are you supposed to do with all those cushions when you're trying to sleep? I can't think of anything more constructive than throwing them on the floor. Susannah, my friend who rents out her luxury home in Helford for about £2 million a week, has only one set of cushions, which she uses for photo-shoots, moving them around for each bedroom shot.

Sashka says the converted barn she now works in has a sunny seating area with views to the sea twenty miles away. One of its walls is made entirely of glass, and its sitting room is longer than my kitchen and dining room put together! She says the kitchen is twice the size of mine, all gleaming stainless steel and granite. So modern that she couldn't find the plug sockets, because they're horizontal, built into the work surface.

Huh! Who would want to come to an immaculate shiny showhouse like that, in the middle of Dartmoor eh? Dartmoor is for MUD.

I have tried to think of a reason why someone would prefer my place to this nouveau barn - and I've come up with one.

At Wydemeet you can shout your head off and no one will hear you except the sheep. Does that count? We've fixed up a karaoke with a couple of mikes coming through Malcolm's PA system, and you can sing to karaoke versions of songs you look up on YouTube via our huge telly screen, resulting in surround-sound underscored by the throbbing boom boom boom produced by the base woofer I bought second hand off eBay for £400. Leave the French doors open and you can deafen all those belted Galloway's placidly waiting outside for my electric gate to break down.

One beautiful gentle balmy sunny evening last summer, Will used our system to serenade a pack of girl-guides practising for their Duke of Edinburgh Gold, camping 1/2 mile away down by the river.

My list of what to do before I say goodbye to my home for the Rental Week appears endless, inexhaustible. My friend Malcolm is being amazing and has arranged for Neighbour to put some of the gravel from the council pile outside my gate onto the drive. Patrick is here, coping with the sticks and leaves. I have arranged for a professional contractor to clean and service the hot tub, called the plumber re the water neutraliser, found a bloke to tidy up the carpets, booked the window cleaner, and my next jobs are to arrange insurance and smoke alarms.

Meanwhile Kathy and Sashka are working double hours together, cleaning out every cupboard, washing every piece of crockery and glass. I hear them hooting with mirth while I'm trying to Get On. They call me Mad Mary or Lady Muck behind my back, and think it's really funny that I'm still saving the tin of fois gras that my Mum brought back from France for a special occasion, even though its sell-by date is April 3rd 1997.

I am increasingly unsure that I could be going ahead with this without my amazing little team. They just pack me off to the health club, arrange their own agenda, and get on with it.

I've planned a little stay on Malcolm's trimaran in Portugal for the second part of my enforced week away from home, but first I've booked a couple of nights in a B&B down the road, at £32.50 a night. That will be interesting. Hopefully they won't see me as competition as I'm charging £40 per head, based on two sharing, for a minimum of two nights. In truth, I'm anticipating letting out my best en-suite for £120 a night in due course, otherwise I'm not sure I can really be arsed with all this B&B bollocks. Early mornings, being nice first thing, frying eggs ... Hopefully I will come up with a solution to such issues if I ever get a customer. No enquiries.

Poisoned!
19/03/2013

Oh help! I think I might have poisoned Malcolm!

He normally has a stomach of iron because, like me, he was brought up on leftovers in a school, where our mothers were at liberty to raid the larder. We share fond memories of giant catering packs of dried 'Chicken Chasseur' enthusiastically served throughout the holidays - in his case on the family yacht, in ours in the camping van.

We both had 'war mothers' who believed in saving everything, no waste. Malcolm's family specialised in Izal, and margarine. We also had Izal and hundreds of little plastic pots of moulding scraps of anything as small as an old pea, stored in the fridge.

We are proud of our inherent embrace of the leftover, and the resulting tiny compost bins.

Yesterday, I came up with the perfect occasion to use my pot of out-of-date Fois Gras. Granny (82) had driven the eighty miles from her home in Dorset to listen to Faye playing "Oops I did it again" on her flute in the school music competition, followed by supper at Wydemeet and an overnight stay.

The little round tin lay innocently, centre piece on the kitchen table. It was so discoloured you couldn't actually read the exact sell-by date (I was embellishing in my last blog), and it had leaked two orange rings of fatty rust. I prepared my version of Melba toast, and opened the lid with a flourish.

There was some brown stuff inside with white, grey and blue marks on it. "Just what it's supposed to look like," I announced, and sniffed. It smelt fine.

I cut off the blue bits and as Granny, Malcolm and I demolished it we discussed how old it really was. We worked out that Granny had brought it back from a trip to France around ten years ago.

It left a weird sticky fatty sort of layer in your mouth, but tasted fine.

Lidl's DeLuxe Three Fish Bake followed next, and then raspberry cheesecake and profiteroles.

This morning Malcolm complained of a feeling of queasiness all night.

I also felt a bit sick and headachy, maybe from mixing Cava with white wine and red wine. Granny was bouncing, as she finished washing up.

Over the past few hours I've left messages on both Malcolm's mobile and landline to no avail. Where can he be? I hope he's not in hospital.

Gravy in the Bathroom
27/03/2013

"That'll be gravy," I advised Kathy, when she reported that no matter how hard she tried, she couldn't remove the stains from the finally finished new bathroom's carpet.

"How on earth did gravy get into the bathroom?" she asked, astonished.

"That would date back to when it was Faye's bedroom, and I took her up meals when she was ill," I explained.

Sashka and Kathy are here every day now. The number of coffee and fag breaks we are enjoying, if that's the right word, are on the increase. I have discovered that smoking in my home is illegal, since it became a public place. I'm not sure the mercury has risen above zero for a week now, and at the moment it's snowing yet again, with a wishy-washy wintry sun peeking through for what feels like the first time in living memory.

Just as in the lead-up to the film company's bed-and-breakfast weekend, I can feel myself, despite Sashka and Kathy's best efforts, sliding back into panic-mode. This morning Kathy felt the waves of it hit her too.

The carpet man didn't turn up, the hot-tub man didn't turn up, the plumber didn't ring back, the gardener didn't turn up, my eBay ad for the Range Rover has been hacked into, or 'fished' to such an extent that I have had to change my password on everything, and the electric gate man, who hasn't returned a call or email in two months, has finally contacted me to say he will pop by tomorrow. Meanwhile, whilst it is relatively straightforward to insure your house for renting out in its entirety, or for running a B&B business in, it appears to be impossible to insure it for a combination of the two. I have three bespoke brokers on the case, who haven't quite got all the info they need. One of them is querying my use of the word 'entrepreneur' as my stated profession. "Well put 'single mother trying to make ends meet' or something," I suggested.

The piles of logs - well actually to be exact tree trunks - outside our house are nearly touching the sky, and it feels as though the house and I am drowning beneath them. I have warned my guests about them - I am so worried that they will be disappointed as they approach the house and see nothing but a huge pile of timber wrecking what was once a beautiful valley, but the wood comprises the livelihood of Neighbour, for whom hill farming no longer pays the bills, so I can't moan about it too much.

Sashka and Kathy's cleaning efforts have now reached the main spare, Faye's and Will's rooms. Every bed has to have a mattress and pillow protector, duvet, ironed sheet and duvet cover, and there are three towels for each guest. I am going to have to leave the heating on 24/7 with this unseasonal weather - a fact which physically hurts! I really don't think I am going to make any profit at all from this first letting - but I comfort myself with the thought that what we have done would all have been necessary anyway.

I am worried about my horse who is coughing - it is too cold to suddenly leave the horses out so somebody is going to have to visit them twice a day, and muck out while our guests are here. I am worried about packing for three people ie Will, Faye and me, each of us due to spend the next week in two different countries; and I am worried about my stupid car which still hasn't sold and is deteriorating outside my house, and which now has another flat tyre.

And then in the middle of all of this, an email arrives from my lawyer which means I suddenly have to get properly divorced this week, before she goes on holiday! The forms seem to be endless. I have signed off whatever she's asking for this time, and hope for the best.

PS I didn't poison Malcolm after all. He's still alive. He caught a bug, meanwhile his phone was ringing away in his next door room.

Everyone's So Nice!
29/03/2013

"When you arrive, I think I will probably kiss you," I breathe down the phone.

A couple of hours later, and Dave draws up outside the house. He is around 5'6" with grey hair and a beard, slight paunch, is wearing baggy old black track suit bottoms and trainers, and is probably around 70. I rush over, almost jumping up and down with excitement at his arrival. He is the eighth and final carpet-man I have called. I was warned he is semi-retired. He has driven over direct from our phone conversation, ready to work straight away, and if necessary, on tomorrow's Bank Holiday Friday too!

Stephen arrives to see if he can sort out the electric gate using the rams I have bought from eBay for £16 (plus £72 P&P). He is very tired and is planning to take off the Bank Holiday weekend this year. Normally his only days off are Christmas and Boxing Day. He says what I have bought are no good, and I might as well put them back on eBay. He won't let me pay him for his time.

Sashka and Kathy are here again, working at lightning speed cleaning up seventeen years of accumulated family clutter and filth, laughing together as they go.

That was yesterday, and today I have a lump in my throat. Patrick arrives in his giant army Land Rover to finish tidying the garden and to replace the twisted, knotted old piece of electric fence with 6' posts he is planning to bury into the rock-iron sod; Dave is back - hating his job of tidying up the carpet where numerous plumbers have repeatedly pulled it up, and also putting down carpet in the new bathroom, against the advice of my entire family and all my friends; Sashka and Kathy are becoming stressed at the amount there remains to do; and I start swearing because the only thing my guests, who arrive tomorrow at 3pm, have asked for, is a DVD player, and it's stopped working.

Sashka phones her friend Carl, who drops everything, drives directly over, and spends two hours going through the maze of wires behind our AV system, in return for a cup of instant coffee. Meanwhile Ken, the insurance man, calls me for the eighth time in his determination to help make sure I have changed my insurance to 'commercial' before my guests' arrival. He, too, is now working on a Bank Holiday Monday.

I don't think I've really done anything to deserve this kind of support. I think people are just generally kinder than I am. I don't think I would be this nice to anyone, ever.

It's 2.30pm and I'm eating the remains of last night's leftovers, comprising a sausage and some spinach, and suddenly there is the most hideous, deafening screech! It makes my ears literally throb! I can't think straight! What on earth has happened? How can I make it stop?!

Agh! It's the panic alarm! Kathy's dusted it and set it off!

Hey - look at this! How proud am I? I've found the key to stop it! But the key doesn't work. Nor does the switch in the airing cupboard, which already reads 'off', yet on and on the sound drums through all of our heads. It's been deliberately designed to drive you so barmy you couldn't even rape someone.

I know! Brilliant! I'll try plugging the code numbers into the burglar alarm! That might stop it. If it doesn't, then I am stumped. I punch the numbers in. Merciful peace.

Blimey, my house is really showing us its tricks today. I pray it will behave itself for the next week. My list of instructions of how to deal with all its quirks has reached three pages!

Maybe this rental won't cover its costs, but it's made me focus on sorting my house out, and we will be much better prepared for next time. If I have any friends left to help me out by then...

Isolation, not desolation
29/03/2013

God. If I were in my twenties, when I was a young and thrusting PR executive in West London, and could see my life thirty years hence. Well, I would have had trouble believing any of it!

Living alone with two young children in the middle of nowhere, tonight I find myself in the pub down the road, listening to Faye's little friends playing the recorder and keyboards, while Alicia, daughter of Neighbour, tap dances to the music, on a square white board placed on the pub floor. I have to admit, the youthful band is jolly good, and so is Alicia, who has now reached Tap Grade 4.

It is the perfect jolly, warm scene of rural idyll, and I have recorded it on my camera to show my guests tomorrow how splendid life is in this remote hamlet.

I wonder what everybody might be thinking, if they notice at all, while Faye and I sit on our own, tucking into a surprisingly good Aubergine and

Feta Bake, the musicians' proud Mums huddled together on the sofa and their Dads standing at the bar, discussing farm subsidies over their Jail Ale.

I feel I'm not such a part of the local community anymore, now that I no longer have a husband, and my children have moved from the wonderful village primary to their posh schools. The rest of our hamlet, who are mostly slightly older couples without children at home, have reconvened onto a long table in the other bar. I'm not included there either.

I can't think of many other women who would have done what I've done, and remained rattling around in their too big family home, determined to make it pay its way. Who might then turn up at the local pub's jollities, with just their small daughter for company, to take part in a social so that they don't mess up their own kitchen.

I know that Malcolm will be thinking of me, as he marks, literally, a million words of his students' dissertations, cosy in the cabin of his clapped-out trimaran, so stable on its mud bank, somewhere out in southern Portugal.

These feelings of mild isolation might have something to do with my current situation. It's been like moving house today, waiting for someone else to take over my much loved home of so long. Faye and I have both retreated to my bedroom - she's on an air mattress, and the things we're going to need over the next week are piled up in the spare room, to be retrieved and packed tomorrow.

Post pub I sit on the floor to watch telly as I don't dare squash or stain the pristine white sofa and its plumped up cushions. (I caught Twiglet lying on it this morning.) All the other rooms are closed to Faye and me, each waiting in its immaculateness for its new inhabitants. I feel as though I am camping in someone else's hotel.

Next time, when we know what to expect and half the things that we've had to worry about this time will have been done, life will be much easier. You never know – getting ready could almost become fun! The weather will be warmer, and we will be going directly off on a lovely summer holiday too. It may not be pleasant right now, but only a few hours to go and we'll be away! Then there won't be a lot to do except work out how to make the most of the next few days of transience. I feel some retail therapy coming on...

Revenge!
03/04/2013

Ex's old office block bit back.

I've always hated what he calls 'The Bothy'. It is the sort of shed beloved by men escaping from their wives. It is where Ex and his team used to prepare polar expeditions. The only time I set foot in it was to deliver cups of tea, or to find things of extreme urgency that had been lost or forgotten. It's totally cleared of everything polar now, but still the waves of stress hit me whenever I open its door.

A year or two ago, Will somehow persuaded Granny to sign the form at the hardware store allowing him to buy cans of spray paint in black, blue and red.

The next morning I discovered that he and friend had sprayed the entire building inside and out with graffiti, including sophisticated slogans such as "Cheryl Cole Shagable" (sic). Ex took the defacing of his beloved old office very well, and a newly matured Will has since repainted everything white, and the Bothy has now become an attractive teen den, housing some old sofas and a ping pong table.

So - I open its door to show it off to my rental guests, and as I talk, the wretched door takes on a life, or death, of its own. A slim panel slowly falls out, landing on the earth below. Then the one above it goes 'plonk' too. I look down to see a third panel slowly sliding earthwards, and then a fourth. By now the whole of the bottom half of the door is missing. With supreme nonchalence, I casually pile up the planks of wood against a nearby wall, and continue with my tour of the house that Sashka, Kathy, Malcolm and I have worked so hard on, for so many weeks, to make look immaculate.

By the time I have finished showing my guests around, left them to it, and driven to Granny's house in Dorset, I find myself very upset by the entire experience of renting my home out to strangers, and am relieved to be spoilt silly by Granny for two days, during which time I slowly regain my composure.

I Met Him!
03/04/2013

Today was the annual Boscastle Football Match between all the boys in Will's year from his old school.

The most interesting aspect of the midday event was either the choice of clothing worn by formerly glamorous Mums, endeavouring to remain warm in the easterly gale blowing across the cliffs direct from Siberia; or the sloe gin/champagne cocktails served in large, real glass glasses by self-styled 'Barman Bill'.

We endured three hours of it, as I cruised car boots scavenging smoked salmon sandwiches, because my life has been too difficult recently to make up a picnic of my own.

Some of us went on to our hosts' home to continue the merriment - remaining revellers comprising, as always, Her, Ex, Me, and a couple of others who, seeing who else was there, made a rapid exit.

None too soon, finally, She disappeared too, so I could relax at last. And then Ex went, leaving me to enjoy myself with my lovely host friends.

But then the door opened. And. OMG - She reappeared, with... Bevan!

Blimey - what a shock! I felt quite wobbly! I'm not really sure why. I was sitting at the kitchen table surrounded by 14 year old boys, with a cup of coffee and a glass of Cava in front of me, a fag in hand.

I found myself competing with host (he, I and Bevan had all been at school at Eton at the same time) yelling, "Do you remember ME?!"

"No do you remember ME?!"

"Oh only my sister? Bugger. Everybody always remembers her.."

Poor chap! What has he entered into?! He started talking Green Wellie Shooting with host so eventually I thought it time to depart in Marv for my cheap and cheerful B&B.

Just before departure, host showed me round a cottage which he aims to let out as a holiday rental via 'Ultimate Home Stays'. We're all at it! "The amount of work I've still got left to do is completely doing my head in," he reassured me.

As I drove to my basic B&B I felt a bit tearful. No home, no Range Rover, no family, no dog. All because of Her, still enjoying herself yacking away to all my friends, introducing the new boyfriend, who, having met him, I don't think is nearly as attractive as Ex, nor, as it happens, as Her ex-husband, who is now a Lord.

But then I thought – well actually. I quite like being anonymous, in my funny old car, playing all my favourite songs on my i-trip, off to some jolly little B&B where someone else will do my washing and cook my breakfast.

I can just lie in the bath and read my new book. It's called "An Unusual Love Story" and I have just bought it from the Co-op. Then I'll spend the evening watching telly, while tucking into prawns and enjoying yet more Cava.

My Luxurious B&B
04/04/2013

The bathroom is along a corridor and, if I wasn't the only guest, I would have to share it with several other people. It has lino on the floor and is painted light blue. The towel rail appears warm, but the room is icy. The bath and shower gel, body lotions, shampoo and conditioner are all in pump dispensers.

I wander back to my room, my modesty protected (just) by the B&B's tiny towel. There are no pictures on the walls, and no telly in my room, the curtains are thin, and the 'tea and coffee making facilities' are shared. I am cold, as the snow starts coming down again, and the duvet is rather small. All is explained when the hosts tell me later that there is no central heating, but only a lovely log burner in the rather plain sitting room downstairs, which you can fill up with logs at will, while you use the small telly there. It is all very simple and surprisingly cosy.

I am totally cheered up. I feel a whole different person from yesterday. This is real farmhouse B&B, and the hosts are delightful, friendly, chatty, easy-going, young, and can't do enough to be helpful. A couple of years ago they won a 'Best Farmhouse B&B' award in the Sunday Times. It's obvious that being a nice host counts almost as much as the quality of the service that you offer.

I put the daffodils I have brought with me into a coffee cup of water, and excitedly ponder upon the fact that I am quite justified in hopefully charging nearly double for my B&B what I am paying here.

Helen, the proprietor, on hearing about my plans, whizzes off to get me her 'setting up a B&B' book, and I discover that what I am offering might just about count as 'boutique B&B'; or 'complete home hospitality B&B' along the lines of the very expensive Wolsey Lodges. I have spoken to a couple of friends about these. They had pulled out of the arrangement when they were told the exact dimensions required for the towels that they should provide. Hmm. Doesn't sound quite 'me' either!

The book tells me that a 40% occupancy is good. My hosts say they're at 25%+; which they're pleased with, and they spend days a week on their marketing efforts and are open and available year round. Um. If I am putting myself forward as the most expensive B&B on the moor, only open on weekdays during school term times, for a minimum two people for two nights; hot tub or no hot tub, we're not looking at a lot of guests. I might have to re-think this.

Perhaps I might need to go cap in hand to Alastair Sawday, for his list of wealthy and exclusive potential clients.

Whatever. Any further action will have to wait until I get back from Malcolm's old trimaran in Portugal. I am typing this up on one of Bristol

Airport's computers at £1 for every 10 minutes internet access. Luckily it's a very nice computer and keyboard, but I'm buggered if I'm going to pay for much more, while Ryanair keeps calling out the Faro flight.

Things seem to be coming together though. I just need to call Sashka and Kathy before I board to let them know ...... oh what was it now?

Scam!
20/04/2013

Look what I got back to after Faye's riding lesson this morning! At bloody last! A nice friendly email from an oceanographer called Diane Joy who is such a loving Mum that she wants to buy my Range Rover at its published price and give it to her son! What's more, she's a Christian, so she won't be trying any funnies!

She writes:

"Hi there, Sorry for the late reply, Well can you assure me that it's in good state and that i will not be disappointed with it.I'm ready to pay your asking price and to be honest, i wanted to buy this for my son as (Gift) and i want it to get to him as surprise gift, but the issue is i am an oceanographer and i do have a contract to go for which starting today and am leaving any moment from now just trying to send you this message" blah blah blah, saying that she'll pay for it via Pay Pal and send an agent to collect it, ending "God Bless You".

I've had the wretched car on eBay so long, now, that the ad has run out, despite reducing the price and taking out the copy and pictures referring to its various dents and scratches. So only yesterday I signed up to AutoTrader for £45, and now it looks as though I've got a keen buyer already! Hurray for Diane!

A teeny weeny little voice in me whispered 'hesitate'. So I forwarded the email to my friend Miriam who is the ex-policewoman. She screamed back "Avoid! Avoid! Avoid!" and directed me to all the websites detailing identical scams, right down to the oceanographer bit.

So I emailed back:

'Hi Diane
I am so glad you would like to buy my car. And how lovely to be dealing with another believer. I very much look forward to meeting your agent.

God Bless You too

WPC Plod'

Sadly I haven't heard back from her, and meanwhile all three of 'Mazza's Motors' continue to block up the drive.

Hello! Real People!
22/05/2013

A big black man with a sticker on his chest saying 'Gift' stands in front of me. What a funny name!

I love Speeding Courses - you meet a total cross-section of the world at them.

We are divided into 'the red team' and 'the green team' and Gift goes off with the reds. They look like the youngsters. I bet they've all done something really bad – not just 32 in a 30.

We troop in silence (apart from a large woman wearing biker boots who is observing loudly what a profit the organisers must be making out of 20 of us paying over £100 to attend this course) into a characterless, very hot, rectangular, off-white room; and I sit down next to a man with a beard whose sticker says 'Anoy'. Oh. Actually it says 'Andy'.

I imagine what a terrifying experience this must have been for Granny, who had been caught by a camera doing her top speed of 34mph, who must have been sitting in this very same room a couple of months previously, wondering what was in store for her, knowing that she has spent her entire life trying to be good, to please people, and to behave herself generally. She's not used to the hoi poloi in their t-shirts, hoodies, surfer shorts, trainers, crew cuts and tattoos.

Meanwhile I've been here before. I know that we're not going to be punished. I've already acknowleged the smiley matey greetings of the advanced driving instructors welcoming us onto the course, and their prolific use of Christian names. And I know that I will stick out as the most glamorous, best educated, funniest, cleverest, most perceptive and best dressed of the motley crew attending.

Or will I? A lady from Essex, also in biker boots, turns to the big lady and says "You ought to be a comedienne on telly you know." Oi – wot about moi?!

Anoy, or Andy, turns out to be cleverer than I am at answering the simplistic questions, and is the natural leader of our little group. I think he probably does pub quizzes. He already knew that in 2004 there had been 2,600 (or something) deaths on the UK roads. He even disputes some of the facts presented by the nice people taking the course!

There is also a funny lorry driver from Newton Abbot who does 130,000 miles a year. His greatest hate is middle-lane hoggers, as his juggernaut has an inhibitor or whatever they're called that won't let him drive faster than 52mph, being a lorry he's not allowed to overtake them in the third lane.

The thing that makes me really cross, which I loudly voice, although I know I have gone a little bit pink with heat and embarrassment at my posh accent, is old people drivers. Like my mum, as it happens. Who make impatient people like me do stupid things and cause accidents.

Oh dear. Now an elderly, shy, foreign lady is standing up and describing how her husband died in a bus station. I did notice that she was looking rather alarmed by my vehemence. Well whatever. They should all take tests at 70.

The jolly man running the course announces that we're the chattiest group he's ever taken, but don't we want to be away on time? The three hours fly. Even the plain digestive biscuit and cheap coffee seem delicious.

And then disaster. I am wearing Jaeger black trousers, high black suede boots, and a top quality black coat from Frank Usher, my wardrobe as ever bought in the half price sales of Clarks Shopping Village. I appear rich - well at least that's what I'm hoping! We wander back to our cars, and there's Marv, waiting patiently for me, in all his ordinariness. The other cars are gleaming Toyota's and Honda's, whose remotes actually work. I fumble with the key in Marvin's lock, dive in and drive off, eyes on the road, the myth of posh bitch shattered, never, probably, to see a single one of those people again.

Someone's Found Us At Last!
23/05/2013

Hurrah! Ex has volunteered to drive all the way to Truro to watch Faye play in the netball B-team in sub-zero temperatures, leaving me free, all alone once again, in my rather large and very cold house, to 'Get On' - the whole day to Twiglet (the dog) and myself, no school runs or any other distractions.

Trouble is, 'Getting On' seems so fraught with problems. It's SO SLOW!

I had been becoming gloomier and gloomier and slower and slower, looking for better pics to pinch off the internet to illustrate my new Wydemeet B&B website with, when - KERRRRPOW!!!!

A very nice lady has just rung. "Are you Wydemeet?" she enquired. My first ever proper bed and breakfast enquiry!

I am raised from my lethargy, bugger the photos - here I am, straight on to the keyboard, to report my success!

"How did you find me?" I asked her. She didn't know - she had been passed my details by her husband, but really - it's only TWO HOURS since the Wydemeet phone number was listed by BT!

How fantastic is that? So thank God I now have an energy boost and can re-apply myself to my desk-top research.

43

Yippee! Actually I think I will go and celebrate with a coffee and a fag, I am so excited!

She can't come, by the way - the lady ringing about Bed and Breakfast, as she wanted to during the school holidays, when I don't really want guests. But who cares?!

Another hopefully constructive thing I've done today is to pretend that my Range Rover lives at my sister's house in Fulham, and I've added £500 back onto the price. It's been a month on eBay, and two weeks now on AutoTrader. I haven't had a single enquiry from Auto Trader that wasn't a scam. Four scams in all so far!

Lying Again
25/05/2013

Champagne three days in a row! Can I really plead poverty?

At my sister's house, toasting Faye's 11th birthday. At Saddlers Hall in the City the next day, beginning a family lunch under chandeliers for 49. And at lunch on Sunday in Wimbledon Village – just because the sun's shining and we're feeling good.

Life continues in its crazy surreal way, not helped by staying up drinking and smoking til four in the morning at my best friend Annabelle's house in Putney. Everything was so comfortable, and I was concentrating so hard in order to remember every sage word that fell from her lips, that I just didn't feel tipsy at all. It took a while to recover again after all that though, especially having shared a bed with Faye, who suffers from eczema, and scratches and kicks.

Three weeks a nomad until I finally returned home from my various travels and achieved three consecutive nights' sleep in one bed. How wonderful it was to fall back to earth at last.

I arrived back to two enquiries about the Range Rover and a man and a woman have now arranged to come and see it. Their visit is timed to take place between Faye's and my horse ride to Princeton, and the first dinner party I've thrown for several years.

I leap off wonder-horse Panda and throw her out into her field in the rain. I rush over to inspect the Range Rover, which I haven't looked at in ages. It has earth all around its bottom rims, and muddy wheels and tyres. I rummage around in the Bothy and find a plastic container full of bottles of car cleaning materials. It's raining though - what good is wax in that? I half heartedly flll a bucket with tepid water and rub some of the mud off bits of the car with a small flannel. I squirt the tyre-cleaner onto the muddy tyres, where it stays in a white goo, and it's time for the potential buyers, armed with £7000 in cash, to arrive.

"I am sad," I explain to the overweight lady, "because if you buy it, I know it's gone and it's worth more than £7000, but if you don't buy it I will be sad too."

They look around it, noting the dent, the scratches and the chewed bit.

Luckily when the man presses the button to make the car go up and down, it seems to do its thing, as I am leaning against it at the time and nearly fall over. They open the back door and all my muddy washing water suddenly gushes out. Then they drive off in it, leaving behind their shiny Jaguar with its personalised number plates.

They're rather a long time. I have been too trusting.

Eventually the doorbell rings. It's the lady.

"I think your car's run out of diesel," she explains.

Not again. That bloody fuel indicator. This time it says there's 100 miles of fuel left. And my hard-won potential buyers have been left stranded outside the garden in the rain. Bloody car. Lying again.

I join them and the wretched car in the hurricane, having happily found a container of diesel to help them get up the last few yards of driveway.

The couple say they will call me in an hour or two, when they've had time for a little think, over a meal at the Plume of Feathers in Princetown, where the horses, Faye and I have just had lunch. The call will interrupt my dinner party.

What a surprise! It never comes.

Range Rover Over
26/05/2013

With butterflies in my tummy, I carefully stuck up the sign reading "£8450, MOT until November, 149,000 sedate miles" in the windscreen of my Range Rover, using the piece of selotape I had prepared earlier, slammed the door shut, locked it, and ran round the corner to Malcolm's house, so that he could drive me home, as I sat shaking in his passenger seat.

I had driven my beloved Range Rover, 'King III' (so-named because Jeremy Clarkson once described the Range Rover as 'The King' of the road) eight miles down off the moor, and parked it on the grass in front of a bench, just behind a bus stop, by the Ashburton junction of the A38, opposite Ashburton Motors, which sells second hand four-wheel-drive cars at twice the price of mine.

'Foolhardy' was how Malcolm described my action, through gritted teeth.

'You're mad!' exploded Sashka, when I told her what I'd done.

But ho ho to both of them. Within 24 hours I received a phone call about it from someone calling himself 'Kouros', and was in a muddle because I didn't know whether he had seen it in real life, or come across it advertised for auction on eBay. I have now been trying to sell the thing since February!

Anyway, Kouros called back and said his friend had seen my car parked on the grass, and that he would come and give it a go on Sunday.

'Fat chance' I thought, by now quite used to no one wanting my adored car. And as anticipated, no further phone call was forthcoming. 'Who cares, anyway − F*** it; I'll keep the Range Rover and flog Bill the Shogun." I thought to myself, gritting my teeth.

But first, I had to give selling the thing one more try.

That evening I asked a couple of friends to bid for King III on eBay, to make it look as though somebody was actually interested in buying him. I did get one enquiry and then countdown began... four hours left for someone to bid £7,500 and It was theirs. Three, two, one .... Nothing. Gone. Auction over. Nobody. Another £17 in advertising costs down the Swannee.

Meanwhile, every time the phone rang I thought it might be the police saying they had towed my Range Rover away at vast expense and added several points to my licence, or Malcolm reporting that someone had covered it in scratches, or that the wipers and/or wheels had gone missing, or, indeed, the entire car. After five days I could bear the tension no more, and Malcolm dropped me off, for me to drive it home again.

Instead I went into Ashburton Motors and asked the very nice staff there if they would like to sell it for me, for a huge commission.

"No one would ever do that," they assured me (very nicely).

So I went to the Country Wholesalers to buy some horse-food and bumped straight into the arms of riding-boyfriend James, and, almost in tears, told him my sad story. James used to own the identical car, same colour, year, mileage and price, only his had since cost him £12,000 in repairs whilst mine, much to James' envy, continued to work most of the time. "My friend John will sell it for you," he said cheerfully. "He sold mine."

And the next thing I know is my Range Rover is on the forecourt of a small country garage in Ugborough, and James is driving me twenty miles home, with a stop for a baguette in the sun at a village pub on the green, as a thank you.

Saying goodbye to my car was like walking away from a much-loved dog or horse. I will probably never see King III again. In the meantime, for £300 John will make it look immaculate, and for whatever it costs more, the rattle in its engine will be eradicated (I hope).

And, young John is only going to take a 10% commission! He's going to call me in a couple of months to let me know how things are going, but in the meantime will thoroughly clean King III on a daily basis. That will make a change. And now, finally, I've got some space in my driveway. And in my head.

Growing Up
28/05/2013

I'm getting really old now. I've got much fatter and much wrinklier this year - my 54th. Wrinkles AND spots. That really is unfair. I'm trying out some new moisturisers to try to reverse the signs - I've moved from Boot's Protect and Perfect, to Neal's Yard Frankincense Nourishing Cream, to Olay's Regenerist 3 which has apparently got special peptides in it. But nothing's working, and they all seem to curdle with any foundation I may try putting on top. I don't suppose my diet of Cava, fags, riding through the horizontal rain of Dartmoor, and getting divorced, would be terribly helpful for anyone's complexion, nor my penchant for deliberately getting sunburnt.

Nobody's commented on my demise in the looks department yet, except my children, who cheerfully let me know that I'm beginning to look like Granny.

Meanwhile Ex is, annoyingly, looking better every day! He appears to be keeping to some diet and regime prescribed by his personal trainer, and anyway, fifty year old men, with their greying temples, do tend to look better than fifty year old women, it would seem. Bum.

I am so grown up that I included him in the dinner party I threw the other day.

I guess this was payback after Ex brought Will home from school to me, with no comment nor demand for exaggerated thanks. Ex is actually just the best company if there are people around, and I was really pleased that he joined us. He helped make the evening go with a real swing, no matter how surprised our friends were to see him there!

I am so intrigued about what his next girlfriend will be like. I think he would be happier with a straightforward outdoorsy-type who camps, than with the manipulative film-star types he has favoured of late.

But it must be quite hard for him (as the actress said to the bishop or whoever) as there is just so much temptation for men in the public eye. During his speaking gigs when he went on about how he 'did it all for his family', women would still pass him napkins with "I want to have your babies" written in lipstick on them.

Honestly. What sisterhood?

Nothing Works Faster than Anadin
08/05/2013

I'm going to make Malcolm Rich and Famous (even though he doesn't want to be).

Just as I did with Ex (who did).

And you heard about it here first!

You see, Malcolm can cure headaches! It's true, because I know! First hand! And it's so, so simple!

That ancient Anadin ad, 'for tense, nervous headaches' has caused SO much misunderstanding. Malcolm explained that your actual brain can't hurt. So my constant, on-going headaches aren't being caused by stress. They are simply caused by my holding my head in the same place for too long - writing this for instance.

He says the little muscles in the back of the neck aren't designed to hold up such a big heavy thing in one place for hours on end. They are meant to dip and dive as you move your head a lot, when you're not doing unnatural things like sitting in front of a PC screen all day. He says everybody knows this already, but I don't think they do. I certainly haven't read about it in the Daily Mail recently. And I've been under the impression for years that Nothing is just as ineffective as Anadin.

I call Malcolm 'Artist of Touch'. He releases these seized muscles by gently putting increased pressure on the 'trigger points' which are causing them to jam resulting in the pain that you feel in the muscles further up around your skull. I sat quietly in a kitchen chair while he exercised his technique on me. It took about 15 minutes, while my sceptical mother, back towards us, carried on washing up the family lunch.

Well blow me down. It worked. I mucked out the horses and came back smiling.

And the next day I consciously moved my head around as I was bashing away on the keyboard (no one was looking, so it didn't matter that I looked like a crazy woman, or 'special', in the rather unattractive words of my revered son, Will). Come 4.30am that night, and no daily dreaded headache appeared. Wow!

AND. Malcolm can do the same thing for backs too. In fact it was problems with his own back that got him into researching trigger points.

He is probably the greatest expert on them in the South West, but is currently too modest to blow his own cornetto. He could change the lives of thousands and thousands of pain-racked people.

So I am going to tell the world about him and his special powers! But I am not quite ready to yet. I've got to market my B&B and House Rental first. Then I will be Onto It. Watch this space!!

Decree Nisi
08/05/2013

If it were as difficult and expensive to get married as it is to get divorced, I am sure there would be far fewer marriages, and far fewer divorces as a result. The lawyers would be out of business!

My lawyer charges £25 for every email sent and received by her, even if it's just one word long! I emailed her at vast expense saying "Sorry I haven't been very polite recently, but I feel I can't email to say 'thanks' if it costs me twenty-five pounds every time."

I have just discovered from some form that a Decree Nisi, if that's how you spell it, was issued to me last November. News to me. I haven't a clue what it means. Or what it looked like.

Anyway, apparently our financial arrangements have been 'sealed' so I am now officially broke, and am about to have to ask my Mum to help me out for the first time since I was 35.

I have also just signed a thing applying for a 'Decree Absolute' which means we should be divorced in a few weeks' time.

Hurray! At bloody last! This has all taken so long - the process started back in October 2009 - that I feel I hardly care anymore.

It must be horrid being a divorce lawyer, or in 'family law' or whatever they call it, because as far as I can tell, there's just absolutely nothing remotely pleasant about anything to do with the whole experience.

The worst bit for me has been listing our belongings, and allocating them.

Walking from room to room writing them all down - it brought back memories of eighteen years ago when life was all so exciting, moving into our new home, deciding where all his antiques and glassware, and our wedding presents still arriving from Harrods and John Lewis, would go best - the years ahead beckoning in a sunny sort of way. We've agreed that he's going to keep all his family's 'wealth' - including six Royal Worcester miniature porcelain coffee sets, and I will keep the modern things you can't sell, such as carpets.

Let's hope he doesn't decide to take everything away immediately, or there won't be anywhere to put things down on.

Being Divorced, Absolutely
31/05/2013

Well. Apparently I got divorced just now. Without noticing. Ex has sent me an email 'truly hoping for only good things' for me.

I say. What an anticlimax! After ALL that! I mean not just the year of planning the wedding and the £10,000+ that it cost, but all the anguish of the split, and the incredible hassle and vast expense of getting all the right bits of paper together from the bottom of old drawers, and making sure we'd got the exact, precise wording onto the divorce forms - and now it's done. Bingo.

I really don't know what to feel - if anything much at all. Is it an excuse to crack open one of the £12 Lidl bottles of champagne I have carefully put by? That would make a nice change from Cava.

Or should I go and smoke a fag at the bottom of the garden by the manure heap and feel sad about the wasted emotion, time and money? I simply don't know.

What I do know is that I must hurry off in Marvin to reach the school in time to hear Faye singing 'For All the Saints' in the school Church Choir.

Perhaps I should first change into a Little Black Dress in which to mourn the end of my eighteen year marriage properly.

3 REAL GUESTS!

Signs of Life
31/05/2013

I bet we're the only house in the world with daffodils still blooming in the garden in May! What a cold winter's tale.

As they're about the only thing that's blooming. Or so I thought. By yesterday lunchtime (spent with my friends = the Jilted Wives Club = at Olga Polizzi's Endsleigh Hotel, the poshest hotel in the South West, total bill £12.50 each for the best sandwiches and spritzers available in the universe) I was becoming despondent.

All my hard work just doesn't seem to be coming to anything.

After that first one, not a single B&B enquiry, despite having spent three solid weeks on creating a fabby-dabby-doo website complete with SEO (Search Engine Optimisation) which means all the things you have to do to get it to the top of Google; which I believe has now become an even more significant skill as part of the marketing mix than advertising or PR.

Breaking about even on my first house rental and no sign of the follow-up cheque, now due, for the second.   A blank in my brain about how to get my website actually seen.

I am now actually overdrawn for the first time in 25 years. And no sign of things improving.

And then yesterday tea-time: Ping! An email from a Swiss couple wanting to stay for a couple of nights in August! And then, Ping! My July rental lady emails to say she would like to drop the cheque round personally! Wowee! There are signs of life after all! Fancy that!

Never mind that I don't want to do August B&Bs because the children will be at home, and that the mower's at the menders, so if my potential rental turns up she'll run a mile if she sees that jungle.

All is not lost. TripAdvisor must have sprung into life at very long last. I will forward the Swiss couple to my friends' fantastic hotel, Prince Hall, just up the road, and perhaps they and I might enter into some mutually beneficial arrangement over time, in case this happens again.

Just when you think there is no light in sight, bingo! It would seem that I just need a little kick up the arse now and then, and off I spin!

Cutting Down On the Lunches
31/05/2013

I've told everybody that now I need to spend some time making money, I am going to limit myself to just one Lady Who Lunches a week. So this week I'm doing three.

Yesterday's was the Jilted Wives Club, and today I simply couldn't resist joining my brother and his two edible male friends on their yacht, as they sailed back from the Scillies via Newton Ferrers in Devon, and on to Chichester. Their dropping by in Devon seems to be becoming an annual event, and as usual they treated me like Lady Muck and took lots of pictures of me looking just that.

In fact it was on the previous occasion that I had lunched with them when they took the picture that I subsequently used in all my internet dating sites, when I was a couple of stone lighter than I am now.

I like sitting on boats in the sun, but am not too keen if they start moving along, over waves. So as the boys fussed over me with delicious 'Bladder Wine' (wine served from the 'bag-box', the cardboard part having been discarded to save space on the boat) and cold meat and salad, I found myself expounding on what had been bothering me during the night.

Once you are no longer part of a nuclear family, you don't fit in.

Jack winningly tried to reassure me that other people's wives are just terrified of a glamorous single woman like me getting anywhere near their husbands. "That's just a silly cliché!" I reprimanded him.

I think people generally like to be involved with others in similar situations to themselves – their own 'tribe'. But I don't have anyone in my position living anywhere near me.

Ex has just bought a two-bed flat at the poor end of Parsons Green in London, and I think he is going to have loads of fun. There are millions of single people like him living within a stone's throw of his new home.

No one at all lives within a stone's throw of my house, let alone someone like me. I'm wondering whether I am mad to be so determined to stay in this large, expensive, worrying, demanding, inaccessible place, especially assuming both my children will soon be at boarding school. I am at a crossroads. Ex has started a whole new life. Perhaps I should consider that too.

The boys on the boat, all in happy marriages, didn't really have any views on this line of thought of mine, and wandered off, slightly uninterested, doing the washing up and preparing to make the most of the sunshine and wind by sailing on to Salcombe that afternoon.

This Thursday my favourite Auntie Rhonda is coming down from Edinburgh to stay with my mother. I feel the whisper of another lunch coming on. Yes. No. Yes. No. Yes! So that's three in five days! Hurray! I'll work at making some money next week instead.

Decayed and Neglected
02/06/2013

The gate is still broken. The logs are still piled up to the sky on either side of it. It's raining again. I squelch out of the car into the cow-shit and in my cream cashmere top and salmon pink manicured finger nails reach around the orange bailer-twine which is vaguely keeping the gate held to, and pull the wooden five-bar structure open, as usual getting the green lichen into my finger nails and all down my front; my 'top stylist at Toni and Guy hairstyle' matted wet to the top of my head, making me look, as ever, like Esther Rantzen.

I have been waiting nearly three months now for my new friend to sort out the electric 'ram' which makes the gate work automatically, for free.

I think I might prefer to just pay a stranger to sort it out, today!

The wind's in the wrong direction again, so I have to lean down and pick up a huge, heavy slimy stone to keep the gate open while I get back in the car, drive it through the opening, get out again, and kick away the stone with my damp, stained suede high heeled boots, lean over the mossy stone pillar to get hold of the twine and shut the slippery gate; get back into the car and gaze with dismay up my potholed drive and the mad jungle that now runs along either side of it, while the house stands above, looking grey and forlorn, the paint peeling off all the rotten window frames.

I pray that my second house-rental hasn't been here and seen it all like this, while I have been out collecting Faye from school.

I collect the post from the box outside the door, and a letter with no stamp or address falls away from the pile of letters. I open it, and inside is a cheque for over £2000 from my July rental, no additional comments.

God she must have been disappointed, I think to myself.

I email her to thank her for the cheque, and to once again apologise for the sense of neglect and decay that must emanate from my wonderful home.

By return she writes: "I thought the house looked lovely, huge, and very pleased that it was straightforward to find and quite close to Ashburton for shopping (I like Ashburton). The dog and I had a bit of a wander down to Hexworthy and around which is also very pretty. My American sister-in-law will love it.

"We are quite serious walkers so some recommendations for good walks close by would be great if you have some. And my daughter and her boyfriend would love a recommendation for a good hacking stables, she doesn't get much chance to ride in Paris!"

Well blow me down. I write back that I never go for walks - that is what the horse is for, so I can sit down going uphill. But thinking about it we could not be more perfectly placed for short, middling or long walks, including pubs and/or total wilderness, north, south, east or west. And I am very familiar with all the hacking stables nearby, each offers something slightly different so that there's a choice for people of every riding standard.

This entrepreneurial life is such a roller-coaster. Depressing, elating, frustrating, all-consuming. Perhaps my home is nicer than I thought! And maybe I'm not very rural. Although I was exaggerating about the cashmere and the manicure. All my jumpers are black! And I don't have any fingernails.

Domestic Drudgery
29/06/2013

I am lying flat out on the dining room floor. I can't even crawl. My heart is thumping. It's 100C and my sweat is dripping onto the carpet. How am I going to manage to cook supper and be charming when I have completely used up every shred of energy I've ever had? My first ever proper B&Bers are due to arrive any second. Followed an hour later by no less than Alastair Sawday himself - The King, no, The Emperor, no God of global B&Bs - aagghh!

It's been a red letter day for me today.

I had to learn how to turn our hoover on.

It's been many years since I did any housework, and the horrible heavy great big red machine wasn't playing ball.

After nearly ten minutes of trying all the switches I could see, I was panicking. Already noon, and my guests due at 4pm.

No customers at all for three months, and then God Himself invites Himself to stay without my even having to pray for Him, and the others choose this day of all days too.

Immediately I received God's message, I was straight onto eBay. I bought 21 things, including a pair of giant ears for Faye, who is playing the Mad March Hare in Alice in Wonderland next week; and a Singer Steam Press, for which I bid £75.

And then, at the height of my apprehension and butterflies, I received an email from the aptly named (in this case) LateRooms (who have, after three weeks of nagging on my part, finally managed to get Wydemeet onto their map), telling me that they are sending me my first proper, paying customers in 24 hrs time, to coincide with God's arrival. I don't even know if, or how, to charge them!

I only have one room ready for B&B, which I have already reserved for my Deity and his wife. The room I must put the proper paying customers in currently has a hole in the carpet, bare walls where pictures belonging to Ex used to be, and domestic flowery un-ironed bedlinen which has been 'Twigletted' - ie it's covered in muddy paw-prints.

Only a week ago, Faye taught me how to use the mowing machine. She mowed the entire garden - about an acre of meadow grass, in an hour and a half, so I gave her £5. I've lived here for nearly twenty years, but have never used a mower. Just banged my head against the wall when endless gardeners didn't turn up whatever the weather, while the grass went on growing, and I looked helplessly on.

Well now I that I've learned what to do I'm finding it quite fun. A bit like hoovering really. I had always assumed that it's man's work, but if an eleven year old girl can do it, I jolly well can.

Nevertheless - the whole experience has finished me off, and I can't move.

Hey ho - Malcolm to the rescue! He is not a trained massage therapist for nothing! He squats down and gets my muscles back listening to my brain, I heave myself up and add a final touch to each room - the last two blooming bluebells from our garden, each stuffed into a sherry glass.

Well, I muse. One fun bit about all this domestic drudgery is that I can get it done how and when I choose, instead of waiting for people who don't turn up, or forgetting to tell my wonderful team exactly what I want, and expecting them to work on telepathy.

If you ever see a fat cleaner, she can't be much good.

Egyptian Cotton
18/07/2013

I'll tell you something. 100% Egyptian cotton sheets with a 200 thread count are a complete bummer. After washing the stuff, its creases look like the complexion of an old woman, and I just don't seem to be able to iron them out.

But. This B&B lark. It's brilliant! I am really loving it! I still simply just can't believe that I ever possibly could!

I mean. You actually get paid for doing your own hoovering and mowing, and making your house look like a show home! Well, you would, assuming you had some customers. Which I'm sure I will eventually.

My freaky scary night with my first guests was really great.

I served Cook's Wild Mushroom Lasagne again, for dinner with God and his especially delightful wife, just after returning from listening to Faye singing 'Swing Low" particularly wonderfully in our local parish church.

I asked God whether he thought it would be OK for me to serve future guests pre-prepared food. Cook is based in Kent and makes home-made food in bulk, freezes it, and gets it to you within 24 hrs of ordering. Most courses cost £3.95 a serving, and taste exquisite - words can't really do it justice. It's delicious, and completely reliable and consistent, unlike my cooking.

"Just be open and honest, and fun - that's what matters," replied God.

Well that should be easy for me then!

"And what do you think about all that hideous wood piled up to the sky right outside my gate, ruining the valley and every body's experience as they arrive?" I wailed.

"It's real," he said. "It's what the moor's all about these days. What's really going on, now that the hill farmers are forced to diversify."

God, his wife, the LateRooms couple and I all sat around the polished dining room table for breakfast the next morning, and it was really like a jolly house party. The freshly baked (from frozen) croissants and pain-au-chocolats that I had found the day before in Sainsbury's went down particularly well. And I was especially pleased that one of my guests had come down in her onesie. I felt that she set exactly the right tone, and I have consequently used the website to encourage guests to have breakfast in their pyjamas.

Later I joined God and his wife for lunch at the Rugglestone Inn in Widecombe – possibly the best pub on Dartmoor - after they had wandered along the banks of the River Swincombe, which winds down the valley from just outside our house, to join the East Dart. They were stunned by the beauty of what they had seen.

I have recently discovered that people who have lived on Dartmoor for years choose my out-of-the-way very spot to celebrate their most special occasions. It is so important not to take where I live for granted. There is truly nowhere else like it in the world!

I had spent the morning filling in God's B&B form, and rushing around tidying, clearing up dining room, bedrooms and kitchen, washing up, straightening flowers in vases and straightening beds, wiping around bathrooms and hoovering. Stuff that I have never really done in my life before - well at least not for about thirty years, since my mother made me do it during the school holidays.

For the price of an overnight stay - averaging £100 a room for one of my three rooms - I really can't complain about this. All the books say that to run a B&B is such hard work. Well, not compared with a proper job, in my probably not as humble as it should be opinion. It just gives you an excuse to keep your house in good nick and hopefully, in the end, to entertain a steady stream of people staying the night, and to cook breakfast for them, and chat to them. All of my favourite things.

Roll on that steady stream!

And in the meantime I'll gird my loins and get experimenting with my new steam press. I got one for £52 in the end, from a very nice lady just down the road from my health club. All the books agree that a decent B&B must offer Egyptian cotton. So I have to have a proper ironing device. But personally speaking, I really can't see the problem with polyester.

The Best B&B
19/07/2013

As you know, I have decided that I am going to offer the best B&B experience on the moor.

By this, of course, I mean the most expensive. But I'm still cheaper than a hotel, and I'm not liable for VAT yet, which means 20% off for guests – or, more accurately, 20% more for me. If I have sufficiently few guests so that I can manage to do all the work myself, I should be quids in!

The reason I have been a bit 'off air' recently is because I have been trying to market the thing. After all these months I have felt as though I have been banging my head against a brick wall until it bleeds. I have become increasingly frustrated and irritable as nothing I do seems to work, and all appears out of my control.

I used to style myself modestly as 'Queen of PR'. I could make anyone famous, and get any crappy old product into the national papers for free. Well such talents now appear redundant. These days I have just one simple marketing goal. That if you plug 'Dartmoor B&B' into Google's search engine, up comes Wydemeet. Simples. Not. Over all this time I have got nowhere with it.

Owners Direct - for holiday rentals - no enquiries since January, despite my putting a 20% reduction on my prices.

TripAdvisor - after three months I still don't appear to be on their map, and I'm languishing at No 47 in their 'Top 166 B&Bs in Dartmoor National Park'. They won't include any contact details in your entry unless you pay them, or do it through another agent. So now finally I've succeeded in organising a link on the Wydemeet entry from TripAdvisor direct to LateRooms. What an effort though! It seriously doesn't just happen!

AdWords - they're the ads that come up in the yellow box, or are listed down the side of your screen when you do a Google search. Every time somebody clicks on an AdWord it costs the advertiser anything from around 25p, according to a complicated kind of auction-system. You're supposed to make up several very short ads, and fill in columns and columns of keywords and phrases (I completed over 200 in the end) to make sure the ads come up according to the various searches potential guests might make (including spelling mistakes such as 'acomodation'). I put my budget at a maximum of a £5 total spend a day, and my ads started appearing on the front Google search page occasionally, but still no one has booked through it, so I have cancelled my subscription.

LateRooms - I spent hours sorting out details of what should go on their website, and subsequently changed to a company called Eviivo, which covers LateRooms, TopRooms, LastMinutedotCom, Expedia and about 30 others, all at once. So I needn't have bothered with the LateRooms-only website after all that. It took two weeks to get up and running with Eviivo - quite quick relatively speaking in this business. They were sensible and efficient to work with. Hurray!

Booking.com – currently operates separately from Eviivo. It insisted on writing its own copy and choosing which pictures to use to advertise

Wydemeet, and in what order. The result was that Wydemeet's greatest asset, according to Booking.com, was its 'easy access' to Torquay, and the first picture they used to advertise the B&B was one of a silver horse and some glasses on the dining room table. Eventually I did manage to work with them to make the entry sensible.

AirBnB - operates differently from the above agencies. The others mostly charge me 15% + VAT commission per booking. AirBnB charges both customers and operators. Canny! And they are flying, judging by the number of enquiries I have been getting from them. And it's straightforward to set up.

God of B&Bs has gone away to France so I won't be on his website until after he gets back.

Search Engine Optimisation. Otherwise known as SEO. Hah! Aren't we modern now, to know that? I have been working on it really hard. As in AdWords, you have to list lots of 'key words' in your copy and behind the scenes in special hard-to-find sections of your website builder-thing, add a blog, use captions with capital letters under your photo's, etc etc etc. Apparently it can take six months for all these little touches to start working to make sure you come high up on Google searches, once Google's 'spiders' have crawled all around them. It is an ancient myth that the more clicks your entry gets, the higher up you appear. Whatever - so far I'm nowhere - not even on page 12 of search results!

YouTube: on one of our rare sunny days I grabbed the opportunity to film the garden and a bedroom I've called 'Dartmeet', and put the results up on YouTube, using as many keywords in the accompanying copy as I could think of, added a backing track of a Chopin Nocturne for the bedroom, and a quick blast of Beethoven's Pastoral for the so-called garden. This has resulted in Wydemeet's appearance on page 6 of a Google search, but somebody not very kind has added a 'dislike' little sign to my bedroom film. Perhaps they thought the use of one of the most beautiful tunes ever written, to advertise a B&B, was naff.

So I have been busy. With zero result. No other accommodation in the area is following up so many marketing avenues, as far as I am aware. So what's the problem? That I am up there too late in the season, that I am too expensive, that I am too dictatorial demanding a minimum of two nights, that the place is let out for a week in July, that I am new, so that I am at the bottom of all the marketing arms with no reviews as yet and have no repeat business? Perhaps it's just me. Perhaps they all hate me. I must admit I am becoming pretty unpleasant with the ongoing frustration of it all.

So any results remain to be seen. At least I now have an online presence.

Which means that I can calm down, get away from my computer for a few minutes a day, and be a bit nicer generally.

And I remain firmly optimistic that very soon all will begin to gather momentum, and in due course I will be over-inundated with bookings. Watch this space!

Cracked It?
23/07/2013

Well, I was going to write about my perfect moment as follows:

Wow! Wow! Wow! I am reclining here in the dark, on my newly-oiled teak sun-lounger, with a full moon gazing down upon me through the gap in the trees, picking on Lidl's 70% cocoa solids 'dark chocolate with raspberries', enjoying a fag at the same time, and a chilled glass of Naked Wine's Mar del Sur; while Will lies back in the hot tub before me, using the moonlight to read a dodgy-looking novel called 'The Vincent Boys', the blue, orange and blood red disco-strobe lights flashing under the water of the tub; his tea, lap-top and i-pod next to him on the shelf by his head, music (some of which I know and actually quite like) blaring across the moor from the ghetto blaster, the gorgeous heavy evening scent of honeysuckle permeating all around.

The house is clean and tidy, the lawn and patio immaculate, the tubs of flowers and herbs still alive, my pots of cooking oil, beverages, preserves, baked beans, herbs and spices all in neat OCD rows in their kitchen cupboards, everything just as I like it, awaiting the arrival of our guests on

Saturday, while we catch EasyJet to Pisa and drive on to Siena, to stay in a luxury converted monastery (the sort of place prime ministers reside in during their holidays) to relax for a week with 14 other members of the immediate family, courtesy my lovely sister.

Tomorrow the window cleaner, telly man, hot tub man, and my 'Mr Fixit Team' arrive to finish everything off, while I live up to my new persona of 'Mad Mower of the Moor'.

I've just received a B&B booking for two rooms for mid-August for a couple of nights from a German family. I've bitten the bullet and opened up my B&B for every night of the year, weekends, school holidays, bank holidays, whatever... I've got to get some business somehow!

So now it feels as though we've finally arrived! We're going to be OK!

And the unforeseen bonus is that this holiday lettings/B&B thing means that I can spend time and money making my home really nice, just as I'd always hoped it might be, guilt-free - and get paid for the privilege. Bingo! All is right in my world!

Or was. I have now spent 45 minutes trying to get my i-pad to log on so I could tell you all about how happy I am and the bloody thing won't work. So I've had to come indoors, up two flights of stairs to my normal computer, and even that took another 20 minutes to sort itself out because we're so far from a proper broadband connection, and it is now well past bedtime at one o'clock in the morning, so I am going to bed in a bait.

Well I Never!
28/08/2013

I thought it would never happen. No one came.

And then suddenly - floodgates!

This is the first moment I've had, since before we went on our uber-luxury holiday in Tuscany, that I could properly put fingers to keyboard.

We've had breakfast in the dining room and in the garden, the weather has been out of this world, and we have developed what we call 'The Wydemeet Challenge' - a twenty mile yomp there and back across the most varied terrain of central Dartmoor, to 'The Warren House Inn' - the second highest pub in England.

I always offer to collect anyone who gets too tired on their walks, but have only been asked to once. The second person to complete the challenge was a Swiss twelve year old boy, who set out with the rest of his family at 10.30am, and returned at 6.30pm, ready for a sumptuous dinner at Prince Hall Hotel.

We don't have plans to start making it into a race at this stage.

Today I served my 100th breakfast since everything went mad. Phew! I am exhausted. I haven't been able to do or think about anything apart from Bed and Breakfast now for nearly a month.

Sashka is laughing her head off to see Lady Muck with her head down a loo cleaning up other people's poo. I have gone back to being a (relatively well remunerated) chambermaid - a job I last did when I was 17.

I thought this B&B lark was money for old rope to begin with.

Wrong! Instead, I have found I have never worked so hard, under such pressure, for such a sustained period of time, in my life! Well actually since I was publicising Ex succeeding in his world record attempt on the North Pole back in 2003.

My current guests comprise a jolly band of six from down the road in Plymouth, who were looking for somewhere remote to stay, so that they could make as much noise as they liked without disturbing anyone, celebrating their 26th wedding anniversary with champagne and several bottles of gold leaf cinnamon flavoured vodka. I wanted to give them an award for receiving my 100th breakfast complete with its 'Very Best Eggs In The World', courtesy Neighbour, but I couldn't think what the award should be, so I didn't bother.

Tonight I get my own bedroom back at last. I have been dossing down in whatever bed happened to be available at the time, with all my things packed into a green Tesco crate, as I moved from room to room. Last night it was Will's bed again (he was away at a party in Dorset, and I am dreading finding out what he got up to there), which is two floors away from the nearest available plumbing.

The past few weeks have proved an extraordinary and surreal experience. Ask me for 'sunny side up', 'easy over', 'egg over hard', fried, poached, scrambled, baked or boiled - I can do the lot.

It has been terrifying, but at last I am gathering up the blobs on TripAdvisor and everybody appears to be having a very jolly time here.

Hurray! I love my home being used for what it does best. A really good party!

I'm a Mole
30/08/2013

I feel as if I'm a mole. That's been underground for a long time and has suddenly emerged into the light and air, and who, all of a sudden, after days and weeks, has space in which to move around and stretch.

I've got time to write, play the piano, have a bath in my own bathroom, and celebrate with my dear little team the clear fact that my B&B and house rentals are, without any doubt at all, a resounding success.

I am such a perfectionist in my work that it has been something of a roller-coaster though. Sometimes it has felt that anything that can possibly go wrong will. And because I suffer from early onset dementia - well it feels like it to me anyway - I always seem to forget something. And I simply cannot bear to make mistakes. Or get told off. I have been moving around in a state of exhausted, permanent, apprehension.

All my guests have been extremely nice about this though, and many have just laughed at the inevitable errors of an inexperienced B&B proprietor.

My first four visitors, post God and the girl in the onesie, all arrived at once, and honestly, they were so nice, and so along the same lines as me, that I really felt, had they lived around here, they would have become close friends.

When the new loo lever went wrong, Robert mended it himself, and when the adapter for the silly continentally plugged kettles blew up because it was meant for 1 amp shavers, he personally drove to Newton Abbot to buy three sensible ones from the pound shop, and refused to accept payment for them.

A more mature couple, with the most delightful little dog called 'Spud', found that despite my changing all the tellies from 'Freeview' to 'Freesat' at late notice and vast expense, they still didn't work, nor did the light switch in their bathroom. Having silently lost my temper inside my head on both counts, I subsequently discovered there was nothing wrong with either - we had simply been using the wrong switches. I wrote down their breakfast requests, but then didn't read my notes and only gave them one poached egg instead of two, and forgot to lay any cups or glasses; yet despite all this I felt they became very fond of, and paternal towards me.

I have repeatedly not quite finished laying the table when my guests appear for breakfast at the time they said they would come down, and on one occasion I forgot to offer them tea or coffee! Sometimes I forget to wear an apron, or even put on shoes!

I have finally learned how not to over-book, with all the calendars I have to complete for every booking; but the worst moment was when I came back to find the kitchen awash. 'Agh, those delightful Swiss children have left the bathwater running with the plug in," I thought. But no - water was pouring through the ceiling above, into my £90 per night bedroom, 'Bellever'.

Meanwhile a car came up the drive, which was the guest that I had already double-booked, and who I had had to move down to Bellever from the poshest room, which he had asked for originally.

We sat at the garden table in the sun, as I had a Cava and a fag and explained the situation to him, while Malcolm hot-footed it over from Ashburton to help solve the problem, as the water continued to pour in.

Uncle Tom Cobley and All
09/09/2013

Tomorrow it's Widecombe Fair. This takes place on the second Tuesday of every September. It's a cross between a kind of Henley for the local community, mixed in with tourists coming from all over the place, even from abroad.

It nearly always rains so hard that the pony area, where we hang out with all the horse trailers, becomes a quagmire. Tomorrow's forecast isn't too bad, I don't think.

We will have to leave at 7.45am to drive around the one way system to arrive at 8.30am and be ready for Faye's first class - Best Hunter/Hunter Pony. She's also in the Best Pony and Best Rider competitions. The showground is very uneven and on a steep slope. Showing consists mostly of going round and round in circles with everybody else, then demonstrating a figure of 8 on your own, and finally standing still a lot.

Elwyn, Faye's bouncy pony, will hate the ground (like last year) but he's so pretty, and Faye has got to grips with him, so he should do well. She is Number 4; so it doesn't look as though the classes are going to be very full anyway.

Sashka is kindly cooking breakfast for my very nice guests, who will be coming along to join in the fun a little later.

What larks! I love Widecombe Fair, complete even with Uncle Tom Cobley in his ancient white smock astride his old grey mare (which I believe some years is a gelding).

Still Busy!
17/09/2013

Now the holidays are over and everyone's back to school I thought things might calm down a bit. But no! The bookings just keep on coming! I am beginning to wonder whether I might soon move back into my (the best, obviously) room, and then someone else books it! Good! I am very comfy in Will's hideaway in the attic, while the money pours in and he is away at boarding school.

I had wondered how logistically it was going to work, incorporating Faye's school run with preparing breakfast. But so far it's fine. If anyone wants a Full English between 8.05am and 9am Sashka is kindly available to help on Monday's and Friday's; and I'm here on Saturday's and Sunday's. Which leaves Tuesday's, Wednesday's and Thursday's for the odd occasion when this might prove a potential issue. In which case Faye will have fun enjoying a sleepover at a friend's house; or flexi-boarding at the school.

So all appears to be working remarkably well to date, and I'm looking forward to meeting six more guests/potential new friends this weekend!

Only Four Blobs!
25/09/2013

I think 'management of expectations' is critical to enjoying almost anything in life.

I was very upset the other day, because a nice, and, I believe, well intentioned, lady called Tina gave me the most fantastic write-up on TripAdvisor, with full marks for everything they list such as room, value, service, sleep quality etc; but overall she only gave me four blobs. This is worse than no write-up, as it will pull down my ratings. It's already made me slip down from No 34 to No 46 out of 172 B&Bs on Dartmoor. And I am determined to be Numero Uno!

I've been battling with myself since, about what, if anything, to do about it. Should I contact her? Was it a mistake? If it wasn't, I just don't want to know what she didn't like about my perfect home. Perhaps it was too quiet and remote for her?

But I've come up with an answer. I must make sure that these lovely guests of mine don't expect to find the equivalent of a Holiday Inn in my family home nestling in the wilds of Dartmoor.

So I've amended my website and told them! "Expect to come across drawerfuls of stored ski-clothes, family photographs and old lipsticks, the odd muddy paw-print and a shower with a mind of its own," I've written on the Home Page. I am very curious as to whether this is going to increase, or decrease, bookings. I don't really care either way, because it is all going so well that I wouldn't object to a bit of a rest. What I really, utterly, absolutely couldn't stand, is the idea of someone arriving with the wrong expectations, and being disappointed.

The most expensive room on offer, which I've called 'Hexworthy', costs a rather substantial £260 (£130 per night, 'including scrumptious breakfast of local produce', available only for a minimum of two nights), largely because it is my bedroom, and I don't want to go to the trouble of moving out of it for less. The result is that it must be the most pricey B&B bedroom on Dartmoor, so I think some of my guests are a little surprised to find themselves sharing my walk-in cupboard complete with underwear shelf, and the dressing table drawers all stuffed with unused nail varnish and body lotion. And to get rid of every carpet stain made by children and dogs over the past fifteen years would have meant re-carpeting the whole thing. So I haven't.

Instead we have to play on Wydemeet's unique location, and my magnetic personality. Seems to be working most of the time. I nearly cried when by chance just today I came across lovely Tracy's review, complete with the full quota of blobs, headed: "Perfection!!! Great Host, Wonderful Setting and the Best Night's Sleep away from Home in Years!!!!"

And I was most gratified by a recent American guest's delighted reaction when I showed him Hexworthy in all its glory. "Holy Cow!" he exclaimed.

Don't Steal Our Dog
03/10/2013

What has caught me most by surprise since I started this business, is how much our guests love our mutt, Twiglet.

They keep smuggling him into their bedrooms, where he leaves muddy paw prints on my best white Egyptian cotton bedlinen; and nearly all the comments in our Visitors Book appear to be more about him than anyone else!

Faye has started a website about him. It is called www.gotwiglet.com; and features lots of pictures taken by our lovely guests.

B&B-itis
10/10/2013

I can't think about anything else! Every spare minute - while Faye practises Ballade on the piano, or gorges herself on Nutella and B&B leftover bread for breakfast - here I am on my i-pad, checking my ranking on TripAdvisor and making myself frustrated and envious as I compare my marks with other establishments' 10 out of 10s on Booking.com. I had no idea I was so competitive. I think it's an addiction.

Further to my last post, I've been tweaking my website daily, so that when guests arrive they are braced to find no hanging space and a total absence of what I have rather cleverly referred to as 'slick, sleek, urban chic'.

As I said before, I want them to realize that I am the most expensive B&B on Dartmoor (I have started losing blobs under the 'value for money section') because of (1) the amazing location, and (2) my brilliant service and personality. Not because I offer immaculate interior design.

I've pulled back from the 'you may find muddy paw prints, and the shower's temperamental' allusions on my website, but I have still broadly hinted at such things.

Anyway, the results of my obsessing about my new B&B are now publicly available for all to see. I am inordinately proud, smug and boring about what I have achieved. Read on.

I had my monthly meeting with my local girlfriends (The Thunderbirds) plus partners last night, and asked them to play my new game. "Type 'Luxury Dartmoor B&B' into Google Search, and see what happens," I ordered them.

Hah hah!!! Up came Wydemeet!! SECOND!!!! Out of 180 B&Bs on Dartmoor!! Page ONE! Along with Bovey Castle and Browns Hotel in Tavistock! How clever am I? So all these hours and days spent giving myself headaches and getting irritable, immersing myself in Search Engine Optimization/SEO, has been worth it! Maybe I have a new career here!

So all is going according to plan, and my next stage will be to sack all the agents who charge me such a huge commission, and wait for guests to come flooding in to me direct through my own website!

Except that they're not. Demand has fallen off a cliff. Null pointes. Zero. I've got two more couples in October and then that's it.

Meanwhile I think I've booked the house out for a week over Christmas, to a lovely sounding extended family with small children and three dogs (eek); as well as receiving my first B&B enquiry for Summer 2014. Directly through my newly highly visible website, as is now usual. Preen.

So dear Sashka is back to working just for Lady Muck, who lies in bed til 10.30am, now she's got the chance to do so after all these weeks. The difference is that I am feeling financially secure again, for the first time since the marriage bust-up. Yes - those children will benefit from an elitist, privileged, divisive education, turning them into people who haven't got a clue about the real world. Why? Why do we kill ourselves to achieve that? God knows.

eBay Addict (reprise)
17/10/2013

Not only am I addicted to looking up Wydemeet B&B on Google and

TripAdvisor.

I am also, as you know, a total addict for eBay. With this new B&B business I feel I have an excuse to buy new (or sometimes old) things all the time, and at the moment I am making about 20 bids a week!

Yesterday I bid £2 for a black and white spotted apron for Faye, who has offered to clear up breakfast and tidy our guests' rooms for £3 per hr on Saturday, while I visit Will at his school because it is his 15th birthday.

My latest approach to using eBay is to press the 'time left' column, so up come all the things that no-one really wants, and with no time left for anyone else to make a bid. Try it - you'll find that eBay is selling a car almost every five seconds, lots of them at silly prices.

Anyway, my latest triumph was buying a carpet. A few years ago, at vast expense I stupidly covered our kitchen floor with that sisal grass stuff, where all the old bits of food go down the cracks, it shrinks if you get water anywhere near it, you can't wipe anything off it, and it stains with immediate effect. Well it did look nice on the first day. So to protect it I bought a rug from Trago Mills for about £90, which very quickly also got stained with all the gravy, coffee and red wine which we habitually spill on it.

Sashka has been desperately but hopelessly trying to make our kitchen look clean and hygienic for when I offer 'tea and cake' to my guests on their arrival. An impossible task. It actually looks a bit disgusting.

So what sort of flooring should I replace the sisal with? And how on earth much would that cost to get it all fitted properly? And then bingo. Brainwave. If I could get a big carpet just the right size, I could pop it on top of all the stained ones and no-one would be any the wiser.

So I measured up and put 'carpet 111" x 85" ' into the eBay search. And do you know what? Up it came! An all wool, earth red, unused carpet from Trago with its £299.99 price tag still attached! No bids, a minimum price of £60, and located not too far away in Truro.

So it's mine now. Malcolm kindly picked it up on his way back from Falmouth, and brought it here, collecting Faye on his way, the carpet sticking through the sunroof of his old Vauxhall Corsa (he had checked the weather forecast before setting off). He was gobsmacked to find it fitted my kitchen perfectly, with a 1/2" margin all the way around. He should have predicted my immaculate planning. With all the mank old carpets still underneath, it's so springy it's like a trampoline. I just hope nothing below goes mouldy and starts smelling.

Love
21/10/2013

"I'm a bit nervous, because I'm going to ask her to marry me when we come to stay," my B&Ber rang to warn me in advance.

"Oh no, now you've given me butterflies too!" I exclaimed. "But I know just the place to pop the question - down at the stepping stones, where the Swincombe meets the West Dart."

So after he disappeared with his girlfriend for 'a walk' on Saturday afternoon, Faye, her little friend from next door, and I excitedly put champagne in the fridge, opened our best Kettle crisps, lit the fire in the sitting room, arranged red roses in their bedroom, poured ice into the under-used Tiffany's ice bucket - a wedding present from my best mate; displayed under-used champagne flutes - a wedding present from my other best mate - on a tray, all ready for Wydemeet B&B's first betrothal.

As we heard the couple returning from their stroll, the girls were jumping up and down, poised to rush out bearing our gifts. "No, no - wait!" I entreated them. "What if she said 'no'?"

"Here they come!" shouted Faye.

"Has she got a ring on?" I asked.

"Yes, no, yes - it's on the wrong hand - oh no - yes, no - it's on the right hand!!!" cried Faye, and we all flew down to congratulate the happy couple.

4 WINTER OF DISCONTENT

Bed Ridden
28/11/2013

I've broken, or cracked, or bruised some ribs. I was walking along in the dark, holding a torch and a bucket, and tripped over a tiny ledge of the ramp up to the horses' barn, my ribs landing on my hand with the torch in it. The world went sssshhwwissshh, and then I was back to normal, and carried on.

At four in the morning, Faye came through to be sick in my loo. I was about to get up to look after her, and found I couldn't move. At all. Not even raise my head.

So despite having contracted some dreadful virus, she found herself having to call the NHS, and a couple of hours later, after driving round and round the Dartmoor lanes in the dark, a bloke turned up in his car. If I couldn't get myself to the loo, I was going to have to go to hospital – my eleven year old Faye wouldn't be able to deal with bedpans etc.

He spent a further couple of hours filling in forms, gave me some morphine, and finally called an ambulance to take me away.

One more try to stagger to the loo before being rolled onto a stretcher, and I made it there, on my own. My God did I feel ill afterwards though. Apparently I am 'drug intolerant'. I would imagine that is a very good thing.

So the ambulance went away again, and here is the result. I can hardly get out of bed, and have to come up with clever ways of rolling onto the floor in order to reach the lavatory. Six weeks they say it will take to get better.

Well call that three. Or two. I am a single mother with children to organise, a business to run, and horses to exercise. I can't afford to be out for one day, let alone 42.

So this morning, after ten days in bed, I have hauled myself upstairs and onto my computer, to tell you how I've been spending my time.

Shopping.

I've lost count of how many pairs of jodhpurs and electric blankets I've bought. So far I've got four pairs of jods, and Faye's got three, and four electric blankets have been delivered. Also a cream coloured set of tea, coffee and sugar tins, and a 'Rock Box' - which is a very groovy very loud amplifier which works with blue tooth so that you can download current backing tracks to accompany Faye loudly, turning flute practice into fun.

I have also been learning things. I now know more about showers than anyone in existence, and we've got the wrong one. That's why it works all funny. So I've bought a new 'second-hand twin-ended pump and thermostatic head' to replace it with.

Satellite broadband! It's coming on Saturday! This will add years to my life, as it will finally put an end to the hopeless service we receive from BT, thereby reducing my stress levels by about 98%! It's only £500 to install with a hideous white satellite dish, and £28pm thereafter for speeds of 20mb/s. That's 153 times faster than what I have now!

Android mobiles! Yeah! You can use your mobile without a phone signal via Wi-Fi! I've bought two by mistake. One will have to go to Faye for Christmas.

Renewable Energy Sources! A windmill, heat exchanger, bio-mass boiler, solar panels? Or the whole lot?! A company is calling me tomorrow to discuss it all.

I am truly a woman of the modern world. With a broken rib or two.

Poor Lonely Me
28/11/2013

This Christmas I shall be all by myself in the cheapest B&B on Dartmoor, while my two children wake up to their stockings with their father in his new luxury pad in SW6, and go on to join their cousins in Sussex for a jolly family Christmas Day.

We originally bought Wydemeet as a 'Christmas Home', which it is perfect for, and swore to spend every Christmas in it, for ever. And now I have rented it out for another family to enjoy.

Hurrah! I am free! I have been struggling to prepare a Christmas meal in a 2-ovened Aga for sixteen years now, without a break. No time to catch the Christmas telly! Not a chance of attending Christmas Eve and Boxing Day meets. Just stress stress stress as to how on earth I will get the roast potatoes brown and crispy in an exhausted old Aga.

So I've organised this arrangement on purpose for this year, and I just can't wait for the 'me time' to begin. I shall be on that horse, jacuzzi-ing at my health club, coming back from parties (if I get asked to any) to someone else's lovely, warm, friendly, cosy house, and having breakfast prepared for me every day.

And on the day itself, lovely Malcolm is preparing Christmas Dinner for me, his wife, their daughter, my Mum, his wife's sister, and any other waifs and strays who knock on his door, I assume. How modern!

So I think it's going to be really, really fun! (Although I do think that I'd like my children back next year.)

Yet More eBay Madness
28/11/2013

I have just bought Faye a flute which cost more than my car. It's solid silver - unlike my car.

I bought it mostly because it was a quarter of the price that I was expecting it to be. Her teacher had told me that a silver one, called a straight, open-holed Yamaha 481 or something, which professionals use, would be around £4000. So when I saw this one advertised for £1100 on Gum Tree I just ordered it then and there.

I'm wondering whether Gum Tree is the next eBay. You can advertise on there for nothing.

But I think, despite its best efforts, it might be a portal for prostitution.

Two people rang up in one morning, directly after I'd posted an ad on it for Malcolm's massage business. Sashka answered the phone, and not being briefed said "No, this is not a massage parlour, it's a bed and breakfast business," and hung up on them.

Aaggh! So that's two even fewer customers for Malcolm then. I returned the next call from a chap called 'Dave' asking for 'Mary'. Well honestly - there's a pic of a bloke massaging someone who's fully dressed in the ad; and the copy is all about long term pain relief with particular reference to backs and trigger points. I left a message on his answerphone saying so, and guess what. Dave never called back.

My final enquiry came from someone trying to get me to pyramid sell health food products. Eh?

I might go back to eBay.

And now, to make things fair, I suppose I'll have to buy Will a new sax. No doubt this will be made from solid gold, and will cost more than my house.

What I Love about Running a B&B
12/12/2013

I have just said goodbye to my latest guests. They have been a complete larf and generally brilliant, and I am going to miss them. I am smiling warmly to myself now, just thinking about how funny they were!

In fact this weekend is going to be my first weekend without guests since

July! Time for a well-deserved lie-in! Except we get those anyway sometimes. Last weekend I served 'my doctor' breakfast at 5pm! It suited us both very well.

I have been amazed at guests' reactions when I ask them what time they'd like breakfast in the morning. They nearly always say, "When would suit you?" I mean WHAT???!!! I am here to serve! That is my job! Breakfast, anywhere, any time, whatever anyone can think of, except kedgeree because it makes the whole place smell.

Sometimes I almost have to force guests to say what will suit them, everybody is so astonishingly nice and obliging. Inside my head I am often trying to convey what I really want them to say by telepathy. I concentrate hard, focussing on their brain, saying "Say 10 o'clock, say 10 o'clock!!" and usually they pause before replying with "Would 8.30am be too late?"

Well now I am sad that my latest couple have left, because I have had to go around the house turning off all the radiators and the wall lights (which I only use on special occasions because they are very expensive on bulbs), and I won't have any more fresh flowers now until my next guests arrive.

It's 'family make do' time again. Horrid cheap plastic longlife croissants, nasty spreadable Lurpac, grotty bland orange juice with no bits in, and processed bread are what we live off when there are no guests around.

Before I started the B&B business my house was becoming a tatty old mess, to such an extent I felt like moving, rather than attempting to get it sorted out.

The very idea of porcelain tea cups, scatter cushions and throws in each bedroom did my head in. Getting everything immaculate with not a single 'curly' anywhere to be seen (a disgusting word I have learned through my recent addiction to Channel 4's 'Four In a Bed' - a reality TV show featuring competing B&Bs), no flaking paint, and no dust even on top of a 7' wardrobe, filled me with utter horror and dread.

But nine months later, I wander around my establishment with its cut grass, swept gutters, filled tubs, clean patio's and (almost) everything working, including the mended glass pane in the dining room window that had clearly once had a bullet shot through it at head height. I'm feeling good.

And also cold, until my next guests arrive and I have an excuse to heat the whole house at 20C all over again.

A Thoroughly Modern Christmas
30/12/2013

Granny sat on the squishy white sofa of the main room in Malcolm's house, sipping a cup of tea, while Sonya, his wife, completed the hoovering. Malcolm basted the venison haunch, I positioned the presents under the tree, and Malcolm's 19 yr old daughter emerged from the bathroom, radiant, to join us for dinner at 5pm.

Malcolm, Granny and I had returned from a hobble along the River Dart in the rain - Malcolm nursing a broken heel; 83 year old Granny with her dodgy ankles; and sulky, childish me, loved and treated as 'tiresome' in equal measure by the sensible adults immersed in conversation pottering along ahead of me, as I fiddled, staring at the ground annoyed at what - I'm not quite sure, with the toggles on my oversized anorak.

I am polar opposite to Malcolm's wife, who is much cleverer and kinder than I am; and she is even more polar opposite to my Mum, being an intellectual liberal, while my mother was quietly at a total loss as to why we hadn't organised the entire day around the queen's speech.

But we all ended up having had a very jolly time, and finally wandered back for a B without the B, 100 yards away, alongside the A38 dual carriageway, where Malcolm had booked Mum and me in for the night.

We were the only people in its 20 bedrooms. It was warm and quiet, with masses of hot water, clean, comfortable beds, and a peaceful view of the carpark directly outside the window, and quite a good sandwich breakfast the following day from the garage next door.

Perhaps that's really all you need from a B&B?

Christmas Hols
05/01/2014

Pandora (13) is giggling on the computer next to me, enjoying her first Facebook flirtation with a boy called Ted (12). Ted says he loves her.

Thi is my first visit for a month, to what's laughingly called my health club. It's neither healthy (we've just shared a chocolate brownie) nor a club (a small glass of wine costs a fiver and members don't get to share out the profits - those all go to that bloke with the woolly jumpers and the beard, who also owns an airline amongst other businesses, and who, unsurprisingly, smiles a lot).

2014 is about to begin. B&B proper.

Since my lovely funny guests, I had a family of rock climbers, and then three days in which to get the house ready for its Christmas rental.

I mind so much that people are happy in my home. I waited for the rental family's arrival with bated breath, having booked myself into my B&B the previous night, to ensure I didn't crease anything or leave any drips on the basins of my immaculate home before my guests arrived.

In the event, they turned out to be the perfect 'fit'. Three siblings, their families, and a grandparent. Just like our own family Christmas of 2012. I was quite emotional about it. "The house is made for you," I said, as I let them in, "I am so very happy that it is you."

I will never know how much I should have enjoyed eight nights of me-time. I wasn't well and had lost my voice for almost the entire break, but despite all of that, I spent most of it talking, and the rest of it trying to get my voice back. Nothing is ever quite as much fun as it should be, when you only feel 90%.

Home Sweet Home
12/01/2014

This is only the second weekend I've had without guests since everything went mad back in August. It feels strange to think I am earning a living from B&B, and yet this week I have been almost entirely uninvolved with the business. It is nice to have my home to myself and use whichever loo I feel like, whenever I like!

My last visitors were a sort of hybrid between guests and friends. I am very fond of them, but hadn't seen them for nearly a decade!

Here was a murky B&B area. Already some best friends have changed their minds about visiting me because they were not sure about coming to see me and taking up a potentially profitable bedroom, whilst strangers wander about the house. The result is I haven't had any friends or family - not even Mum - to stay since it all took off.

I also rather foolhardily gave away a free night at a recent charity pledges evening. I begged my mate Richard, who was attending the dinner, and who had persuaded me to part with the night in the first place, to bid for it.

Thankfully, he kindly did - he bid £90 for a night in my Dartmeet Room, which hopefully is good news for everybody. Why I was so keen for Richard to win it was so that I could get away with providing domestic worn-out un-ironed sheets which I wash at home, no 'hospitality trays', and a relaxed supper and breakfast with cheap orange juice in the kitchen with me. Otherwise my little gesture might have turned into a rather time-consuming, expensive, generous one!

Richard is looking forward to his visit very much I think, and in the meantime, I like to believe my friends-who-paid had a nice time too. I gave them rather a late dinner on the first night (there was just so much to catch up on!), and they took Faye and me out to the local pub on the second. I provided them with my best quality ironed Egyptian bedlinen, designer toiletries, and hospitality trays complete with ground coffee, cafetieres, and fresh milk-in-a-thermos and biscuits as usual, but didn't do the room-straightening thing, as it felt more intrusive with people you know.

Our final evening was spent in our cosy sitting room in front of its log fire, listening to their son playing some of the hardest concertos ever written for the flute, as a YouTube backing track streamed through Faye's RockBox - a rather successful new use for my satellite broadband.

Grumpy Old Woman
19/01/2014

My phone's been down for over two weeks now.

I have sued BT twice before, and won both times - £3000 altogether. It's cheaper for them to give in and pay the fine than to cover the fees of a solicitor to face me in court.

My satellite broadband has come into its own bigtime. Not only have I been able to download or stream or whatever you call it Christmas Day's Downton, but also it has meant that despite BT's best efforts, I still have internet access, retaining both my sanity and, hopefully, an acceptable route by which potential guests can reach me.

However, I am shortly going to lose my temper.

They told me it would be mended last Tuesday, but that day they mended everyone else in Hexworthy but me. So then they accused me of an internal fault which would set me back £130. I don't think so. Then they kept telling me to phone them to confirm an engineer's visit tomorrow.

How can I, Dear Liza - my phone's down! They sent seven texts to this effect, and then an eighth saying that actually they're coming on Wednesday. And then a ninth to say actually they're coming on Monday. All communication via some chap in a call centre in India called Edwin.

If I lose my temper, I've discovered a new way of causing trouble, which is much simpler than going through all the Small Claims hoops. You just condense the story into however many words and stick it on Twitter. I've already tried this with great success with Hertz, who refused to answer my emails. They got back to me within 30 minutes!

My next victim is likely to be Tesco's.

Tesco has advised me that they are automatically going to take £504 out of my account to re-insure Marvin, my Ford Focus. Well a quick check on Go-Compare reveals that I could insure with Tesco again for literally half that amount direct online, or with Swift Cover for £245.

I think this automatic re-insuring for twice the market rate thing is a racket.

So I've paid Swift, but, without a phone, how do I prevent Tesco from going ahead and gnabbing £504 off me? There is no email contact address anywhere on their banking/insurance site, and if I post a letter it will arrive too late.

So I emailed the Tesco Beds & Linens department advising them of the situation and requesting them to forward my email to the relevant department. They've refused, citing financial directives or something. Well you can email any other insurance business. So I've told them no wonder everyone's turning against Tesco, and I'm feeling another Twitter coming on. I just need to ask Miriam, my ex-policewoman friend, to remind me of the procedure. I've already forgotten how to work Twitter.

Taxi Service in Jaipur
19/01/2014

Very occasionally I receive a comment on the endless drivel I write on my blog, which I find very exciting!

The other day, I clicked on each of the comments, to find out who of my friends had been supporting me with lovely uplifting responses to my various observations.

I discovered that every single one was simply an ad for a taxi service in Jaipur. So I have deleted them all. Dejected of Wydemeet.

Who Hates BT The Most?
04/02/2014

BT has seen fit to leave me with no landline service now for over four weeks.

No less than three of my 'charm' of men-mates have been shouting at them, all thwarted by nice ineffectual chaps from India, who continually send me texts with conflicting messages that I can't get because there's no mobile signal here. Various representatives from BT also try calling me almost daily, surprised to find that no one answers the mobile - because there's no signal. As they have been told on so many occasions. You can't return any of their calls, as surprise surprise, BT doesn't seem to have an answer phone. And anyway, I don't have a line to call them on.

No one from BT has turned up for three appointments now. One text that I eventually received, (I had to drive through the elements up to the cattle grid to get it), told me it's an internal fault, the next that it's an external fault which will be mended within a couple of days, and the next that it is an external fault which requires planning permission, is affecting a lot of people, and there is no date given for repair. On one occasion I received 45 identical computerised texts running, acknowledging receipt of one of mine.

Funny how BT or Open Reach or whoever they are, have managed to mend Neighbours' phone (they live at the end of the line 100 yards away from me) twice, the van driving straight past my gate, while all this has been going on.

Thank goodness for my satellite broadband which battles on through the gales, snow and hail, and allows people to contact me without too much trouble.

Everything else, apart from the electric gate, is withstanding the worst weather that Dartmoor has thrown at Wydemeet in the 20 years that I have lived here, really rather well. A part of me is pleased and relieved, and a lot of me is delighted while Faye and I snuggle down to watch telly in front of the fire in the cosy sitting room, as the rain lashes against the window.

There was snow on the way to school this morning, it's just finished hailing, and now the sun's out, with a chill wind.

I couldn't face my regular Tuesday ride, and am preparing for this weekend's guests instead. They will be ably looked after for a couple of nights by Faye (11), her Dad, and Twiglet, while I see my seven best friends from university in Somerset.

We've Won an Award!
04/02/2014

Faye and I have won a prize in the Scoot Headline Awards!

We are to be presented with our trophy and certificate by someone famous called Ebony Feare at a glittering ceremony on April 28th at Milbank. And if we attend that ceremony, we qualify to win another award for 'National Business Leaders', and go to another presentation, as well as getting our entry included on a CD!

We were very excited at the prospect of going up to London for a sit-down dinner surrounded by lots of other successful and knowledgeable B&Bers, all dressed in their best lounge suits and frocks. We thought we'd pick up even more tips than we have already from watching Four In A Bed!

But then I realised that, as far as I am aware, no one from Scoot has ever visited Wydemeet to check us out, nor, I don't think, has anyone ever booked Wydemeet through them.

What I do know is that I enjoyed completing their competition form in my best PR speak, and that appears to have done the trick! Hurray!

We thought we'd still go, until I read that, as far as I can gather, the event just offers light refreshments, and it's during a school day, and it costs £150 + VAT for two, so we thought we'd give up and let them post us our award instead.

I'm still wondering what we've actually won it for?

£5000?
05/02/2014

Last night I sued BT again, for the third time, on this occasion for £5000.

It takes about five minutes to sue someone, if you go through the online small claims arrangement. You're allowed 1000 characters to describe what's happened and why the defendant owes you however much you're asking for. I need 1000 pages to list all my grievances against BT! The stupid computer wouldn't let me send my completed form through for ages, and eventually I discovered this was because you're not allowed to use a '&' in your copy. So I changed it to 'B and B' but the finished version came out as 'Band B' so I hope they don't think I'm a rock group.

I claimed for pain and suffering - the worry that I have been through, and the misery Ex has suffered, unable to make his daily night-night call to Faye; lost earnings and reputation for my B&B business, the cost of my satellite broadband dish, my HTC Orange mobile with its special built-in Signal Boost app, wages for Sashka to wait around while BT failed to keep its appointments, and an Orange 'Signal Box' which I'm going to be forced to buy at this rate. Trouble is - I can't call anyone at Orange, or what's now called ee for some reason - to ask them whether their new Signal Box thing will work here.

The summons gets sent direct from the Court to BT's head office in London. This exercise has cost me £100. Even if I don't win anything, it will have been worth doing, just for the satisfaction of knowing that I have caused them some inconvenience!

Tree Down
05/02/2014

Wydemeet is probably the most remote B&B on Dartmoor. Or possibly, even, south of the Watford Gap!

At least that's what I have written in my advertising blurb. I expect it is - we're at the end of a 3/4 mile dead-end lane which looks private, but which is actually a 'public highway'. Occasionally snow ploughs with 'Motorway Maintenance' written on the side can be seen making their way along it, just outside our gate. I think uniquely, we have footpaths and bridleways stretching in every direction from our house, and we're 800 feet or metres (I forget which, but high enough to be bleak and cold) above sea level.

The school run to Faye's place of learning, just outside Tavistock, is a twice daily, 26 mile round trip of absolute pleasure. We start by going up a steep hill, and then we go down an even steeper, very windy one, over a bridge, and after a couple of miles we meet the main Dartmoor B-road that crosses the moor.

This is primarily used by prison officers who fly up and down along it at 100mph, even though it's got '40' written and circled in white at regular intervals on the tarmac, bright enough to make the horses shy.

So I need to have a 4-wheel drive in case of ice, hence Bill.

I have never seen anything like this weather, and have been out digging ditches in the field to divert the water and preserve what's left of my drive; thrusting my arm down pipes and gutters, pulling out gunk and leaves, to stop the water flooding over into bits where it's not supposed to go.

This morning Faye and I nearly reached Huccaby Bridge, to find a tree fallen across the power lines and over the road. This resulted in a 30 minute diversion to the next bridge available, and meant for the second time Faye was unable to be presented by the headmaster I mean head teacher with her certificate for 'Musician of the Week' in Morning Assembly.

The phone, obviously, remains down, but so far broadband, oil and electric power are intact. We have a couple from Norfolk arriving to stay tomorrow. They are bringing wellies and macs. I'm hoping they're not going to need torches and a gas burner as well! In the event that we do lose power, ironically we will have no water (it's electronically pumped up from a borehole and pure enough to sell!) so I expect I will have to find us all alternative accommodation.

Two and a Half out of Ten
19/02/2014

We've just received a score of 2.5 out of 10 for 'service', on Booking.com.

That would have been the couple who booked Hexworthy at 1pm, for a 4pm arrival the same day. Hexworthy is our most luxurious room, costing £130 per night. Worth it, I hope, because of the comfort and spaciousness of both bedroom and bathroom.

I have been personally using Hexworthy for months now, so it needed a very urgent deep clean, which normally takes me three hours. Without the use of the phone, with minutes to spare, using my clever HTC app, I succeeded in arranging by text for some neighbours, who are also in the B&B game and therefore understand the problems, to kindly collect Faye from school while I did battle with my Marigolds.

So my guests arrived to no phone. No mobile signal. No electric gate. Weak Wi-Fi. And then to cap it all, Tesco's, with various ingredients of my guests' vegetarian breakfast on board, came and went without delivering anything, neglecting to ring the bell (the battery had expired) or shout for me, despite the fact that there were three cars parked outside the house, and three people inside it.

Through the window I caught sight of the Tesco van slowly disappearing out of the gate in the rain, and Tesco (who I couldn't phone) ignored the urgent email I sent, imploring them to send it back.

So fair do's. Sometimes you are just jinxed, especially living out in the wilds of woolly Dartmoor. Incidentally, my guests did describe their visit as "Welcoming, homely, awesome location, really quiet, would go again" so it can't have been all bad. I'm just relieved they wrote their review on Booking.com's site (we still rate '9.1 Superb') rather than on TripAdvisor, where we have slowly climbed to the No 14 Slot and rising, out of all 182

B&Bs on Dartmoor.

Phone Back!
19/02/2014

"BT's here!" shouted Faye. Odd. They hadn't made an appointment as far as I was aware.

Hey Baby I'm the Telephone Man leaped out of the driver's door.

"You've taken your time," I said rudely, and offered him a cup of tea.

It turned out that he's visited Wydemeet many times over the years, and knew exactly where all the boxes are. He solved both problems in a jiffy - a blown socket and two burnt out wires, caused by lightning on January 4th.

Meanwhile Neighbour next door has now enjoyed three visits from 'Open Reach' or whoever, who could easily have popped by and sorted us out, and all this nonsense about broken telegraph poles requiring planning permission with an open ended date given was just clap-trap sent in an automated message to us from a BT computer in India.

So now I was able to hear all twenty messages left on 1571 in the first week of January, one of which was a potential booking of the entire house for a week in the summer, sum total: £2500. I called the lady back and they've booked somewhere else now, no surprises.

Anyway, so now I am finally able to book an appointment at the hairdressers.

Broken
19/02/2014

It's half term, with lots of lovely horsey events booked for Faye at the pony club.

On the last school day, I drive home and just as I reach the garden gate there's a terrible stench and smoke pours out of the front of Bill the Shogun. I leap out before he explodes - he's petrol so he'll go up big and fast. The nice man from the AA joins us for breakfast and follows me to Super Sexy Dick's garage, where the problem turns out to be simple – a stuck brake pad.

The next day, Faye is entered for the Intermediate Trec competition, which includes some people who represent Great Britain. I've put her in this grown ups' class so that our slots are at about the same time, so we don't have to wait around too much. And so that we don't have to get up too early.

Faye comes fourth out of six - not bad! We also enter the Pairs together - it is a very special thing to be able to participate in the same sport as your offspring. The weather has an extraordinary window and it is just beautiful riding across Woodborough Common.

The next day is a fun ride and another early start. While I cook our guests' breakfast, Sashka prepares the horses for Lady Muck (me) and my daughter. We are just about to set out through the horizontal lashing rain, to discover the trailer has a puncture. Ever resourceful Sashka swaps the wheel, and we are still early for the start. Faye's pony, Warrior, decides he is in charge, and he'll go wherever he likes, at his own pace - the gallop. On a scale of 1 - 10, one being a disaster and ten being brilliant, the day scores three.

After that is a show jumping lesson, oversubscribed and booked three months ago for £20. Bill overheats at the top of the hill and Faye has to ride home, while I am visited by the AA man again. This time it is a simple leaking radiator.

On the fifth day we have a Fun Ride of around eighty horses scheduled. I have been looking forward to this for months. I'm all dressed up and ready to go, to find that my wonderful mare, Panda, has lost a shoe, so that's the end of that idea.

Instead I drive to Newton Abbot to collect Will from the station after his daily parties of sex, drugs and rocknroll, or whatever they do instead these days, and Bill hardly moves, going through half a tank of petrol, and overheating again on the hills, as a funny orange light flashes. I limp into Super Sexy Dick's again and swap Bill for Marvin, who is waiting for a new clutch.

So much for Faye's next horsey event booked for tomorrow. We'll never get there now. I hope it pours so that we won't be too sad.

I think I might have had enough of old bangers off eBay. Next time I might buy a new car.

5 IT'S A NEW LIFE

Oll at the Weekend
21/03/2014

My Mum is the most supportive Granny in Faye's year group.

Funny. When I was at school she only came to one of my sports events in the whole time I was there - to watch me in the swimming team. But she arrived late and missed my 13.2 seconds of fame as I won the 25 yards U13s Freestyle, battling my way through the icebergs floating around in our unheated school pool.

But now, even though she lives 1 1/2 hrs away in West Dorset - call that two if it's her driving - she attends lots of Faye's events, and it is a real pleasure for us all that she makes the effort to come.

As we drove home in convoy after last Friday's Evensong (Faye was singing in the choir), as we entered the house I growled: "No one make any mess. We've got visitors arriving on Sunday, the house has been cleaned at vast expense, and we have no Sashka coming between now and then."

Within five minutes, dear Granny had walked a splodge of mud at repeated intervals, starting from the back door, across the hall carpet, up the stairs, and all the way along the landing carpet to 'Bellever' at the far end of the house, where she was sleeping.

I made myself scarce to a place in which to quietly lose my temper, while Faye somehow made the mess disappear.

I thought the kitchen was smelling increasingly of oil, while Granny and I caught up with each other's news over turkey breasts in white wine and

95

grapes - a signature dish I copied off Bridget Jones.

And by the morning my worst fears were confirmed. Both Aga and boiler were out of oil.

No oil means no hot water, no heating, no cooking facilities = no guests.

I have something called a Top Up System with the local oil suppliers, which I assume means they top up the tank every time they visit.

Apparently not.

Poor Granny had, again, to see the worst side of her middle child, as the air turned blue with my anguish. She gave up and went home.

This has happened once before, last time on Christmas Eve when the house was full of family, so I already knew that putting things right was not going to be easy. The oil supplier has no emergency number. There are no other local companies on the internet who supply oil during the weekend.

I called Malcolm, who said there might be a drop of oil in the second tank that I could run through to the first. Guided by his instructions, Ex dropped in to B&Q on his way down to Devon, after watching Will playing hockey, to buy some special spanners to bleed the system, but all to no avail.

Astonishingly, at 6.30pm on Saturday night, I tracked down a plumber new to the West Country, who came to sort it all out at 8.30 on Sunday morning. £150 later - Bingo! Lucky I dye my hair, or you would have noticed it turning grey as we speak.

Angry of Wydemeet (not again)
21/03/2014

I had a brilliant idea of how to get my own back on BT today.

In response to my £5000 small claim, they sent me a forty-ish page legal document, direct from their team of specialist lawyers, which was enough to scare the living daylights out of anyone, even me!

I am reluctant to travel all the way to Northampton to face these professionals in court, when I have every reason to believe that BT's Terms and Conditions cover them for every complaint I have made, not helped by the fact that mine is a residential, not a business, line.

Did you know, for instance, that if you fail to be at home for an appointment with them, they will fine you £139, whereas if they fail to attend the appointment, with or without warning you, you can only reclaim £10? How fair is that?? Anyway, I really don't want to be bothered to read through all the blurb to check the various ins and outs - as I expect there's nothing we can do about them. I bet BT and all the other Big Boys rely on all of their customers being equally lazy, and anyhow, what alternative supplier do we have?

But I was impressed by how spending £100 on suing BT finally, finally brought out their engineer straightaway.

So I have written to Sean Poulter, Consumer Editor of the Daily Mail. He must have been at the paper for practically thirty years, as he was on my contacts list when I used to do a proper job - PR for sunglasses, skis, sports watches, you name it - back in the days when I was a yuppie with a red golf GTi, living in Fulham.

I suggested to him that my plight might strike a chord with many of his readers, and that we are all bullied by the Big Boys and helpless in the face of a near monopoly supplying a necessary product which is not fit for purpose. That a normal person can't begin to understand the gobbledegook that comes back from their legal department if you try having a go at them; eg "The Defendant therefore seeks that the Court exercise its case management powers in striking out the claim pursuant to Parts 3.4(a) and (c) of the Civil Procedure Rules", but that these big corporates all start grinding into action if we invest a little in suing them through the small claims on or off-line.

I haven't sent the letter, but have forwarded it to BT News Office (who haven't replied yet) suggesting that we settle out of court rather than going to any further trouble and expense over the matter. Included in my email were links to two recentish articles remarkably identical to the one I am proposing Mr Poulter might run, if BT doesn't play ball. They are:

www.theguardian.com/money/2012/jun/01/get-bt-listening-visit-hq#start-of-comments;

and

www.theguardian.com/money/2013/oct/13/bt-openreach-broadband-phone-fault?INTCMP=ILCNETTXT3487.

I'm feeling a bit nervous now, as it's possible I might have broken some law(s) over this, but what will they do to me? Fine me? Caution me? Or send me to prison? I've always thought it might be interesting to go to prison if I wasn't incarcerated for too long. Better than girls boarding school anyway. Free heating, ensuite facilities, food cooked for you, and the washing up done. And I bet there are some other inmates in there who would be all too happy to join me in a moan about BT.

Bags I Lidl
21/03/2014

The people I bump into most often at Lidl are my fellow local Dartmoor B&B proprietors. Don't tell anybody!

I generally use Lidl to stock up on chocolate, scent (it's called 'Suddenly' and at £3.99 for a bottle was highly recommended by the Daily Mail recently), smoked salmon, gravadlax, individual steamed haddock with broccoli dinners, frozen paella, kangaroo, ostrich, reindeer and crocodile steaks, and stuffed duck.

But the best moment of any Lidl visit, is if I succeed in accurately guessing the number of bags I've got to buy in advance at 4p each, to pack away all my goodies in. Four were enough to carry £120 worth of groceries, as well as a broom and a rake, last visit.

Queen of the Road
21/03/2014

Sometimes it feels as though everywhere I look, just nothing, absolutely nothing, works.

After six weeks of no telephone landline; all four 'new' handsets bought off eBay turned out to be faulty; three months of no electric gate; outside lights with minds of their own; no oil; pipes requiring bleeding; leaking overflow causing mildew in the bathroom; blocked macerator; stupid shower; leaks under the bath; the electric plug has come off the horse trailer which also has yet another puncture; Marvin the Focus needing a new clutch; and Bill the Shogun seems to be on his last wheels, so that despite the fact I own two cars, I am stranded. I did actually begin to shed a few tears about all of this, which isn't like me at all.

And then a little glimmer of light began to twinkle in the distance.

The first amazing thing was that the Princetown Mower man came and collected my mower and strimmer the day after I asked him to, and a couple of days later brought them both back, fully serviced! That's a first! Normally it takes a month!

The landline eventually got sorted out (it went down again last Sunday, but one look at my file and BT fixed it again within hours!); I bought a fifth handset for £7 - a Binatone for deaf and blind people which has big buttons, and is very loud; the gateman is here right now; Godfrey has replaced the bulb in the outside light; Super Sexy Dick's son, plumber George fixed all the bathroom things, and Super Sexy Dick himself has just brought Marvin back £550 later as good as new, and sorted out the trailer. Which just leaves Bill - not mended - sitting outside a garage in Okehampton.

Meanwhile, 'Queen of the Road' me, is driving 'The Beast' - all 4.2 litre engine of it, at a stately pace, averaging 28mph whilst consuming 22.3mpg of diesel - that I've been lent as a courtesy car by the Okehampton garage, while Bill is mended.

99

Desperate to get Faye to her horsey events, I rang all round Devon in an attempt to hire a 4x4. Nothing nearer than Exeter at £200pw. And then I found this garage where they offered to mend Bill while lending me a 2004 Toyota Landcruiser Amazon for nothing!! Well I asked them to take as long as possible over Bill, and they've still got him, over a week later. I am chuffed to bits with my fantastic alternative. I looked it up on AutoTrader and it's worth around £20,000! I rang the garage up and implored them not to hurry with Bill and kindly, they still haven't started work on him!

Things are looking up!

Are You a Clamp Silage Man?
23/03/2014

Sometimes my B&B guests very kindly give me presents. Occasionally tips even - that's particularly nice!

But last week I was given something much more valuable than that. £750 worth of chemicals for making silage with! Packed in little silver foil pouches.

So I immediately offered them to Neighbour, expecting to win lots of brownie points. But unfortunately they make the wrong kind of silage. It has to be clamp silage. I tried my next neighbouring farmers, but the same story.

So the little foil pouches continue to take up space (and I think they're supposed to be refrigerated) on the 'this needs to go elsewhere' table by the back door.

Twiglet in the Dark
07/04/2014

"I wonder how airlines deal with changing of the clocks?" I mused out loud to Faye. Our flight was leaving at 6am, and we had to catch the coach to the airport from Faye's school at one-in-the-morning.

She and I were enjoying a typically disgusting unhealthy lunch prior to a swim at my awful health club, now that term was over, to commiserate the fact that after all our efforts, she hadn't made it into the school's music competition final. Which, incidentally, was won by an excellent cellist, aged eight, playing a Grade 1 piece immaculately. Meanwhile the school's top music scholar went home with nothing, despite a particularly impressive advanced performance on her violin.

But who am I to judge.

"The flight's tonight - the clocks go back tomorrow," Faye casually replied, finishing off her microscopic 'for adult tums' spag bol, ordered off the kids' menu.

"No, it's tomorrow," I said.

"No, it's tonight," she said.

"Well I'm going for a swim and we'll find out when we get home," I said calmly, rattled.

And so it was that I found myself driving around central Dartmoor at 10pm, with the dog and his food and cage, mobile in hand, desperate for a signal, running out of petrol, trying to find someone prepared to look after him for a week, to whom I could deliver him immediately, two hours to go before we had to catch the coach booked to take us away on our school ski trip. My landline down again, thanks to my old mates, BT.

Gloves Off
07/04/2014

"My ski gloves are older than Matthew is," I declare.

Matthew is one of the teachers running the school ski trip. He is twenty-eight. My gloves are twenty-nine and still white(ish). They still work too.

The school ski trip comprises 32 children and nine adults. I have been clear throughout the planning of it, that I am not here to look after children, and all promises have been kept to, rigorously. I have nothing to do but be told when and where to go. No decisions to make. No responsibility. I don't care what the weather's like, what the hotel's like, what the skiing's like. It is just heaven being able to relax for a week. Even though it feels odd that there's been no break between attending the school music competition, swimming at the club, finding a home for Twiglet, coach, plane, coach, hotel, ski-hire place and revolting supper in the very basic hotel's very basic dining room somewhere in Italy, surrounded by eight year olds who've also been awake for 48 hours. I've rarely been happier.

Dancing on the Bar
07/04/2014

Eleven year old Douglas's parents, who live in France, arrive to find all the grown-ups gyrating on the bar, enthusiastically 'moving like Jagger' in the routine some of them put together last night over a few bottles of Prosecco, while the rest of us were engaged on a galati hunt with 32 children, two of whom are acutely allergic to nuts.

Soon Douglas's big brother joins him on the dance floor, to demonstrate 'Gangnam style', while ten year old Wilbur does an Irish jig to 'I am Happy". And we all are. This eclectic mix of adults and kiddies have bonded so well that no one cares who they find themselves sitting next to over the unremitting daily supper of rock-hard white rolls, cos lettuce, radicchio, olives, and tinned chopped carrots.

Prior to supper, evenings comprise two lines of adults and children sitting on their bums, back to the wall, legs in everybody's way, in the hotel passage, gaming, running their businesses, gambling, or checking out the talent on Encounters, as the free Wi-Fi doesn't work in our rooms.

Days involve forty-one Brits racing around the mountains on skis, from the first chair-lift up, to the last chair-lift down. It is extraordinary that every single child appears to be mad about skiing, however much crying takes place in between runs. Meanwhile the adults oversee the action from the centrally located mountain cafe, tucking into something called

Bombardino - an orange kind of advocat that you mix with coffee and cream - discussing children and parenting.

'Benevolent Neglect' appears to be our most favoured approach to the bringing up of our little loved ones.

The sun is hot, the sky is blue, the snow is perfect, the runs are virgin, there's no one else here. The mountain is our very own.

On the last day we are all such experts that we ski to France. Here we find noise. Hundreds of English people clogging up the chairlifts, all colour coordinated. Some wear orange caps, lots of tiddlies are crying, some young teenagers sport purple sweatshirts, others have sky blue ski jackets, all with the names of their schools emblazoned on the back. School ski trips have clearly become big business. The Bombardino's cost nearly double over here. We are glad to get back to the peace of Italy, where even the first-timer seven year-olds are now leaving me behind, as they ski their bittersweet last run, after a week of universal hilarity and joy.

It Never Stops
07/04/2014

My son Will has just broken his thumb, from punching someone.

The game is called 'Bum'. You form two lines opposite each other, and then individual children run down between the lines, as the others punch them as hard as they can. The modern version of 'Strip the Willow'. The kind of thing you expect your children to learn, if you are stupid enough to pay for them to attend private school.

This is bad luck because Will has been playing rugby all season at regional level, and is now engaged on an outward bound adventure course outside Barnstaple, which is clearly being run with all the ElfandSafety small print crossed, ticked and dotted, but the small print clearly doesn't cover the playing of Bum. So much more dangerous than rugby.

And now he's gone and punched someone in the hip, broken his thumb joint and so can't go skiing. Which means neither can his father nor his two friends, one of whom, it turns out, isn't insured. That's £1000 wasted for his poor mother.

So while I'm living it up in Italy with Faye; Will and and his Dad, Ex, have moved into Wydemeet, which, frustratingly, I have failed to let out either for my skiing week, nor for Easter. The result? No £2,500, and no B&Bers booked in either.

It is an odd thought - having Ex back living in what is now my home, while I'm away. Where will he sleep? Will, now fifteen, refuses to sleep in his own attic bed, as we found a spider on his lampshade in there last week. So he is currently in Bellever. No one is allowed in Dartmeet as it's made up all clean and ready, by Sashka, for our next visitors. I don't suppose Ex will want to go back into my luxurious, rather pink, bedroom, but I'm not too bothered if he does.

Also odd is that I have had more communication with Ex during my Italy stay, than with anyone else. First he is organising for the puncture in my courtesy car to be mended, then the third puncture on my trailer; then the dishwasher blows up and needs to be repaired; the landline goes down again twice more, and Twiglet is retrieved from the couple who took him in with a smile with one minute's notice at dead of night for a fiver.

Meanwhile both Will and Ex are clearly quite ill, with colds bordering on flu. In the end it becomes apparent that they have had a very happy week, chatting, bonding and relaxing; finally leaving me a bottle of Premier Cru Chablis and an immaculate home with everything working in it again.

So Much Fun
07/04/2014

We arrive at Grenoble Airport three hours prior to our flight home, to ensure there is plenty of time for a party of 41 to check in.

We discover that our plane hasn't even left England yet, and will probably be delayed by around four hours.

I don't care. I am still in a state of bliss. No decisions, no responsibilities, I will just do and go and be wherever, and whenever I am told. I am a remarkably obedient person for someone who is so cussed.

The airport is entirely choked with school skiing parties. 'Unicorn School' seems to have nearly fifty children, all in matching brightest blue.

The people at check-In are clearly like the ones in 'Airplane', enjoying mixing up and matchmaking the children from the different schools. Our coolest kid, Jonny, who went from nought to skiing helicopter turns in the air in just one week, is horrified to find himself seated between the window and a strange 13 year old girl from another school. He can't sit down, crouching against the wall of the plane, his mouth open in abject terror, until a teacher takes pity on him and swaps some children around, and he is next to a boy he already knows.

We are finally dropped back at school in a pitch black gale of horizontal rain at 4am, to find our cars without the aid of a torch or an umbrella.

Twiglet Hotspurs
07/04/2014

Up again at 9am to prepare a picnic to rival and beat that of Nemesis, at the annual football match of 21 of Will's friends from his old prep school, on its exposed cliff outside Boscastle. It is important to me that my picnic is sufficiently tempting to lure all the players to my car boot, in preference to Hers. The rain, as last year, is bucketing down and I have never seen the West Dart more torrential.

As it happens, it doesn't really matter how good my picnic is or isn't, because Will is captain of his side, broken thumb and all, and his friends crowd around him at the back of my cool courtesy car anyway. Will's team, "Twiglet Hotspurs", has won again, for the fourth year running, and this year, I promise Nicola, the organising Mum, that I will definitely get the huge silver cup, lovingly polished by Ex, engraved. The adults hover around, quaffing plastic cups of chilly Cava, as their hair sticks to their heads in the downpour, and the hard-core, which this year turns out to be only Nemesis (Bevan appears to be history already) and me, repairs back to Nicola's house for more.

Racing home afterwards, we still haven't unpacked, done the post, nor replied properly to B&B enquiries, risking the disaster of double-booking. But no, we can hardly sit down before it's the next morning and Faye's first official ride on Perfect Panda, my wonderful horse, in thick fog, high winds (only on Dartmoor do you get both at the same time) and rain so heavy it's as if God is pouring an endless giant bucket of water over the whole of Devon.

I have given myself a couple of days' grace from the B&B to squeeze in some fun – even more riding scheduled for tomorrow - and then it's back to work.

Hopefully I will have a shower that works properly installed before our next guests arrive on Thursday.

Scary Boiled Eggs
16/04/2014

How many ways are there of cooking an egg?

This morning I did my first omelette, complete with bacon bits and cheese. It worked fine, thank goodness, despite my little non-stick pan feeling rough after I've used it for lots of poached eggs. I have just ordered another, off my mate Miriam's highly successful website: www.onestopcookshop.co.uk.

Yesterday I prepared Eggs Royale - toasted muffins with smoked salmon, poached eggs and hollandaise. I also offer Eggs Florentine (with spinach) but not Benedict, as I don't always have ham to hand.

Another speciality on our menu is the 'Wydemeet Special' - one egg made as an omelette, the other broken into it like a poached egg. Nobody has asked for this yet, which is a shame, because it's a lot easier to prepare than it looks.

Most people ask for fried, poached or scrambled, even though I encourage everyone to ask for anything they can think of.

One of my guests, who was a mixture of Thai, German and American, made a special request that I cooked his scrambled eggs 'properly'. I was a touch insulted but hey ho.

The next morning I served him up what I considered to be properly cooked scrambled - soft and rich - and of course I had totally misunderstood him. He meant 'well done'; and ordered 'hard easy-over' for the next morning. I had to look that one up on Google.

Oddly, the most demanding thing anyone can order for breakfast is a boiled egg. Did you see that episode of Gordon Ramsay laying into a chef, yelling: "You couldn't even cook a f.........g boiled egg!!" Well poor bloke. They are very difficult to get right. Especially here, because I cook on an Aga. One plate is too hot to simmer water, and the other one is too cold. So I have to keep moving the pan around, which means that one minute it's boiling its head off and cracking the shell, and the next it's not boiling at all.

I have invested in various gadgets, including that pin-thing to let the air out, and a plastic oval thing which supposedly tells you whether the egg's inside is soft, medium or hard; but the main problem is that you simply can't *see*. I get butterflies every time I have to serve a boiled egg, wondering what my guest is going to discover when they crack it open.

I have been conducting 'taste tests' for best eggs over the past few months; involving eggs from down the road, eggs from up the road, eggs from a recent online date who subsequently dumped me by email, and eggs from Mum's neighbouring farmer. For size, taste and value, I couldn't fault Mr Dumper's contributions, but now that he's history, Neighbour's eggs are proving to be my mainstay. They are large, rich, orange, and very fresh. No one can fail with such eggs.

I have a lot of guests who say they can't make poached eggs, but they're easy if the eggs are fresh enough. My ultimate goal is to produce poached and fried eggs so perfect that, every time, they look like pretend plastic ones.

Ein wahr gewordenes Märchen
09/06/2014

Well I haven't a clue what it means, but I think whatever my latest lovely, review says, it must be nice, because as a result we've finally made it!

We're in TripAdvisor's 'Dartmoor National Park B&Bs' Top 10! Out of 183!

Hurray! At last! Thank you so very, very much everybody who has helped Wydemeet along in this journey!

The significance is enormous. I am massively excited, not just because now I can preen myself at my brilliance as a B&B hostess. It's mostly so that I can kick the expensive agents into touch, which means that my booking process is massively simplified and streamlined.

My goal is to run Wydemeet in the most efficient way possible, whilst not skimping on anything. Except marketing costs.

The downside of the review system is, of course, that every time someone comes to stay, I feel as if I'm being judged for an exam. It's critical that all my TripAdvisor reviews are lovely or I'll slip down the league again, and out of sight. How exhausting!

I quite approve of all this reviewing stuff that the social media are so keen on though. I think it works for raised standards all round.

This weekend we had eleven people and two dogs sleeping in the house.

You would never have known, as I tiptoed down three flights of stairs for a glass of water at 3 o'clock in the morning. All was completely silent, bar the occasional snoring of a slumbering guest.

The three rooms were all booked out, as they were last weekend, next weekend and several more times over the summer, leaving nowhere for me to sleep.

Faye and I found ourselves in Will's room in the attic, Ex slept in Faye's room, and Will (currently known as 'Tank' by his friends), and his mate, ('Little Man') both aged 15, slept outside in the teenagers' Den of Iniquity. All of us had to share the downstairs loo, which has no shower. Faye hasn't washed her lustrous golden locks for very nearly three weeks!

Faye spent the night thrashing around scratching her eczema, while countless enormous spiders, kept landing 'thump!' by my head on the pillow. So the morning's order of three Eggs Royale, three Eggs Florentine, two poached eggs on muffins with smoked salmon but no hollandaise, and two full English breakfasts, all at once at 8.30am on a Sunday morning, while Claire Balding discussed her faith with Rhydian on Radio 2, did my head in. I found myself sweating over the Aga, rather unattractively.

So I've made a major decision. Today I have booked out my smallest room, Bellever, for the whole of the rest of the summer, just for ME! (except for those nights when it's already been pre-booked).

How much is this going to cost me? Do I know? Do I care? What sort of a life is it when I'm moving around my own home living out of a Tesco's crate with no bathroom to call my own? So I've 'closed' out Bellever on my Freetobook form and now I am going to get some sleep.

And also, to preserve my sanity, I'm going to say 'non' to dogs, which are a total pain whining away when everybody else is trying to enjoy breakfast. I'm also going to ban sticky fingered children who leave jam patches on my mahogany table, and hot chocolate stains on my new chairs.

Will anybody ever book again?

The White Company
10/06/2014

'Added Value'. That's what I do. It's the most fun and efficient way of earning as much money as possible in the shortest time frame. Stack it high, sell it cheap, is not for me. Sounds like much too hard work. And more often than not turns out to be for ingratiates.

Non. The fewer customers the better, paying as much as I dare charge, means less work for yours truly. And happier, nicer customers too, don't ask me why.

I love The White Company's products - they're very added value.

When first setting up, I spent a long time trying to source their specialist trade B&B toiletries on the internet, getting nowhere.

After fruitless hours, I finally tracked the company down, under the umbrella of a distribution channel called Pacific Direct, which also represents Asprey, Conran, Floris, Elemis and Penhaligon's. But they wouldn't let me become a customer! Not good enough for them eh? What a bloody nerve!

Anyhow, last week I called them again, and now I'm allowed to stock their high fallutin' products! Hurray! I've clearly Arrived!

So I'm sitting here in my attic office, buried under 100s of titchy bottles of shampoo, conditioner and soaps. It smells fantastic!

The odd thing is, though, that however gorgeous I think the stuff is that I provide, most of my guests still use their own, and no one ever takes my lovely freebies home. How come? If I stay anywhere nice (those were the days) I throw everything available into my suitcase. OK sometimes I leave behind a dressing gown, or a sheet.

I turn up the heating, open the windows, leave all the lights and the telly on, and throw the damp towels with their mascara stains on the floor.

Wake up call Mary. My guests are so tidy that sometimes it's difficult to know quite how to 'refresh' their rooms!

Anyhow, my visitors get proper fresh orange juice with bits in, unpasteurised so it only has a three day shelf-life and it doesn't freeze properly, at £2.49 a pint.

Their Christy's bath sheets (not mere towels) weigh 650gsm (no idea what that means, but it sounds good). Sausages come from my mate's down the road and she feeds her pigs on leftovers from the Princetown brewery. My bread is artisan, and looks home-made. The other day I spent £40 at the local fete's cake stall, on five home-made cakes and six pots of strawberry jam.

I don't want to do the sums but with laundrette bills, shop-flowers, Sashka's hours, heat, loads of hot water etc I guess everything adds up to quite a lot. But so what. The cost of anything and everything pales into insignificance compared with agents' commissions!

And yet, despite all my best efforts, a particularly jolly Russian couple who stayed last week have just described Wydemeet as 'rustic' in their TripAdvisor review.

Death on Dartmoor
10/06/2014

We're going to be famous!

Peter's film is really happening! He's managed to get the money together for it, and it's being shot this afternoon. A proper feature film - not just an episode for telly! And Faye and her friend Julia are going to be in it!

The people involved with 'Dartmoor Killing' are all mega! Not only does Peter have a Bafta, bus so does his co-writer, Isabelle Grey, whilst his producer, Jayne Chard, and production designer, Amanda Bernstein, from Star Wars, are both Bafta-nominated. Wow, wow, wow! How glamorous all this is! Hurray! I hope it turns out to be a blockbuster!

Faye and Julia are to play two friends who are 'led into a web of mind games, sexual deceit and betrayal, on a weekend trip to Dartmoor.' We have to be on location later today at Poundsgate, at 5.30pm. We'll drive there direct from the girls' school rounders match.

Yesterday I had to pop into Tesco to see if I could find a pair of '90s-looking jeans for Faye to wear for the film. I discovered that Tesco stocks 'skinnies', 'very skinnies', 'boyfriend' (severely oikish), 'cut-offs', 'bootleg', and 'flared'. I was forced to buy flared (at £16!), as bootleg wasn't available in a Size 10, so Faye will look as though she's from the 70s, not the 90s.

Taking on Babbers
16/06/2014

Yesterday I bid for four Nespresso machines on eBay.

Guess how many I won? Four. Oh dear - where shall I put them all? And I don't even like espresso coffee that much.

They are called 'Pixies'. Two are Krups, and two are Magimix, and I got them for around £50 each, instead of the £100+ charged for new ones by companies such as Lakeland Plastics.

These machines are part of my drive to improve the 'product', or 'offering' of my B&B.

I have been looking at pictures of Babington House on their website, so that I can copy what they provide. Babbers, near Frome in Somerset, is where the pop stars go, or used to go, to pretend they were enjoying a country break, complete with borrowed willies, I mean wellies. It costs up to £400 a night without breakfast, and I am hoping to meet someone via Encounters Online Dating who would like to take me back there. It's my favourite hotel, and it's been many years since I was lucky enough to be able to visit it.

So, in my bid to emulate, or, of course, to outdo them, as well as the

Nespresso machines, I have also bought three white candles from Morrison's, some cotton wool balls, and a really nice little box to hide the tissues under.

A see-through bath in the middle of the room, and a TV the size of a garage, complete with Dolby surround sound, remain beyond me at present.

Rationalisation
27/06/2014

Hmmm. I might have made an error. In my extreme efforts at rationalising the marketing of my burgeoning new business, I appear now to be empty for most of July. That wasn't exactly the plan.

Having closed out 'Bellever', I now just have the two larger, more expensive rooms available: 'Hexworthy' with its morning sun, huge bathroom, private shower cubicle, bidet and trouser press; and 'Dartmeet' - evening sun, twin option, and lovely private view across the garden to the moor.

I've sacked all the agents – and now, well, this.

But honestly - with their commission, if someone were to book Dartmeet for a week, say, the agents would take a whopping £150! Mad!

And another problem. Those guests who come via the agents don't always seem to quite 'get' what Wydemeet offers. Not surprising really, considering the main agent is based in Amsterdam or somewhere, and it's staffed by people who have never heard of Dartmoor.

I keep being sent extremely nice Germans who erroneously believe we are a convenient central point for exploring the West Country, and are surprised and a bit concerned that there are no signs to the B&B, and that we don't have things such as wardrobes, and that our albeit satellite broadband is nevertheless still rubbish and only works in half the house.

The next most expensive items after the agents are Sashka's hours, and laundry, which come to half what the agents charge, and are absolutely vital for my sanity, or at the very least to keep me in a good mood.

TripAdvisor's doing its best, but it's a challenge to stay in the Top Ten when you've only got two roomfuls of guests writing up-to-date five-blob reviews.

And to maximise my visibility, I also need to keep coming up first in the Google Search Engines.

On top of all of this, what with originally 'closing out' much of July in an attempt to let out the entire house, and banning large bouncy dogs and sticky-fingered children, perhaps I've gone too far!

So I've just re-opened lots of July, updated this website to help with SEO optimisation, and crossed my fingers.

How the Hell Does She Do It?
30/06/2014

Help!

My rationalisation has definitely gone too far! I am STILL empty for the whole of July! Now I'm panicking!

OK - I have let the house out for the week of July 26th which means closing the B&B for a couple of days either side.

But I had thought that my marketing expertise was so splendid that my two glorious, luxurious rooms would fill up with last-minuters. Wrong. Nothing. Not a squeak.

On the other hand, I am really, really tired after a frantically busy June. I might get a lie-in on Friday morning when Faye is boarding overnight.

That will be my first, including weekends, in probably a month. So it's odd having our house suddenly back to ourselves after such an ongoing round of guests, especially with my lovely huge sunny Hexworthy room empty, waiting for someone else, instead of having me in it.

Yesterday I lay for an hour in our hot tub, which has been completely renovated at vast expense. As a result, today my ancient skin is even more dry and wrinkly than usual. Faye didn't even bother getting dressed all day. And we forgot to feed the horses.

I guess business is bound to pick up soon. We have been given yet another cry-worthy fantastically fantastic review on TripAdvisor so we retain our place in the Top Ten, and now I've fixed it so that you can book us direct via TripAdvisor too. I'm not sure how much that will cost, but I'm very interested to find out.

Tonight on telly it's "I Can't Believe That She Does It" or whatever the name is of the book by Allison Pearson. Ms Pearson once met Ex at some talk, and sent him home with a copy of her book for me, with a message inside saying "I can't believe how you do it."

The other day she was speaking about her sequel - a book about her teenage crush on David Cassidy - at Dartington 'Ways with Words' literature festival. I really love 'Ways with Words'. It's so beautiful, calm and peaceful in the glorious grounds of Dartington College, and everybody else is white haired and over seventy, so I'm made to feel young and glamorous too!

I went to see Allison, and told her that I hadn't managed to 'do it' after all. She commiserated, and wrote me another lovely message, which went something like "All men are bastards", on the inside cover of the David Cassidy book.

Actually I've checked, and she's much too nice to have penned such a thing. In fact she wrote "I think I love you" (with the 'think' crossed out and changed to 'know'). "Better Luck Next Time."

Going Up
12/07/2014

Sometimes, when I read what people have written about me, Faye and

Twiggy on TripAdvisor, my throat gets all closed up and chokey.

My lovely, lovely, lovely guests' enthusiasm has meant that, despite only being properly open for less than a year, and now only having two bedrooms available, so by definition having limited numbers of guests who could have written anything, we have risen to the grand position of Number 8 out of 183 Dartmoor B&Bs, and we're still rising!!

There isn't any real reason why we couldn't hit the Number 2 slot! We will never beat the Apple Tree in Tavistock into first place though. They've got over 200 rave reviews, whereas we've only got 37. The only negative comment they've ever had is that the car parking is a bit tight.

My latest wheeze is to make a hair appointment with the lady who runs The Apple Tree (according to my hairdresser she runs a salon in Yelverton, as well as being a B&B Proprietor), and have a chinwag with her and pick her brains about how she does everything so well, while she gives me a trim.

Renting Your House Out Is Hard Work
31/07/2014

The first time I rented out Wydemeet, it took Sashka, Kathy and me nearly two months of preparation, stress and worry, thinking through what needed to be done, tidying up the garden, the field, mending things, painting things, deep cleaning; sorting out and emptying all drawers; throwing things away etc.

We were treading on each other's toes, with one person turning radiators off and another turning them back on again; one person putting things away and another getting them out again; all my precious beyond their sell-by-date pots being thrown away and me picking them back out of the bin; Kathy providing me with a pair of curtains to hide my extensive plonk cellar from prying eyes; Kathy hiding what's laughingly called my jewellery so that I couldn't find it; Sashka worrying about children going into the horses' field in case either party gets hurt; me writing out extensive notes on how to work the Aga, the heating, the water, and what to do when everything goes wrong; Tesco crate after Tesco crate of the family's belongings all cleared out to be stored away in safety...

Well.

Last Monday I sat down for my usual coffee and fag with Sashka and her wonky knee (it's just her and me now, as Kathy has moved), and said,

"They're coming on Saturday. Please could you do everything so that I don't have to panic about it. I've just remembered we're meeting friends in Polzeath today; we're shopping and swimming tomorrow; I've got an internet lunch date on Wednesday; and lunch with Mum and my brother in Exeter on Thursday."

"That's fine," she said, and hobbled off to make up the first two of five bedrooms.

Wydemeet, being on Permanent Alert for guests, is in a totally different state of overall repair now, compared with how it was 18 months ago. This is one of the many upsides about running a B&B business. But there are limits.

11.00pm Wednesday: Faye, who was leaving imminently for an outward bound weekend in Wales, whispered, "I am so tired from all that clearing up that I feel dizzy, I can't do any more."

"No worries, I replied, I'll finish clearing up your Hell-hole room tomorrow."

6pm Thursday: Guests called to ask if they could come a day early.

"That's fine," I told them - I offer a platinum service. I replaced the phone handset and immediately called Sashka.

"Help! Help! They're coming a day early! What are we (you) going to do, wonky knee and all??"

"That's fine," said Sashka, "I'll rope in my daughter and niece to help."

11.00pm Thursday: I started murmuring to myself, "I am so tired I feel dizzy, I can't do any more," and lay back on Faye's unmade bed.

11.00am Friday: I came in from mowing so hot that I couldn't see through the sweat streaming down my face, bringing with it stinging mascara and sun cream sloshing into my eyes. To Sashka, who arrived at 7am and had just finished the strimming: "Sashka, I am so tired I feel dizzy, I can't do any more."

"That's fine," said Sashka; "Get out of my hair and go to your Mum's."

So here I am. Having done virtually nothing at all to prepare my home for a week of visitors; and yet, if they have read the blurb properly and genuinely enjoy remoteness, mostly thanks to Sashka they should be having a jolly nice time. Well I hope they are. I don't even know whether they're leaving a day early, or have just got themselves an extra free day simply through asking!

I'm sitting typing away, looking out through the rain and pine trees at the most exquisite part of West Dorset. My horses are happily munching away at their livery in Mapperton - one of the most beautiful spots on earth, with high, deep, steep valleys of pasture, woodland, and winding river, long gallops and views across a patchwork of undulating fields over to the sea.

I have just enjoyed one of the best rides of my life with Mum's delightful next door neighbour riding Mad Vegas; and the old banger Nissan made it from Exeter to the livery and back to Mum's house, a miracle in itself.

I haven't spent eight solid days with my mother since I was at school, but the only spat we have had so far was when she tried to make me eat some seven-day-old ham when there was a perfectly good quiche in the freezer.

This is truly one of the most enjoyable and relaxing holidays I have ever had.

And every minute that I sit here twiddling my thumbs - the money is rolling in!

I think I had better just pinch myself!

I'm Scared Stiff
08/08/2014

I am so nervous that I haven't been able to sleep properly for the past few nights.

I have entered Faye vs me in a horsey competition to take place in the middle of a forecast hurricane, on top of one of the highest hills in Dartmoor, this Sunday.

I've booked Sally to make breakfast for our six guests, while Faye and I rise before light to hitch up the trailer, prepare our horses, and arrive at the venue for not long after eight in the morning.

The list of other entrants has now arrived, and, as I expected, the rest of the people in our class are aged nine, like Faye's friend, Willow, on her pony Twizzle who is very hairy and slightly smaller than a Great Dane Dog.

Of the total 16 competitors, only three others have 'undisclosed ages' - meaning old. Although I did tell the organisers my age, and I wouldn't mind at all if they'd printed it. Personally, I think they ought to have a cup for the oldest combination of horse and rider, as well as one for 'Best Under Ten'. In fact I think I will donate one to next year's competition.

There are three stages to the 'One Day Event'. We have to learn by heart, and perform a dressage test, which means walking, trotting and cantering around in circles. Faye has never done one of these before.

Then we have to jump some painted poles, which fall down if you touch them.

And finally we have to canter a mile or two around a cross country course jumping brown fences, which don't budge however hard you hit them. In Faye's and my class, the jumps come up to your knees.

Both of our horses are big, scopey, talented and experienced professionals for grown-ups, used to jumping huge, solid, wide jumps 3'6" high from the gallop, and to doing all sorts of incredibly complicated gymnastics in dressage. So both of them can easily manage what we are asking them to do on Sunday, with their eyes shut, asleep.

But the big question is, with us two riding them, will they?

Six In Three Beds
10/08/2014

Yesterday, after cooking breakfast for six B&Bers, clearing it all up, and then preparing rooms for six more - missing the local fete as a result because I'd run out of time/energy - Faye and I finally reached Widecombe as the sun began to set, to walk the show-jumping and cross country courses, while Sashka's niece, young Maggie, plaited up the horses back home for £15, ready for the One Day Event today.

I was so tired I could hardly stand up. How Sashka does it day after day I have no idea.

The show jumps came up to our ankles, but the cross country course was quite a different story. Several of the jumps were too large for me to step over. Terrifying!

Finally, as we got back to the carpark, having walked two miles up and down vertiginous hills, a cry went up. "It's been cancelled!"

Thank God, in a way. Breakfast for six again this morning and I am a walking zombie. I think three rooms, or six guests, is too many if you are operating a B&B on your own, are over 50, and trying to do anything else as well. I have no regrets regarding my decision to restrict myself to two rooms in future.

Readership Breakdown
10/08/2014

Wow! I think that there are now at least eight people reading my blog!

The thing of particular interest about these readers, speaking as a marketing person, is their demographic profile.

About six months ago, after a year of searching, I think I finally began to find 'my blogging voice' - a sort of Bridget Clarkson hybrid - part Labrador, part Rottweiler.

And I thought I was addressing people like me - posh single mums,

Well it turns out not a bit of it!

My sense is that about 70% of my readers are dry, clever, witty men. LOVELY!

About 10% are my friends who live abroad and want to stay in touch.

About 10% are my lovely B&B guests.

And finally there appears to be somebody who is the mum of a schoolfriend of my son's. Eeek! Better be careful!

Home Run?
17/08/2014

Yesterday I bought eight slabs of home-made tiffin tea cake for £5 from the local Bring & Buy sale - all they had, in fact.

I've packed it in cling film and put it in the freezer. Tomorrow I will buy some 'cookie jars' - if that's what you have to call glass containers for biscuits these days - and display my teacake in our Hexworthy and Dartmeet Rooms. I hope people don't eat it too fast, or that could get expensive.

I've done this because the B&B at the top of TripAdvisor's Leader Board of Dartmoor National Park's 183 B&Bs features a lovely close-up pic of a jar of bits of teacake, with a brown hand-written label attached on a ribbon, saying 'home-made chocolate biscuits'. And all its reviews refer to these delicious titbits. So I am going to copy them (only mine appears to be a bit on the soggy side).

Otherwise on the face of it, there doesn't appear to be anything particularly special or outstanding about Dartmoor's new Number 1, which has somehow taken the place of the Apple Tree.

So my suspicion is that its owners are utterly delightful, and that they must offer an immaculate service, with delicious breakfasts including home-made compotes changed every day. And these nice owners, just like me, have presumably got wise as to how TripAdvisor works, and are using it to promote themselves for free. Good on them!

Meanwhile Wydemeet has been stuck in the Number 4 slot for weeks!

If you'd told me a year ago that we would reach Number 4 in just twelve months I would never have believed you. But now I know how TripAdvisor's system works - ie the computer checks out who's received the largest number of 5-blob reviews most recently - I am beginning to dream of the unimaginable possibility that Wydemeet might become Number 1 shortly!!!!!!!!

Wouldn't that just be completely amazing?!

Coca-Cola
27/08/2014

TripAdvisor is like Coca-Cola, the sensible South African woman at the other end of the phone told me.

I had rung the TripAdvisor helpline to ask how to award myself a five-star rating; and to qualify for the 'romantic', 'family friendly', 'luxury' etc categories that line the top of their page.

The nice lady and I were chatting about how they measure the blob rankings, and she was explaining that it is down to a secret coding which nobody is privy to, just like the recipe for Coca Cola.

Meanwhile, to get myself a five star rating, I have to contact Expedia, she told me. And to get categorised, you need to have lots of the appropriate words quoted in your reviews. TripAdvisor's computers look for these key words, so the more reviews you have, the more likely you are to get categorised.

I contacted Expedia regarding the star ratings, and five days later they got back to me, and advised me to ask TripAdvisor about it.

Meanwhile, Wydemeet continues to languish in the Number Four slot, and I'm not sure what else I can do, other than entreating an entire family of four to write individual reviews for me (providing they enjoy their stay, obviously) and see if that gives us the boost we need! Or should I simply give in, acknowledging that there must be something in the Coca-Cola mix that we're never going to overcome, and we'll never achieve that Number 1 slot.

Uncle Tom Cobley and All
10/09/2014

One of the purposes of the blog is to help make sure Wydemeet's website remains high up and prominent in Google's Search Engines.

But I think that in order to do that, blogs are meant to feature on the front page, and to provide useful information. No matter. We're high up enough already.

So, in order to do things properly, I should be including helpful info such as "On the second Tuesday of every September it's Widecombe Fair! Come and stay at our wonderful B&B from which to visit this Special Event!" (Never mind that to get there takes 45 minutes round the one way system.)

Well I forgot to include this useful tad of info in advance, so if anyone wanted to visit the Fair I'm afraid they're too late. It happened yesterday. You'll have to go next year instead.

At least this year Uncle Tom Cobley's mare was a mare and not a gelding. I think the last old grey 'mare' was so old that it died. This one belongs to my mate Venetia up the road, and was in her first year of standing around the large, noisy country fair, watching Morris dancers, and horses in fancy dress, from 8.30am til 5.30pm. She was very well behaved.

Anyhow, the point of this story is that Mad Vegas of the Rolling Eye, won A SOLID SILVER CUP for 'Best Local Hunter'!!

And my nervous little Faye, having begged "Can Louise (Sashka's daughter) ride her?" (to which I said, "No") came second in the Best Rider class! And, again, no tears either! Things are really looking up!

It would have been a perfect day, if only Twiglet hadn't bitten Carl's Racing Spaniel during the terrier race. Carl's dog had been winning up until that point. I've a feeling Carl's not ever going to speak to me again.

No Dogs is Good!
28/09/2014

Guess what. Someone wants to ask my advice! A first!

Whitelady House is a stunningly beautiful house near Lydford Gorge. It sleeps 12 people, and is run by my friend Kay, who has extremely high standards, and she has never received fewer than the full five blobs on TripAdvisor.

Well Kay invited me to meet her friends the other evening at the Trout and Tipple, so they could pick my brains about running a B&B.

I started talking to this couple, but found there was nothing much left to say, because they had already read the blog and I've put everything I know into it. But they said it was helpful. Hurrah!

I have had one or two further thoughts recently, though.

One is that I have discovered my new 'No Dogs' policy doesn't keep people away. Quite the opposite! It attracts them! Other People's Dogs are a nightmare! Worse than Other People's Children! They bark throughout the night. They whine during breakfast. They have to be taken out at 6am, the tramping around disturbing everybody else who's trying to sleep. They smell, and pant in your face. They poo in the garden. And completely distract their owners who can't relax in somebody else's house even worse than if they'd arrived with a two year old toddler! Who wants to stay in a B&B stuffed with horrible stinky, hairy, muddy, Other People's Dogs? Yuck!

So the answer is - borrow ours! Hello Twiglet!

Something else that has recently come up, is that not only is Wydemeet probably the best centre in Dartmoor for walkers, but also for fishing!

Apparently you can spend a day happily trout-fishing the Swincombe, which is 100 metres from our door, for just a tenner, while your wife relaxes in the hot tub, reads a book, or chats to me. And I'm told that all the best seatrout and salmon pools, such as 'Queenies', are within a walking radius of Wydemeet. No need to get in the car. No wonder the original owners chose this spot in which to build this fishing lodge! And I never knew any of that!

Yet only two fishermen have ever come to stay here, to take advantage of this extraordinary facility. Where are they all? I even have one of ghillie Brian's last home-made 'green flies' for anyone to try!

Another small point of interest came up recently, when some guests badly wanted to stay for only one night, despite our minimum two night policy.

I suggested an extra 50% charge, which they were happy with, and so was I!

And what should I do about single people staying? Normally I don't deduct anything from their bills, but try my very hardest to ensure that everything possible is provided, and they can use the house as if it was their own home. I will even go out specially to do any extra shopping that they might need. Not a trivial matter from this location!

I guess I might have my arm bent if circumstances decreed.

I so love the fact that in running a business like this you're completely free to make your own decisions/mistakes, responsible to no one.

Every guest who stays is quite unlike any other - each has his or her own totally new agenda and requirements.

I'm sure some hideous nutter is bound to turn up and rape me, tread mud up the stairs, knick all the silver, and award Wydemeet one blob, sooner or later ..

One Happy Return!
14/10/2014

Google Analytics sent me an unsolicited email yesterday. It had some very interesting statistics in it (I think). They're rather complicated to understand, so I don't really know if they're good or bad.

The email informed me that last month, out of 657 visitors to my website, 243 'exited' direct from the diary page. My blog clearly can't be very good then. What an insult! Except presumably those 243 visitors must have read a bit of my incoherent pointless ramblings, before exiting in disgust.

Unless most of those visits were from me, checking that no unsuitable comments from readers had been posted beneath my pros, requiring instant deletion.

So I still don't know exactly how many individual readers the blog is generating, because I can't work out which button to press to find out.

But even bigger news than that:

WE'VE GOT OUR FIRST RETURNS!!!!!!!!!!!!

So after a little over a year's operation, our first returning visitors have re-booked for a weekend in November! We can't be all bad!

They are one of our favourite couples. They were so kind when we knocked their drying gilet (one of North Face's best, worth £120), onto the Aga and it melted.

The whole thing is a birthday surprise, and represents a turning point. Some of our guests voting with their feet - in through the door, rather than out of it. How wonderful!

Just as well, because it would appear that I really have over-rationalised the marketIng, so business is a bit slow and I'm going to go overdrawn again soon, unless some miracle happens. I've re-signed up with the agents, so they can start taking all my money again. This is such a flexible business - you can turn it up and down, on or off, like the knobs on a radio!

Smells
27/10/2014

"Your house smells nice".

These were the first words that my friend's autistic son addressed to me, as he walked in through Wydemeet's back door.

Ahhh! Just one of the greatest compliments! I wish more people said things like that, when they visit other people's homes. I think different smells can be as mood-changing as different kinds of music, and I am verging on the neurotic about smells in this house.

"Dead mouse" is one that makes me freak out the most.

Our best cloakroom, that all our guests come into the house through, has been smelling quite strongly of dead mouse recently. What a way to greet them! The smell just wouldn't go away so I went mad on eBay, bidding for 24 bottles of pot pourri reviver, and three packets of rose, autumn mist, and lavender pot pourri's. Oh dear. I won the whole lot.

So I'm going to make quite sure that any smell of dead mouse is drowned out by dried bits of flower in future.

Living where we do, a mouse invasion is a constant threat, and they like to come in - between the inside and outside walls - when the temperatures are sub-zero. An immediate assault with poison seems to be highly efficacious (God I sound like Lily The Pink!). Apparently, having gobbled up the poison, the poor little things go off somewhere to drink, and die by the water source, and mummify in some strange way.

Normally under our cloakroom floor it would seem.

I have also been becoming increasingly nervous about the smell of mildew finding its way into the main body of the house from my private bathroom.

I favour carpets in bathrooms in this back of beyond location, to keep us all warm and cosy - which is fine until the overflow gets loose and starts leaking. My bathroom has a roll top bath, a silver-grey deep pile carpet (top of the range remnant from Trago), a silver and blue chandelier, and bright yellow blind. It is featured on my website and is much admired. I think bathrooms should smell as lovely as they look.

So I cut away the mouldy bit of carpet and slipped an ice cream container under the offending leaking pipe, only for the smell to get worse! After many, many days of this, shutting my door, persuading myself that I was making things up, I made myself have another search around for the offending source, and discovered that all this time the radiator has a leaky joint. Which also accounts for the fact that I am having to constantly prime the central heating.

And then I realised why the front cloakroom was smelling so horrid - a waste paper basket full of old McDonalds left-overs from the car, combined with a pile of horse rugs waiting to be washed in the utility room next door!

So I have spent weeks worrying over something that could have been put right in minutes. And now I've got to think of what to do with the 23 bottles of pot pourri reviver I have left ...

Useless Booking Agency
10/11/2014

Hmmm. I'm wondering whether business could be brisker? Is it just that it's November and it's raining again?

Or could it be something that I've done?

"You never want to see how laws and sausages are made," said Plato, or was it wise Malcolm, the other day.

Re-reading what I have written recently - well its hardly how you would normally advertise a B&B is it?! And I call myself a sales-person!

Nevertheless, 47 x the full five blobs in just one year, although still not giving us TripAdvisor's top ranking for any B&B in central Dartmoor (if not the entire National Park) - well. Golly wow!

Here is the thank you letter sent by my 'Returns' shortly after their second stay (for those graphologists amongst you, you may be interested to know that the writing is of the highest possible form level, it shows a narrow stroke, it's written in black ink pen, on two pieces of thick A4).

November 2014

Dear Mary, Faye, Panda, Vegas & Twiglet

I just wanted to say an enormous thank you for helping to make Amanda's birthday weekend such an amazing experience. We both came down believing it would be impossible to top last year's experience, but we certainly did manage it. Despite the appearance of a B&B, the weekend felt like home from home and was like staying with friends – which we now consider you all are!

Thank you so much, and in particular for supper on the Saturday. It was lovely to be able to eat with you in the 'heart' of Wydemeet, especially after such an exciting day on the moor. A 'Cook' meal and wine is an unbeatable combination.

My biggest thanks go to Faye for looking after Amanda whilst out riding. Amanda might be a good horsewoman, but without your expert reassurance that galloping over such rough ground was OK, she'd certainly be worse for wear, and I'm sure would have popped off!

Have a wonderful Christmas and New Year and look forward to meeting up again, hopefully, in the depths of Dartmoor sometime next year.

With love...

I am so massively proud of our home and the service that we offer. Our little team tries its absolute hardest to make sure that everything is immaculate at all times.

Meanwhile, attempting to provide light-hearted, quirky advice for anyone thinking of setting up a B&B, which is what the blog has been mostly about, and then putting it on the same website as marketing that very B&B, was actually, in retrospect, a bit stupid.

The second explanation for slow business is because of the inefficiency of Booking.com. I have just discovered that they haven't actually reinstated me on their site, despite my having rung them five times begging them to do so. I have even told them that I won't pay their latest invoice unless they do, and had no response as usual.

Well yesterday I discovered why their company appears to have gone a bit wonky. It was national news on the radio that they are being targeted by fraudsters claiming to be accommodation providers, taking deposits for bookings, and disappearing. Well. Fancy! But right now I need them! Please reinstate me! All is forgiven!

UnCensored
10/11/2014

I think the Search Engine Optimisation of the website site is now pretty good, so it probably doesn't need a regular blog to keep it high up there - and if I find out I am slipping down the rankings by not contributing any longer, I can update it with banal observations on the changing seasons of Dartmoor. All is going golden brown at the moment, by the way.

So I have just had this brilliant idea. Why don't I hereon stick to keeping a secret, fewer holds barred, diary instead, and not go publishing it publicly where everybody can read unsuitable things all the time? Here goes! Hold onto your seats guys!

6 FOUR IN A BED – WHAT THEY FILMED

SCHADENFREUDE
22/02/2014

Wow! You know how Four in a Bed - the programme where lots of
B&Bers get together and make each other cry - is my favourite, after
Downton?

Well. Blow me down - I've just received a very polite email inviting me to
be on it!! I am absolutely chuffed to bits that they've found and targeted
Wydemeet, out of all the millions and trillions of B&Bs that are out there,
especially since we're not on any official lists except for TripAdvisor.

I have often daydreamed about what being on Four in a Bed might be like,
as I embark on my fourth pre-recorded episode of an evening, once my
guests are all cosily tucked up in bed upstairs. And now the offer has
come direct!

As a professional PR, my advice to me would be that going anywhere near
it would be complete madness. The only reason ever to get involved with
the media is if you think they might be able to help you in some way, eg
marketing something for you that you want to sell.

Well call me complacent - but judging by last year I will already have
sufficient demand for B&B this summer. So why would I proactively wish
for the humiliation endured by every B&Ber who goes on that
programme, purely for the entertainment of the great unwashed, as they

133

get a buzz out of my distress? Schadenfreude, my clever 15 year old son Will called it, as he bent over his lunchtime baked beans earlier today.

Because I'm a show-off, and it's a long time since I was last on telly, are the reasons. Also I would be very interested in watching the process of making the TV programme, and finally, hopefully, there might be some money to be made afterwards.

So I've emailed them back, questioning their assertion that Four in a Bed 'Celebrates the Great British Bed & Breakfast and its owners', drawing their attention to all of the above observations, and we'll see what happens. I think the idea of a fat Blackpool landlady visiting Wydemeet, falling off the nearby stepping stones into the river, and off tussocks into bogs, will be too tempting for them to resist.

I will probably live to regret this, but at the moment Faye and I think it will be a great wheeze, and hopefully hardly anyone we know watches the programme anyway.

Coming Back as a Dog
20/04/2014

"I'm Coming Back as a Man" may be on Radio 2's current playlists, but upon further reflection, I think I'd like most of all to come back as a dog.

This thought first crossed my mind when I heard that I had been accused of treating Ex like a dog. "Lucky him," I said to myself. Every need catered for, unconditional love.

Then, when one of my online dates pulled up outside my house, and an ancient, crippled black Labrador hobbled out of the back of his Subaru Legacy, to tender encouragement and soppy tones of endearment, I thought, "That's how I want him to speak to me too." Alas, it was never to be.

So, on to my next crazy adventure...

"That's the best possible reason for taking part in Four in a Bed," wrote charming Jackie - one of Channel 4's reality TV show's producers. "Of course you must be in it."

I received this potentially life-changing email 30 minutes before I was due to host a fancy dress party for 20 twelve-year-old girls, after preparing B&B breakfast for four, and taking Faye and her horse to a Pony Club Rally.

An Easter Egg Hunt, Fashion Show, Quiz, Jacuzzi, Dancing, Supper and Sleepover in Will's joss-stick/tobacco reeking, teenage den of horrors, complete with semi-naked calendar of Kelly Brooks, lava lamp and flashing fairy lights, all still to be got ready.

I had written to Four in a Bed saying actually I didn't want to be in it after all; and then contacted them a third time, wondering whether it would be too late to change my mind back again, as I had a new objective in mind.

My new approach had come about after I'd spoken to a previous contestant who I rather liked the look of. I had emailed him asking him whether he might be gay, and we had subsequently had a nice chat and discovered we were both on internet dating sites. I looked him up after our phone conversation and found that he was 48, looking for (female) partners aged 26 - 46. Not me then. I'm 54.

But lying in the bath afterwards I came up with my cunning plan. The Encounters dating site, that I currently subscribe to, appears to be replete with fat, old, bald, dull men, whose lifestyles I have almost nothing in common with, and who live 100s of miles away. I'm fed up with it.

What about giving up on that, and putting myself on Four in a Bed instead, and see what happens? 2 1/2hrs of Me, on global TV! That's much better than anything any online dating service can offer. And even if my Perfect Match isn't likely to be watching Daytime Reality TV, his Mum or his sister might see me, and urge him to get in touch! Especially if I make it really obvious that I'm out there all alone looking for someone! What could be better? How can you fault the logic?!

So I jumped out of the bath, sent off my email to Four In A Bed explaining my reasons for changing my mind, and hey presto! They like it!

So maybe I'm going to be famous again! The last time I was on telly was 25 years ago, on a show hosted by the then virtually unknown Carol Vorderman, when she was testing my ability as a graphologist, but that is another story.

B&B For Everyone!
30/04/2014

"Do it! Do it! Do it!" is what I seem to have been saying for the past 24 hours.

Over a year ago I went to look at a friend's B&B nearby, and came away totally depressed by how impossible it would be for me ever to aspire to his standards. The result was a toss-up as to whether I should stay here, with my house crumbling around my ears, and two children who never venture out of the garden gate onto the moor, or downsize into something smaller, newer and cheaper, which is draught-free and comfortable, where everything works, near a bus-stop and a Costa's. And normal people.

I can't remember why I didn't put Wydemeet on the market then and there. It may have been Will saying how much he loves coming home to relax, turn his music up to full volume, and proudly entertain his privileged school friends in his dreaded 'Bothy'; or Faye becoming increasingly involved with the local pony club; or simple inertia on my part.

But I recently attended a hunt meet at my friends' hotel down the road, to discover I knew and felt welcomed by over half the people there. A result of living here for nearly twenty years and becoming a part of the community, I suppose. However bonkers they may all think I am, it doesn't really matter. It is a scenario that I will never be able to recreate anywhere else, and I treasure that feeling of belonging.

Last night my friend with the B&B came to dinner. He and his wife arrived at the same time as my latest B&B guests, and were immediately enthusiastically immersed in discussions about where to go and what to see around Dartmoor, looking at maps together, and admiring the evening sun setting behind the hill.

My friends are absolute natural B&Bers. Their home is well located outside the most desirable village on Dartmoor, it's beautiful, their garden is outstanding, all is pristine, tasteful, and comfortable.

But they're not marketing themselves properly, so are not getting the bookings. They're tired, are losing their nerve, and concentrating on other things which are less profitable, more time-consuming, and more exhausting.

"You need more rooms," (they only rent out one) I advised, "get yourselves properly SEO'd on Google - you can do it yourselves; rent the house out when you're not in it (they're off to Greece for two weeks); and charge double for holding more weddings. Bingo." (I'm not bossy, smug or complacent at all.)

Then this afternoon one of the school Mums came over to see if I thought she should be B&B-ing.

"You're in the middle of the moor, while we're nowhere, really," she said. "We're about equidistant between Dartmoor and Bodmin, and quite near to lots of beaches on both the north and the south coasts, only about 10 minutes from the A30," she continued. Well - there you have it. Centre of the South West. "You really must go for it!" I said to her.

Running a B&B is so much fun, and gives you such a feeling of achievement. The guests are so nice - I've never had a dud - and there is nothing more enjoyable than hearing people admiring your home and knowing that in effect you are getting paid to make it attractive. I feel I've turned full circle - from chambermaid to graduate, to yuppie, to professional, and now I'm back to cleaning loos again. But at least they're my own.

Anyway - the proof of my particular pudding will presumably go public on Four In A Bed. They're coming to visit tomorrow afternoon to check me out. If they decide to feature Wydemeet, I think it's going to be soon! Eeek!

Gold Winner Scoot Headline Award
14/05/2014

Something new to put on the wall in the downstairs lavatory - my 'Certificate of Achievement' for winning the 'Scoot Headline Award' arrived in the post today.

A couple of days ago, I received a letter from them, informing me that the plastic plinths that the certificates were originally presented in kept breaking in the post, so they were sure we would understand why our certificates were now being sent out just in paper form.

Hmmmmmm. And who is this 'famous actress, Ebony Feare', who presented the awards at their ceremony in London? As you, a loyal follower, are already aware, I don't know anything or anyone, so she's probably really well known, but I've never heard of her.

Meanwhile, a few days ago, Four in a Bed's delightful Jackie drove down and interviewed me on camera. She felt like an instant friend. The most dangerous kind of media person! I trusted her absolutely and told her all sorts of things that I shouldn't have, I am sure. She feigned such interest in me and my B&B that I fed into her hand, giving her such an endless monologue that I started boring myself, quite apart from her, let alone her bosses who will ultimately be judging whether I am interesting enough for their programme or not.

So will we be on it? I have no idea. Jackie's footage was delivered for her bosses' summit meeting last Friday. After that, it is down to working out who will match best with whom, and whose locations and available dates fit in with everyone else's.

If they film me, I am going to be in so much trouble for my plumbing that it doesn't bear thinking about. My worst terror lies with the lurking macerator - otherwise known as 'Mazza-rater' - a joyful play on my name.

Whenever the Dartmeet loo is flushed, this potentially lethal monster gives off three grinding explosions and sends the effluent slooshing down a pipe which runs along the side of a thin wooden partition wall, past the sleeping heads of any B&Bers in Hexworthy, the more expensive room next door.

Throughout the house are pictures and photos of family, ancestors, friends and pets; and ski clothes, old lipsticks etc are stored in various drawers. The tellies need someone with a Mensa-level IQ to turn on.

All this, yet I charge more than anyone else on Dartmoor.

Because my guests are paying for our extraordinary, unique location. Our footpaths and bridleways stretching in every direction from the garden gate. And for my amazing chat. And for Faye's general loveliness. And for the honour of taking Twiglet out for walks, of course.

But the Four In A Bed contestants won't know any of that. And anyhow, the score sheets don't cover that kind of thing.

The other day a couple of Lithuanian shop fitters arrived for breakfast with beer, at 9am, slept through the day in Dartmeet, then had breakfast again at tea-time, and went off to re-fit a fast-food cafe overnight, during Plymouth's annual International Fireworks Extravaganza. They were brothers. One was covered in tattoos and spoke no English, while the other is a keen fisherman and says he's going to come back with his family for a fishing holiday. Anyway. This unusual arrangement caused us no problem at all. And then they paid me what I'd normally charge for a two night stay. Result!

These days I'm receptionist, chambermaid, front of house, marketing person, gardener, waitress and chef. A Lady Who Lunches, rides, and swims, a chauffeur, serial online dater, single Mum, and now an author too! No wonder I suffer from IBS and a juddering left eyelid!

And one of the plusses of staying at not-so-immaculate Wydemeet is that you can break a chair, knock over your tea, leave mud on the stairs, and I won't blow a gasket, provided I'm in a good mood. Wydemeet is a place to sit back and relax in.

Which is not necessarily what the Four In A Bed contestants are looking for. I'm beginning to feel just a tad nervous about all of this!

I've Got a Little List
19/05/2014

"I think I'm going to be featured on Four in a Bed," I said.

"Oh I don't think you should do that," my Australian guest replied, and he meant it. He and his wife are celebrating their 40th wedding anniversary by going on a tour of all the places in the world they want to visit most, and are investigating his Dartmoor heritage. They have stayed in ten different hotels and B&Bs so far, so they jolly well know what they're talking about.

"Would you like us to provide you with a list of all the things you might need to do before going on television?" queried his wife.

"Errrr, ummmm, yes, it would be useful to have a friendly, objective view," I said. "One can get too close to it all."

The macerator and the gurgling of its effluent seemed to have been particularly noisy that day, and the telly especially difficult to turn on. I hoped they would forget their offer, and I thought that they had. But when it was time to say goodbye, his wife said,

"Would you like that list then? Do treat it with a pinch of salt."

I said that that would be very kind, and she handed it over. It was two pages long.

Sashka and I went into the garden with a fag and a cup of coffee each, taking the list with us, filled with dread. Sashka read it out slowly, point by point.

"Take the staples out of the new rug; provide tissues; a mug for toothbrushes; instructions for the TV, ensure the kettle's flex reaches the plug without having to put it on the floor; replace the too large, wobbly

140

table lamps (these were a sentimental wedding present from my graphology mentor); replace the towels daily ("We always used to do that at the Forest Inn anyway," commented Sashka); and a couple of other minor comments.

Well. All eminently do-able. And probably obvious. Incredibly helpful. I am massively grateful, and immediately emailed the couple saying so. I wish they could come back and do the same for another room!

Meanwhile I am going to bite the bullet and put soundproofing in the party wall between Dartmeet's bathroom and Hexworthy, so at least I can sleep guilt-free at night, knowing that I've tried, whether my efforts cure the problem or not!

And bloody Hell – I'm clearly going to have to buy a whole load more towels.

Value for Money?
19/05/2014

Am I? Value for money I mean.

On last night's recording of Four In a Bed, a dour bloke from Yorkshire, whose B&B features flowery purple wallpaper, maroon sheets and red bedspreads, said, "No B&B room in this world could ever be worth £130."

Oh dear. If I ever get to be in it, that'll be me then.

The B&B that this chap was referring to, that charged £130 a night for a glorious room with a wonderful four poster, was absolutely gorgeous. It had an immaculately painted grey front door with a brightly polished brass knocker. Then inside all was proper quality interlined thick curtains, real antiques, but, worst of all, light coloured, plain carpets with no stains. It was clear to me that the owner (who looks as though she's a real hoot and I would love to meet her, speaking like Princess Anne, and everything being 'ghastly' and giving her 'the heaves') has never had a child nor a dog set foot in her house.

Over a decade ago our nanny's two year old toddler spilled an entire bottle of black Indian ink over our brand new coral coloured deep pile 100% wool sitting room carpet. We laughed at the time (she was on the verge of tears) and have finally nearly managed to get rid of the stains, but we never replaced it. Perhaps we should. I prefer to cover the grey areas still left with rugs, and hope for the best.

Similarly with some of the bedrooms. Do you really have to replace a whole carpet the minute a guest spills a cup of coffee on it?

And the plumbing. Every time I hear a guest turn on a tap upstairs my heart starts thumping. There is not one tap, one shower, one loo flush or one over-flow which has not gone wrong at least once since they were fitted not long ago.

And in the meantime, Four in a Bed has raised its head again. Only this time it might be Three in a Bed. During the time slot I gave them that we could do it, they're going to be filming in Scotland. However, they have now emailed to say that 'they all like me' and could I be in their new series in early Autumn?

Well their new series is changing back to the old format: three B&Bs competing against each other, to be screened in a one hour slot at 8pm - peak viewing time - on Channel 4.

So that's much better. I was beginning to panic at the thought of providing six breakfasts at once, to people who will be determined to test my mediocre, amateur, limited cooking ability to its limits. And envisaging deep-cleaning three bedrooms to such a degree that we could guarantee not a single 'curly' inside or outside a mattress protector, nor bog brush, nor underside of a plug-fitting, was filling me with dread. And where would I sleep with all my immaculate bedrooms full? Back in Will's attic room I suppose.

Yikes! It Could Happen!
3/12/2014

I've just received an email from Four In A Bed saying they definitely want to use Wydemeet if they get commissioned for another series. I am quite pleased about this, although I am quaking in my Size 9s if I'm going to have to cook loads of different breakfasts at once, depending on whether we're talking three in a bed, or four in a bed.

I feel that between us all, my little team and I have now got most things working quite nicely, and looking quite good. My latest eBay purchases were two pretty little teapots to go in the two best bedrooms - rather than expecting my honoured guests to make tea from a teabag in a mug.

It Should Have Been Andrea!
18/12/2014

I am desolate. I have been gunning for Andrea of the big voice, short legs, beard and jolly Christmas jumpers, but he's just lost to white van man Ben in X-Factor. Boo hoo!

And if not him, then Fleur, who did a faultless rendition of Bruno Mars' current Number 1 hit.

And my favourite in The Apprentice – the nice Irish girl who was planning to launch a range of delicious-looking, upmarket, low calorie, ready meals - has also just lost out to someone else.

I'm afraid to say that Reality TV is what I like best. So I am delighted to inform you that Channel 4 rang yesterday to let me know that (surprise surprise not) 'Four in a Bed' has been commissioned for yet another series, and they were just checking that I am still available.

A Bit Of A Day
26/03/2015

Four In A Bed is (or is it are?) definitely using me! Wow! It's been over a year, now, since they first got in touch. They're going to film Wydemeet on Wednesday May 6th. Yikes! They've just called to confirm. They're putting me as last visit on the programme itself - no surprises there - they always put the posh people on last, when everyone is really tired and hating each other.

So I've just emailed my great mate at Prince Hall Hotel, and also Clydesdale Adventures (who provide treks on massive carthorses across the moor), inviting them to save that day if they want to be involved, and I've also warned the school that my daughter, Faye, who is determined to star in the show, will need the day off.

The whole project will take up two weeks, from April 27th, staying at the B&Bs in the competition, interspersed with other accommodation between filming. I must think about how I'm going to handle running my own B&B side of things during that time.

So that happened this morning.

Also - I have just sent a draft of my potential first book, all about setting up the B&B, to all those most involved with what's in it, including Ex. I am quaking in my Uggs about what their reactions are going to be. The pressure is on now, to have it ready for purchase by the time the Four In A Bed thing gets aired.

Aaaghh! I really am on the edge of making myself famous. How scary! I wonder how famous I will become?

Also this morning I have spent a long time discussing with Ex the pros and cons of Will's current school. Should we move him? That would be a simply huge and extremely difficult decision to make.

Decisions, decisions. At least Ex and I agree on almost everything regarding our children, so I am not screaming in the wilderness.

And then this morning Faye was playing in the School Music Competition, for her last ever time before she leaves, and the new regime wouldn't let parents in! After all my weeks driving 70 miles each way to her flute lessons because the school's teacher makes her cry. And then my having to find her a sax to borrow - she's having a go at that this term - because the school couldn't provide one! I am furious!

Just when I'm off to Austria on the school ski trip in two days' time, and am about to rent the house out for a week for £2,500. I've done nothing at all to prepare it. I must go and mow the grass for the first time this year. It looks like a field. Bloody moles.

What would I do without Sashka - my right arm, left arm, and both legs?

A Sad Ending to A Happy Holiday
06/04/2015

Lying on a picnic rug in the sunshine, after a ritualistic lamb shoulder lunch at my mother's house, is my definition of Heaven.

Except I feel a bit funny.

I can't really move properly.

Arriving at Mum's, on our way home to still-rented-out Wydemeet, after our wonderful school ski trip, Will, Faye and I found ourselves in her small kitchen, shoulder to shoulder with three octogenarians all fighting over how to cook the broccoli. Will even started flirting a little, with scary, 80 year old, Auntie Rhonda.

I had offered to drive her to the station this morning, to save Mum (82) the effort, and to achieve the event in half the time Mum would take, but I had to give up on my offer because I felt too strange.

The holiday itself had felt almost character-changing.

During the last few days' freneticism prior to departure, I think I developed IBS. That's what the internet told me when I checked out the symptoms, which I'm not going to go into here, because I'm too embarrassed to.

I think it was caused by stress – something that is not supposed to be on my repertoire.

Anyhow, over the first few days' of my break – which I hadn't gone on for the skiing, by the way - more for the chat; the IBS symptoms gradually disappeared, as I became happier and happier and happier.

It seemed as though everybody loved my presence and wanted to be near me. I have never felt so special. It was absolutely brilliant and I was encouraged to behave as badly as possible. I felt surrounded by warmth, trust, support and love.

All the men who came along were extremely attentive and I felt free even to practise a little flirting! I haven't done that for a couple of decades!

The whole thing has worked to be the best possible confidence-builder in advance of the looming filming of Four In A Bed.

But I appear to have caught something on the last day of the trip. If I have, I do hope it will go away soon. With my stupid lifestyle, I absolutely cannot possibly afford to be ill.

Ill, ill, ill
22/04/2015

I am screaming.

But no voice is coming out. Just a hoarse, moaning, rasping sound. There is no air.

The wire for the toaster is too short so I can't plug it in. It's just one thing too many. The last straw. Too much to bear.

Tears trickle slowly down the side of my face.

I haven't unpacked everything from letting out the house two weeks ago.

But my next B&B guests are due at teatime, and I'm not confident that even a 'hello' will come out of my voice box!

I crawl up the stairs to my unmade bed, meanwhile the enticing bright sunshine through the window laughs at me: "Come and ride your horses! It couldn't be more beautiful on the moor! They need looking after, exercising and enjoying!"

My head flops onto the pillow and I am virtually oblivious to whatever Jeremy Vine's yacking on about on Radio 2.

This feeling just won't go away. It's been days and weeks now. I have so little energy I can't think straight, let alone plan stuff.

I have no back-up support. Sashka is as ill as I am, but with something different.

I call up Ex.

"You know you offered to help? Well I need you."

And on top of all this, it appears that my friends don't appear to be very impressed with my book. Bugger. After all that. What am I going to do about it? I can't just give up, after so much time spent on it. Eerrgghh. And now, looking back through everything I have written, it is clear that I seem to be constantly ill these days. How many times have I felt that the option of dying might be preferable to mowing the lawn before my guests arrive?

I always used to be completely robust. Something's going to have to change. As things are, life is proving a bit terrifying. I am responsible for my guests having the really happy time that they've been looking forward to for months. I've got to be all jolly on TV next week. And then I need to rewrite my book, leaving out 40,000+ words of boring, repetitive and irrelevant Introduction, according to my many amateur critics.

I need to be firing on all four, or is it eight, cylinders if I am going to pull this lot off.

But all I want to do is to lie in bed moaning.

Four In A Bed - the master interview
22/04/2015

Five hours!

Of that, I expect they will use one minute.

They are going to portray me as the mother from Hell.

The camera's whirling, and I'm excited to bits, shouting at Faye:

"Cinderella - make sure there's not a single curly to be seen on that bed! Each one will cost us a fiver!" as I pretend to polish the mirror over and over again, and she keeps straightening the already straight duvet cover. How we luuurve that camera!

The producer from Four In A Bed who has come to interview me tells me that she has also worked on The Apprentice and X-Factor. Respect!

She's only done a couple of Four In A Beds so far, which were in fact Three In A Beds, but the episode she was involved with, that I saw, featured two posh girls, both of whom seemed delightful. God I hope she can pull off the same for me!

I haven't the faintest idea of how I'm coming across, saying what seems to me to be the same thing over and over again.

I'm sure we'll come last, whatever happens. I think the B&Bers the programme sends won't be able to sleep because it's too quiet here. They'll hate the intimacy of the layout of the house, and all the personal stuff in their rooms, and they won't be into walking, which is really what Wydemeet is all about.

My B&B is priced to reflect its location and my utterly totally fantastic unbeatable immaculate 24hr service. Would I wash my guests' feet with my hair? Probably – if only my hair were long enough, and provided I hadn't just returned from carefully blow-drying it at the health club.

I'll even make guests' kiddies fish fingers for nothing – or go out in the car to collect fat people who can't quite make it back from their over-ambitious walks!

148

This sort of thing looks good and generates blobs on TripAdvisor, without causing me much trouble at all. But you can't really measure such acts of kindness on the telly programme – they don't count in the scoring system.

During the endless interview, I'm trying really hard to be utterly hilarious, but that would be easier if I wasn't on my own talking to myself, sitting on a sofa, feeling half dead.

I'm wearing a fake-silk light pink top, white straight-legs from Per Una, and pink high heels. Faye wouldn't let me wear cut-offs because she tells me that my legs have gone purple with age, and need hiding.

I had originally slapped on a new No 7 'Beautifully Matte Mousse' foundation in 'cool beige', but luckily, just before going on film, caught sight of myself in a mirror. Aagghh! I looked like a ghost with a face covered in deep ravines. I've had to do something drastic to repair it, with no minutes to spare! I feel as though I've gone back in time, as I used to prepare for a teenage party trying to hide my spots with Clearasil!

I wonder what I look like on camera? Guess I won't know until the programme's finally transmitted. "Next January" they said. January??!!! God – I'll be dead from flu well before then!

I am absolutely freezing by the end of my interview, rather wishing I'd stuck to my normal black merino/cashmere.

Too late to change now though. On to another 'housework' scene.

Complete with Faye's miniature frilly black apron, I pretend to wash around Dartmeet's loo. I casually lean on its rim, forgetting for the moment that proper cleaners would probably wear some Marri's if they're anywhere near one of the guests' lavatory bowls.

"Yah," I drawl. "I've turned full circle. I was a chamber-maid at 17. Went to probably the best school in the world. MD of a PR consultancy. Now back cleaning lavatories again." I grin manically at the camera.

"They call me Lady Muck around here.....Blue wellies or pink?" I hiss at Faye.

"Pink!"

So now we're filming in the garden, and here I am, resplendent in fake Victoria Beckham sunglasses, pink silky top, spray-on white trousers and bright pink wellies, struggling along behind an ancient rusty red rotary mower, attempting to cut the grass between the ubiquitous mole-hills, dog-poo, fallen twigs and stones.

I can't wait til the filming proper starts. I'm longing to be told what to do by somebody else, from dawn til midnight. It will be a total holiday.

I've got to visit the Isle of Wight, Cambridge, and Shropshire. Driving for miles! I hope I make a massive great profit on travel expenses! I'm off to Super Sexy Dick tomorrow to collect some new tyres for my Golden Monster truck, as I think the truck, rather than me, is going to be the biggest star of this show.

Today's experience would all have been huge fun if I wasn't feeling so terrible.

After the five hour filming marathon I lie, drenched in sunshine, on a sunbed - trusty Cava and fag by my side, feeling as though I would rather be dead for the rest of the day, even though I now have to drive Faye back to school, together with huge suitcase and laundry bag for her first and last term of full boarding. Blimey – her lovely little prep school costs not far short of Eton's fees!

Faye is on a total pedestal at the moment. Outside of filming, she has spent nearly the entire weekend sewing on fifty name-tapes for her new Big School next term. The one occasion some years ago when I had a go at one, it made my finger hurt, and I've never tried again.

"My time's worth around £40 an hour, so I would rather buy a new sock than sew a name-tape onto an old one," I gasp at her. And collapse back into bed.

Boring? Moi?
29/04/2015

I hurl myself off my Wetbike, which is travelling at 40mph, and dive into the sea, just in front of a Red Funnel ferry. The assembled crowd on Cowes Promenade roars.

That was in 1980, and now here I am, back again at what used to be the Groves and Gutteridge Boat Yard on the Isle of Wight, thirty-five years later, even more excited!

I had spent the most extraordinary summer 'Demonstrating Wetbikes' during the university holidays when I was twenty. Wetbikes are very noisy 50hp motorbikes that travel across water on skis instead of wheels –much to the displeasure of the Cowes Royal Yacht Squadron.

I love the Isle of Wight. For me it is boiling over with happy memories. Earlier I had parked my truck, the Golden Monster, in an 'immobile home' carpark, crossed a quiet lane, and made my way to what appeared to be a rather ordinary house, with a little fountain in the front garden, and exquisitely manicured borders.

"Ring the doorbell," ordered a cameraman filming from behind a bush.

There was a real old-fashioned bell hanging next to the normal push-button one, so I ding-donged on that.

Lots and lots of times, while the cameras followed me from different angles. "Lucky there doesn't seem to be a guard-dog barking on the other side of the door," I thought to myself. "It would have been driven mental."

After an eternity, the door finally opened, and there, framed, stood a smart-casually dressed bloke of about 50, smiling "Come in! Come in!". He quickly shut the door behind me so the cameramen could no longer see us, and -

Oh my God! There's another bloke in there! They're a gay couple! Of

151

course! How typically Four In A Bed!

"SSSSHHHHHHHH!!! SSSSSSHHHHHHHHHHHHHH!!!" they grinned and giggled, giving me a group squeeze and a kiss. "We're only in this for fun! It's going to be really good," they enthused, and I fell in love with both of them on the spot, my feelings and views never to change over the next, intense, fortnight.

They showed me upstairs to a bright, light, pristine room, all coordinated and sparkling clean, with a chandelier made of what appeared to be glass bubbles. The loo was clean enough to eat your dinner off, and I could do my make-up in the reflection off the bathroom floor. £75 for the night including breakfast is miles too cheap!

As we were about to be whisked off to our 'activity', the boys looked doubtfully at my high heeled black suede boots.

"Would low, brown leather boots be better?" I suggested, but still no enthusiasm.

No one was prepared to even hint at what 'the activity' might be, and I've got to look my best at all times on this show if I'm to pull – that's the whole point! So, belt and braces, as it were, I lugged my entire suitcase onto the minibus provided, and off we set.

And now, here we are at the old boatyard. And how glad am I that I brought everything I've got!

I disappear into a café lavatory, and substitute my' black' for a navy blue top, white jeans and a pair of white trainers that I have never worn in ten years. I'm terribly pleased, and immensely relieved, about my sudden nautical look.

There's a rumour about, that we may be kayaking. Yuck.

But the activity turns out to be tying knots, on the boys' old yacht. Callum demonstrates 'the bowline'.

I hate knots. Always have since I failed my 'knot badge' in the Brownies.

And now I finally get to meet the other two sets of 'contributors'.

Introducing Tessa and Ivor. Tessa is Sharon Osborne, but made of flesh and blood rather than silicone. It turns out we're the owners of identical horses -Tessa even has a photo on her phone of herself hunting! Ivor is a great big northern bloke with tattoos, who, holding hands with Tessa, suddenly does a skip to the side, like Piglet.

The other pair are Joan and Thomas. They have been listening carefully to Callum's instructions and are now tying their bowline, very efficiently and expertly. Oh my God. They're 'In It To Win It'! Tessa and Ivor mess up theirs, and it's my turn.

"I'll do a horse knot instead," I say. I tie something known as a 'quick release', and give up.

"All aboard," we heave anchor, and off we potter along the lovely river that I knew so intimately, thirty years ago. Soon the producer asks me to take the helm. Hurray! I'm centre-stage and star attraction, perfectly turned out in my boaty kit - the sun's smiling, there aren't any inconvenient waves nor wind, and I'm lurving that camera!

Back on land, and we're each ushered off for our first, of many, many, many 'LittleChats'. These provide us with the opportunity to slag off all the other B&Bers behind their backs. After all – they'll never know what we said about them until the programme is shown months away!

"Isn't Joan feisty? Isn't she good fun? Isn't she centre of the party?" asks my interviewer.

Eh? Instead of saying that I think quite the opposite – that in my opinion she's predictable, unimaginative, irritating and boring - I say that it is too soon to comment. I am also bland about the knot-tying and sailing experiences, because nearly all my friends in Devon have a boat, so I can sail whenever I want to – ie, never.

So I mutter, "I can't quite be doing with all this clapping."

Everyone else is gathered up together by the telly crew, but I am taken to one side by the producer. Oh good. Something else special for me to do!

"You do realise that I can't use anything you've said," I'm told in an urgent hiss. "You of all people understand what we need for television. If you don't say anything more interesting, we can't show you."

Oops. That wasn't quite the reaction I had expected.

Let's hope I can pull off something better over supper.

Loving the Camera
30/04/2015

They've put me nearest to the two hand-held cameras, towards the front of the table, next to the boys.

I can tell, or am I imagining things, that the programme makers are aiming to use me as 'the character' in this show.

I rise to the occasion.

I am hilarious. I am interesting. I am to the point.

"Pilot!" I explode. "You - uniform - travelling and all that!" I shout, pointing at Don. "You're a pilot!"

"I wish," he replies. "Purser."

"Oh, you mean head air steward type thing?" This fits. He looks the definition of one. "On Thomsons? My children love Thomsons - you have tellies!" I cry.

I am so noisy that I am worried that I am becoming overbearing.

"What does Tessa think?" I ask, and push my chair back out of the way, so that the camera can see the others.

It has been a brilliant evening, in a restaurant set on the banks of the river. Quite beautiful as the sun sets across the water. As I complete my last LittleChat of the day, various middle-aged, middle-class, rather drunk yachties wobble past. They are fascinated by the cameras, and clearly want to be included. I am worried that they are going to fall into the river.

"Much better," says a relieved producer, later on in the evening, as I turn out the light.

Sobbing On Telly
30/04/2015

AAAAAAGGGGGGGGGGGGGGGGGGGGGGGGGGGGHHHHHHHHHHHHHHHHHH HHHHHHHHH!!!!!!!!!!!!!!!!!!!!!!!!!!!!!!!!!!!!!!

That's me gasping out really loud - not quite screaming - I've only genuinely screamed once, and that was giving birth to my beloved Faye.

But - I think with what's just happened, I am likely to go viral on YouTube!

I am absolutely so shocked! Shocked to pieces! I leap back in abject terror! I can't believe it! I can't look! Aagghh - I feel sick! Urrghh! I clutch my tummy!

I have been checking out my new mate Tessa's gaff. It is immaculate - totally, utterly pristine, just as I would have expected of her. She is the ultimate professional. Everything is white. And new. Even the mattress! And mattress protector. And real soft white leather sofa and chair (well we are on the Essex border). And a carpet which looks like the most enormous sheep that was ever bred, or a rather small polar bear. So I lie down on it and find, as anticipated, it's fake. Jolly sensible. Dartmoor real sheep carpets are too small to be any use, and smell.

Anyhow, so I walk confidently into the perfect bathroom, complete with plastic roll top bath just like mine, but much better quality. Tessa's bath still has its silver feet, whereas I have painted mine gold. I nonchalantly open the plastic white shiny lid of the white shiny loo - and - OH MY GOD!!!!!!!!!!

There's this thin red worm about six inches long wriggling around in the water!

OH MY GOD!!!!!!!!!!!!

Well. It's all caught on camera.

"It's a fix!!" I shout.

Which it actually couldn't possibly be, and which is an incredibly dreadful thing for the tv crew to have recorded. It could get them into terrible trouble with some 'compliance' thing or something.

But what dawned on me immediately, being a marketing/PR-type person, is that this is disastrous business-wise for Tessa and Ivor. It is worse than never having appeared on the programme at all! They will have been investing so heavily into preparations for weeks, to get the place looking like it does. Tessa has even handmade a massive - I mean literally ten foot tall - 3-D wraparound headboard!

"We've got to tell them - I mean I've got to tell them - what I've found," I whisper to the crew.

Tessa and Ivor are summoned, and I start:

"I..I...I.. I... there's a THING in the loo," I manage to get out, and suddenly I am in tears. Streaming down. They are going to hate me now. I always felt I liked Tessa more than she liked me, and now she is going to hate me!

The pair peer into the loo and are entirely calm, professional and smiling.

"I can't believe it! It should be you crying, not me!" I wail hysterically.

Me. Tough old me. Who never cries. I didn't even cry about the divorce.

And now it's all on celluloid. Or digital or whatever they use these days.

To be repeated on global television over and over again, for years to come, all around the world, to the vicarious amusement of literally millions of happy viewers.

Speed Freak
01/05/2015

Big, big, slow, wide yawn.

"Is that really the time?" I sigh, checking my watch, and rubbing my eyes sleepily.

Joan and Thomas are driving a beaten up old Discovery, achingly slowly around a chicane, manoeuvring the car so that it doesn't touch any of the old tyres marking out their path. Joan, in the driving seat, is blindfold.

We've already watched Tessa and Ivor kangaroo-jumping along the course, and Callum and Don making rather an expert job of it, Callum guiding blindfold Don as though he were on the Golden Shot - "Left a bit, right a bit..."

I'm bored. And also slightly shaken, jittery, sad, and upset about 'Wormgate'. But it's not allowed to be discussed with anybody now, not until the denouement at the end of filming in eight days' time. I must concentrate - it's my turn to drive now.

I choose Callum as my navigator.

I have to stick on the blindfold and somehow climb into the car. I fumble around for the gear stick, clutch etc.

"Right - I'm used to driving these things - I used to have a Range Rover," I challenge Callum. "Let's go fast!"

I find a small lever at the bottom of the driving well, and Callum assures me that it says 'L' for low range gears at one end and 'H' for high range at the other. I shove it towards what I hope is 'H'. I've got butterflies. I've no idea whether the car will even move now!

"Hurry up!" I'm thinking. And finally we're off.

I haven't a clue how fast we're going, but it feels quick enough to me. If we knock down a tree or a portacabin it doesn't really matter in this old banger.

"You need to go much faster!" says Callum. I put my foot down. We're still in first gear, but it feels as though we're flying, and I know that the other three couples only used the lower register.

"Right, right, right, no left, left, right, left," cries Callum. I appear to have done two circles, and then I have to leap into reverse for a bit, and then another circle and suddenly it's all over.

I get out to find that the guiding tyres are lying scattered all around the arena, but we appear to have completed the whole circuit quite quickly, if in a rather maniacal sort of a way.

The others are laughing. Phew. I think it was a success.

Ugly Bug Ball
01/05/2015

Charlene is filming me going to bed.

I have bought three new pairs of pyjamas especially for this bit. Two are polyester, meant to look like silk, and the third is a rather pretty floral cotton print. Tonight I am in the shiny baby blue ones.

Wormgate has been sorted as far as is possible, and I go back into the bathroom to go to the loo and on to bed.

Oh, NO! NO! NO! "There's a spider in here!" I involuntarily cry, before I've given what I'm saying any further thought. The spider is about three inches long and very spindly, making itself a little web in the ceiling corner over the bath.

"No, you're not getting this one. I won't have it. They've suffered enough," I yell at poor Charlene, who's hovering with her camera just outside the bathroom door. And I do one of the bravest things I've ever done in my life. I don't like spiders. But I grab some bog roll, climb into the bath, and aim to grab the spider.

But aagghh! It falls to the floor! It's still alive! Eeek!

Quick as a flash, in one movement, I jump out of the bath, stamp on the spider, pick up the gunge which is what's left of him with the bogroll, lift up the top of the loo, and flush.

Charlene doesn't quite know what to do. She leaves to ask the boss, and the matter is closed.

Unbelievably, in the early hours of the next morning, when I am caught short as is my wont, I hobble into the bathroom - and this time there is a woodlouse crawling along the floor under the basin! I ignore it, do my business, and return to bed.

Unusually for me, I don't tell anyone about it.

In the morning there are more grim-faced words.

I'm in trouble over the feedback forms. "You have been nothing but gushing about the boys' B&B," I am admonished. "You need to say something more interesting." It hasn't gone down well that I have paid the boys £15 over the odds because I think their B&B is worth £90 including breakfast.

Next, it appears to be a real problem that I have decided to give Tessa and Ivor nine out of ten for cleanliness, despite Wormgate.

"Obviously I can't give them ten, but the room is absolutely spotless, and you can tell it's always like this," I insist. "Wormgate did not make it dirty, it's not the result of it being dirty, and it's a one-off. The room is pristine."

And then comes the biggie.

"How much are you going to pay them?"

"You can't do that."

"I can, and I am. Their place may be a little impersonal for my taste, but in my opinion the room is worth £115."

So there.

The Horsehair Worm
01/05/2015

"SHRIEK!! Live worm in the toilet bowl! I don't suppose there is any chance it didn't come from someone's bottom is there? About 2-3 inches long, fairly thin and it was WRIGGLING. Bleurgh. Stool samples all round I think"

I've googled 'Worm In Toilet' and this is what has come up on mumsnet. Looks like I'm not the only one who was so shaken by my wormy surprise...

"Eewwwwww , it could just be a stray worm gone the wrong way on its mid-afternoon walk..."

"2-3 inches long is far too long to be a pinworm/threadworm from what I know. Pinworms look like little tiny threads not "fairly thin" and 2-3 inches long. Does it look like an earthworm?"

"Did it look like an earthworm or not??? (Running off to puke in a non wormy toilet)"

"Looked thinner than an earthworm. Too big for a threadworm and no itchy bums in the house. Feeling a bit sick since I saw it......."

"Erm hate to say this but where else would it have come from? Or have you got an 8 year old boy who might have dug up some earth worms and put them there for a joke?"

160

"Didn't look like a tapeworm (have been researching worms frantically since seeing the ruddy thing) but am clutching at the "maybe it got there another way" straw"

"Don't google human worms - one image is horrific!"

So I've done a couple of hours' research, and I think I now know what it is. I think it's a horsehair worm. They can come up from the sewer, but live on insects. Apparently they tend to turn up after particularly heavy rain when the sewer is high, and wriggle their way into downstairs or basement loos which haven't been flushed for a day or two.

This would all fit, even though it is the most unbelievably bad luck and coincidence that it landed in Lady Muck's Special Loo, on the one day of filming by Channel 4. I dare say that a large proportion of the television viewing public will simply assume that the worm was put there. But I am satisfied that it wasn't. And it is actually so sad that it has happened. It's going to affect everything. It's not really funny at all.

The Wheels on the Bus
02/05/2015

I'm sitting in the minibus between Don and Callum, waving both my arms in a circular motion, and merrily singing along at the top of my voice to 'The Wheels on the Bus'.

It is only after several verses that I suddenly jerk back to my senses. "Could someone please turn that racket off!" I yell to the front, but it is too late.

My weak moment has been caught on film. Indelibly. Forever. What an idiot I have made of myself to the global television viewership.

Apart from that, I think I have survived the first week of 'Four In A Bed' without saying something I will regret for the rest of my life. But you never know. And they do very funny things with the editing.

So far, it has been a blast!

For me, it is like reading a fairytale and then finding that you are living it for real. All the images you thought were just imaginary have come to life, and are all around you.

ShagFest
02/05/2015

"There've been some issues, but they're all under control now," says Sashka's message on my answerphone, the first time I have heard from home for five days.

What????!!!!!!!!!!!!!!!!!!!!!! The stupid electric gate? The Aga again? The boiler? A burst pipe? The bloody Mazza-rator? Ponies on my lawn? What could it be? I lie awake all night in trepidation as to what has gone wrong with my wretched house this time.

"Hya, yes. A colt stallion escaped from a nearby farm, got into the field, and has been shagging Vegas and Panda senseless, over and over again, for the past 24 hours," Sashka informs me, when I finally get through to her.

"Lucky them!" I exclaim. "I am so glad - Panda's nearly eighteen and has been longing for it all her life. What fun they must both have had. So what happens about the morning after pill then?"

I gather from Sashka that this kind of incident is so rare that immediate post-coital contraception doesn't really exist for horses, but Veronica, our vet, is sourcing an injection which has to be carried out within the next fortnight.

"I hope the farmer's paying," I say, and of course Sashka has already sorted that.

I wonder whether both mares will be suffering from morning sickness by the time I get home?

Getting to Wales
03/05/2015

We're very modern here.

Ex and his girlfriend and her two daughters are staying for the weekend, in order to help get Faye to the horse show on Monday.

Meanwhile my great mate Alice's husband is also joining us for supper - he is staying at nearby Buckfast monastery, a Dutch couple has just arrived to stay for three nights, and Faye's lovely friend Vivian and her Mum are coming in the morning to do some riding.

Just when Sashka needs to get everything ready for the descent of the Four In A Bed cameras in three days' time.

We are all suffering from mild hysteria, while I'm rushing around writing this before I forget what I think; trying to pack so that I look reasonably attractive doing whatever the next activity turns out to be - it might be basket weaving - prior to setting off for Knighton, just beyond Hay-on-Wye, which, according to the AA will take me 3 1/2 hours. The thing is that judging by previous experience the AA man drives faster than I do, so I think it will be more like four.

I've washed all my black gear (that's all I've been wearing so far, apart from for the knot-tying activity). Louise, from the crew, who is permanently dressed as Marilyn Monroe, calls my black look my 'signature'. I've also washed my white trousers so that hopefully they can rival Tessa's for brightness. But they're still wet.

Most of the horsey girls involved with these episodes of Four In A Bed (and it would appear that there are now an incredible five of us, including the crew's Marilyn and Charlene) possess exactly the same kit, which is tight white trousers tucked into long brown boots, and a blue top. I am worried if I put on this uniform that everyone might think I'm copying Tessa and Charlene, so I may just stick to black. They are all so going to love my 'activity', but I'm not allowed to reveal what it is yet.

163

I am now having to be chaperoned at all times, because we have discovered that I am a real chatterbox, instinctively interrogating everybody I meet without even realising that I'm doing it! Whilst I am finally aware that you're not allowed to talk to anyone off-camera on this programme, I don't seem to be able to help it. It's absolutely not deliberate. So I keep getting into trouble, as everything has to be a surprise so that the camera can capture the contributors' genuine reactions to anything that's said.

I keep trying to second-guess what is going to happen next, but have so far been completely wrong every time.

I am chuffed to bits that Joan appears to 'get' me, rather than assuming I'm a posh bitch. "You and your one-liners - you should be on the stage!" she said to me over breakfast at Don and Callum's. Oh how I preened! Oh how I warmed to Joan!

I've trawled through TripAdvisor, and I'm fairly sure that Joan and Thomas's place is going to be a small cottage with a music/craft/writing studio, in beautiful surroundings, with not great bedrooms. I think the activity is going to be either making sort of folk music, or learning a Ceilidh. I don't hate Ceilidhs as much as Morris Dancing, so I won't mind too much if it's that, provided we don't have to dress up. I hope it's not boring basket weaving. I would love to learn to play Frere Jacque on Joan's accordion, which she calls 'Flora', and takes with her everywhere she goes.

All will be revealed soon enough. I can't wait. I am permanently so excited in my Four In A Bed bubble that soon I am going to get a tummy ache.

Sorry Seems to be the Easiest Word
09/05/2015

Plop! The £1000 mike falls, splash, into my wee wee. Quickly I grab it by its wire and pull it out dripping wet, and wrap it in some bog roll.

I am festooned with wires and furry bits stuck to the inside of my jumper, attempting to go to the loo without any of the clobber falling off - forgetting that I am wearing two mikes, not just one.

"Oh no, Sixties Steve is going to be really cross with me now!" I panic.

Something about the stress of all this filming has turned me into a deeply clumsy person. First I threw chocolate powder all over The Boys' white carpet, having mistakenly thought it was a delicious low calorie chocolate mint,attempting to rip it open with my teeth.

Next, I tripped over the leg of the TV crew's light, and sent coffee flying all over Ivor and Tessa's Farrow and Ball immaculate stone coloured wall.

And now this! All in just a couple of days' filming!

I have never said 'sorry' so often in my life! About once an hour, on average, I think. If I'm not bumping into things, breaking things, or making things dirty, I'm saying the wrong thing.

There is a technique to this interviewing business. You can never say 'they' - you always have to say "Tessa and Ivor" or whoever, as being a 'talking head' no interviewer is ever shown, and otherwise the thread of the story doesn't make sense.

Likewise, you must never look into the camera lens. "Sorry, oh so sorry, oh sorry silly me," I am saying, over and over again; until it is my challenge to myself to ensure that I am the quickest and easiest of the contributors to interview, requiring the fewest 'takes'. I will never find out whether I manage this, but I so want to come across as professional.

Sixties Steve has long straight hair, long curly sideburns, and dresses from head to toe in black. He is the soundman and initially has appeared rather reserved. He carries a big box around his neck with hundreds of aerials sticking out of it, and hides behind doors, listening to us chatting away all at once. I am intrigued as to what he has heard that he shouldn't have.

Gradually over the days, as I drop more and more mikes on hard floors (I find it entirely impossible to go to the loo with my elasticated pencil-line mini-skirt riding up above my bum, whilst at the same time retaining the mike in its place on my waistband) his expression begins to soften.

Steve originates from Shrewsbury; but I refer to it as Shroseberry, and tell him that there is a jolly good school there.

"It depends which side of the tracks you come from, whether it's Shrewsbury or Shroseberry," replies Steve. "Michael Palin went to the school there. I know because I've worked alongside his daughter who's great!"

Bog Snorkling
09/05/2015

Suddenly I snort out loud to myself with laughter.

I recognise this place. It's near where I once came to compete against Ex in the famous 'Man vs Horse' race.

Ex had been asked to start the event.

"This is the first time I'm going to beat my wife in public," he announced to the large crowd of runners, and off they set - hundreds of them.

Half an hour later, the horses trotted off from the car-park just outside the centre of the little town of Llanwrtyd Wells in central Wales, where the event is held every year, quickly catching up with the slowest of the runners.

The race is 26 miles long, over four mountains, taking place that year in 80 degrees Fahrenheit. Neither Ex nor I had done any preparation for it, and towards the end my horse, Foggles, could hardly move. I kept getting on and off him to give him a bit of rest, but I had to lean against him as we went on, as I could hardly walk upright!

That year the race was won by a man, with the first horse coming in third. Foggles and I did quite well, not all that surprisingly completing the race an hour before Ex. But Foggles wasn't a great horse for Dartmoor, and I managed to sell him to some other race participants, returning home with an empty trailer, legs so stiff I could only walk up and down the stairs backwards, and a cheque for £4000.

Anyway, the organisers, a company called Green Events, also stage the annual 'Bog Snorkling' contest.

So now it has suddenly dawned on me what our next activity is going to be.

"Oh no," I think. "How very Four In A Bed. They are going to completely humiliate us. Oh yuck. How disgusting – they're going to make us swim through mud."

I am otherwise so happy and excited by my whole Four In A Bed experience so far, that I find I am singing "He's a walking miracle; oooh oooh!" very loudly, as I merrily drive the 179 miles from Dartmoor to the third B&B in the competition.

'That would be a good sing-along to include in the programme,' I think, but remember they can't use any modern tunes at all, even in the background, because of licensing and copyright issues. Presumably accounting for why there is so much more classical music used by the media than is probably reflected in real life. I quickly change to 'Men of Harlech', but can't remember any words other than 'gaily prancing'.

By now I am just on the Shropshire/Welsh border, and suddenly all along both sides of the road are pictures of my old mate Peter Downe – who was the best looking boy in my school. He would now be 56 and appears to be standing for the Conservatives in the election in a couple of days' time.

I meet with the TV crew at an impersonal hotel for another LittleChat, and then follow two of them to the third B&B, doing a few 'drive by' shots as we go. As ever, curious passers-by gather - dying to know what's going on, half-hoping they might get included, and half-hoping that they won't. This one looks like a rather threatening indigenous Forest of Dean type of person, shaking his fist at us.

On we go through countryside that looks like the cover of my not-the-original copy of 'The Sound of Music'.

"Aagghh!" We have just driven past a large blue sign saying "Therapy Centre for Humans and Animals, and B&B".

"I don't want to be therapised!" I mumble. "I like me the way I am!"

So we're here, driving up a steep rough track to a rather tumbledown looking collection of sheds and a farmhouse, past an elderly-looking horse grazing calmly in a field.

As ever, I have to reverse, and then drive up to the house again several times, so that they can take shots of me arriving from different angles, 'tight' and 'wide'.

And finally I am allowed to meet up again with Thomas and Joan - tonight's hosts.

It turns out that the pair met when Thomas was Joan's temporary bank manager. "Oh dear - I do my banking online" I wail. "No wonder I find it so impossible to meet anyone!"

They take me up a narrow stairway to a small, pretty bedroom. I am very agreeably surprised. It's called 'The Lilac Room' even though everything is blue, and there is a picture of a hyacinth on the wall.

The twin beds appear to have new mattresses, bedlinen and pillows. "Not bad," I think. And then I am told that we have 'shared facilities'. There's a loo along the passage, and a bathroom down the stairs, through Thomas and Joan's kitchen, past a couple of large, rather smelly dogs in big cages, and through another doorway or two.

I am filmed examining the bathroom's cleanliness, and discover lots of drip marks on the shower walls and door, an old bath mat with hairs underneath it, and some very healthy-looking plants hanging over the edge of the bath where your head would normally go.

"I probably won't use this, as I had a bath this morning, and it's a rather long way to come from the bedroom," I say to the camera.

If talking to yourself is the first sign of madness, any viewers of this programme will think I'm completely barking, as I do very little else. And I return to my room to prepare for the 'activity'.

We are led into Thomas and Joan's smallish sitting room where Joan kneels with a fluffy welsh collie on her lap.

"We are going to be learning shiatsu for dogs today," she starts.

She shows us where all the energy lines are along the dog's back, an inch or so away from each side of the spine, and then each B&B is presented with a dog of our own.

They're quite nice dogs, and I have a go, but I find really it's just easier to stroke mine. I am partnered with Thomas, so when it's his turn to massage the dog I say, "Presumably you've massaged dogs millions of times. Why don't you massage me instead?" and I lie down on the rug which has been put down for the dogs.

Joan is not amused and inadvertently calls me the name for a female dog in front of everybody and on-camera. "Do you really want all the men to lie on you?!" she exclaims.

Ooops. I pretend I have hardly heard, but really - she does get it wrong sometImes!

Come morning I realise that I must wash my hair yet again, if I'm going to continue to be of universal appeal to all mankind once this programme gets aired, and I wander the 1/2 mile down to the bathroom in my fake silk polyester dressing gown. Cold water! Aggh! My pet hate! But I just have to wash my hair, so I do it quickly, leap out of the bath, and am so cold that I run back upstairs, forgetting to leave everything nice for the next person, or to pick the mat up off the floor, while the hairy grungy tepid water slowly runs out of the bath.

Trying to blow dry my hair is tricky with a mirror of a 2" diameter – that's all there is in the bedroom. I have to keep running from the hairdryer to the bigger mirror in the upstairs loo to sort out my fringe.

Thomas and Joan don't serve a full English breakfast, just their own eggs and continental everything else.

"Oooh that's a big one!" I hear myself saying, as I help myself to the largest croissant that I have ever seen. Meanwhile Ivor, who likes his bacon, launches into a discussion about which is least healthy: a grilled cooked breakfast, or a sugary fatty croissant, sugary cereals and sugary yogurt.

Joan, meanwhile, is in a state because she has prepared her cooked eggs for the agreed time of 9.30am, whereas everything is running late as ever, the eggs are all going hard, and her hens haven't laid any more.

The feedback form is tricky. I haven't slept for weeks, last night mostly because of the mild, invasive smell of dog which I simply can't stand.

Mine looks as though it's a new carpet, but I can't help wondering how many different visiting dogs have slept on it. At 4am, or anyway some time well before dawn, an insistent cockerel started up and wouldn't stop. I'd always thought I would like to keep chickens, but this one I hope we'll have for breakfast.

I mark Thomas and Joan's 'facilities' with a 5, and circle the 'No' at the bottom of the form, to let them know that I don't want to come back.

Having said that, at £55 for two, this is the perfect place for impecunious dog-lovers. Cheaper than staying at home, utterly stunning location, and interesting hosts too. Joan is a very qualified horsewoman and animal shiatsu expert, while Thomas is president of some Carp Fishing Society and drives cars between destinations as his professional occupation.

If you don't like a fair amount of animal dirt, shared not immaculate facilities, and hundreds and thousands of animals everywhere you look, however, steer clear of this place by five miles!

Playing the Game
09/05/2015

The original verbal agreement with the programme's producers had been that I was taking part 'in order to find a new boyfriend'.

But it seems that the people involved in the programme change almost by the hour, and this time's producer wasn't party to the original discussion.

Which makes things difficult for both of us, because, in retrospect, I don't think that she would have supported the idea in the first place.

As filming progresses, things seem to be becoming increasingly tricky.

After all – it is supposed to be a competition. I am a bit paranoid that I am constantly doing or saying the wrong thing.

It's beginning to drive me nuts that I'm not allowed to ask anybody anything except 'have you seen the weather for tomorrow?' Perhaps I am affected particularly strongly because I haven't got anybody with me to share my experiences.

But it's a shame, because I think it means 'Wormgate' is beginning to fester.

The camera crew members however, are absolutely delightful, cheerful, interested and enthusiastic, and so easy to talk to that I am beginning to wonder what I have found myself saying to their cameras. The more charming they are, the less discreet I become. I am playing for laughs and I love those cameras!

But one of my concerns now, is that by being so keen to please and 'play the game', dear Joan is unwittingly turning herself into the fall guy.

Charlene asks during one LittleChat: "Are you afraid of Joan?"

I explode with spontaneous mirth, gasping for air.

"What are you on? No, of course not! But I am afraid of hurting her."

I am beginning to think that Joan is a well-meaning, straightforward, rather vulnerable and fragile person, however loud, bossy and opinionated she might be.

I have always felt that it would be in my interests to be nice to, and about, everybody in this show – I even wrote to the original producers saying so - and I'm sticking with my decision, however hard it is sometimes. "Be nice, nice, nice, nice, always nice," is my daily mantra to myself.

It is confusing being in a competition which you've never had the slightest intention of trying to win. "Don't you think that's a bit defeatist?" I am asked, when yet again I state with conviction that I am going to come last, because the competition criteria simply don't fit my niche business.

But I just won't compromise my integrity by saying something that I don't mean.

"If it were called 'The happiest remotest luxury B&B in Southern England' then I might go all competitive on you," I explain to the producer.

The format just doesn't seem to work smoothly with me being more interested in selling myself, than in selling my B&B.

Eventually I am clearly advised that the programme cannot include the fact that I'm looking for a boyfriend in the final edit. And by now, as it happens, I have reached the same conclusion myself. There are just too many weirdos out there, and I am too vulnerable, living alone with my young daughter in the middle of nowhere.

The thing's not going to be transmitted until next January anyway, and who knows what will have happened by then?

Meanwhile, taking part is proving even more fun and interesting than I thought it would. My biggest worry now, is that if Tessa and The Boys get any funnier, I am going to wet myself in front of 10 million people all around the world!

And then Chazza, the most junior member of the crew, suddenly asks me whether I have considered appearing on 'Gogglebox' - an incredibly popular television programme that his company also makes, featuring normal people (if you can call them that) sitting on their sofas watching telly and commenting on what they see.

"Well of course I have," I reply, monumentally flattered. "Can you get me onto it?"

Like Gogglebox, one of the most endearing characteristics of Four In A Bed, I think, is its quirkiness. While the contract states that contributors should adhere to 'the spirit of the game' – it's not spelled out anywhere that I can find, what this actually is. We carefully complete all the feedback forms, yet the marks and comments we give have little or no bearing on the final outcome of the competition. We're not allowed to use half-marks on the form – but God knows why not. For instance, I wanted to mark Tessa and Ivor 9.9 recurring for 'cleanliness', but wasn't allowed to!

Meanwhile, in my experience, the low-budget generalist types of accommodation tend to do better, though not always, than the niche operators such as Joan and myself.

Each participant's interpretation of what a 'best value B&B' should comprise is just so wonderfully personal, individual - and unpredictable.

And it's all these imponderables and constant surprises that, for me at any rate, give Four In A Bed its uniquely addictive charm and appeal.

At Home to Four In A Bed
09/05/2015

"It's just beautiful!" I breathe down the phone to Sashka.

I am home from Shropshire and have examined, in microscopic detail, the three bedrooms that our guests are going to use. The only fault I have picked up is a forgotten coffee pot in one room. Sashka has achieved a miracle!

I can almost feel the determination and stress that she and Godfrey have undergone as they've been touching up this, and mending that - even repainting an entire wall in the dining room - because the congealed food stuck to it over the last decade, behind my grandmother's rusty old plate heater (I've replaced it with a new one off eBay), looked so unedifying.

I race out into the garden, through the howling gale and rain, in the dark, to do the mowing, while Faye is ordered to sweep up leaves off the steps, clean the weird stone sculpture, and put away the garden chairs' dripping cushions. As I chug my way up and down last week's stripes in the lawn, I pause to stuff torn up bits of old rag, drenched in petrol, down the mole hills - perhaps that will finally stop the blighters in their earthy tracks.

That night, I have to choose between sleeping in Will's room in the attic, or on the sofa in the sun (or more appropriately named rain) room. I opt for the latter, and at last Faye and I bed down, leaving the three immaculate bedrooms and en-suite bathrooms ready for the TV crew to invade at 8am the following morning.

I am not at all surprised that I don't sleep - as usual - and to make things worse, the light floods in through the skylight early in the morning.

The producer can't include me raving on about Sashka in the programme unless she is actually filmed, as it doesn't make logical sense for me to refer to someone that the viewers don't get to see. So, rather reluctantly, she arrives too, just as the film crew draws up.

We all stand in the kitchen and I am given another friendly warning about behaving myself – rather similar to what I'm in the habit of receiving from Sashka – but she has known me for ten years!

Sixties Steve wanders in, wondering, apologetically, whether he might exchange his instant coffee for real. He appears to be something of a coffee connoisseur, buying his own brew from Regent Street and preparing it in a Nespresso machine, he explains.

My first B&Bers are about to arrive and I am genuinely excited and looking forward to entertaining them! They are so nice! I am longing to show off my lovely home to them!

The first pair to arrive are Tessa and Ivor. "It's exactly what I thought it would be!" exclaims Tessa, hugging me and jumping up and down.

"Good - she's got me," I think to myself, relieved. We film their arrival, including Twiglet bouncing around, a few times, and then I take them up to Hexworthy, and we have about three takes of that too. Ivor and Tessa appear to be OK about the room. Ivor's not quite sure what the genuine Corby trouser press thing is. Meanwhile I think to myself how glorious the large south-facing, pristine room looks, with sunshine (all of a sudden) flooding in.

I retire downstairs and twiddle my thumbs for a while, until The Boys arrive. How I love them! I show them up to Dartmeet a few times for the cameras, and then retire back to the kitchen to twiddle my thumbs some more.

Finally Thomas and Joan turn up in their old banger. (Ivor and Tessa drive an enormous, white, bling truck, very like mine.) I have been worrying about Joan. My sense is that she has been annihilated on her feedback forms, and that she will be very upset. But she seems perfectly sanguine and cheerful, and I give her a long, hard, meaningful hug - which has to be done again because we have squashed the microphone.

I take them up to Bellever and start twiddling my thumbs some more.

I am extremely troubled because Sashka disappeared without saying anything, while I was completing my first LittleChat of the day. I am anxious that she is twitchy and tired from working so hard on my behalf, and possibly upset that I asked her to make a different kind of coffee, and has gone off hurt after all that she's done for me, and now I can't credit her in the final programme, which will really matter when it's on air and all this is over.

I can't really think or concentrate on anything else actually. If I have inadvertently made Sashka unhappy, this is miles more serious than appearing on a TV reality show.

Suddenly the pressure is on, and I'm no longer enjoying things quite so much.

Adventure Clydesdale
10/05/2015

"You look like someone from a Jilly Cooper book," says Thomas.

Ooops. Maybe I have gone a bit far. I am wearing Christmas stocking present brand new bright white spray-on jodhpurs, long black riding boots, a well cut tight brown shooting jacket, hairnet and hat, and swishing around a very long, very whippy, dressage crop. Maybe I'd better drop the whip.

I've displayed a couple of fishing rods by the entrance of the house, to put the contributors off the scent of what we are really going to do, because - of course - we are going to be riding for our 'activity'!

But not just any old riding. We're off to see the magnificent Clydesdale horses who live up the road. These are huge heavy horses, originating from Scotland. They look quite regal, striding in a line out across the moor. A couple of weeks ago at the local point to point, I won £8 on 'Tom Parker' who came in first, in the special Clydesdale race.

How incredibly fortunate we have been, regarding the 'activities' on this programme. Boating, off-road driving, 'dogging' and riding. No silly dressing up, no humiliation, all genuinely interesting, sensible on the whole, and enjoyable things to do. What a relief!

We climb into various cars, and enjoy all the normal guessing games as we approach the horses' yard about, "I wonder what the activity's going to be?" Finally we're led into four roomy stables, each housing a horse for us to groom and prepare for hacking.

Tessa gets on with the job in hand, while Ivor looks on, meanwhile Joan goes into mega horsey-woman mode. "I am a qualified whatever in this, and an advanced thingy in that," she informs Tarquin, the owner. She grooms her horse in two minutes flat and then looks at me.

"Not like that Mary! Is that all you've done?" she cries, and comes into my box. My horse is called Cyril.

"You'll be kicked if you brush the tail that way," she says. "Look, I'll show you!"

So she puts the not very clean thick tail across her thigh, facing the back of the box, brushing it vigorously. "That's how you do it!" she says triumphantly.

"But I'll get my new jodhpurs dirty if I do that," I wail, and go to rub Cyril's forehead, as I have seen Monty Roberts, the horse whisperer, do on telly. "Actually, it's a good thing to work with animals slowly and quietly," comments Tarquin, as I softly murmur "who is this bossy lady?" into Cyril's ear.

Joan is now busy doing all my work for me, as I go to lean against the side of the box. I am knackered. "How is it that I so often, and so easily, get other people to do everything for me?" I wonder to myself for the millionth time.

And now we are ready to mount these enormous, gentle creatures. It is extraordinary how you can tell how good a rider is, almost right from the moment they first approach a horse. I am not disappointed. It is clear that both Joan and Tessa know what they are doing. I am in love with Tessa's lower leg position. Heels down, feet steady. I wish I could ride like that.

We proceed in a stately fashion to a nearby field, and walk around it, with Callum on a leading rein, astride the glorious Tom Parker. I am fairly scared. Panda and Mad Vegas are the only two equines I have ridden in six years! Riding a new horse is much more frightening than, say, driving an unfamiliar car.

To start with, everything is sort of OK, but then they want us to walk away from the TV crew, and canter back, towards them, which is also slightly downhill and towards home for the horses. Oo-er. If I were organising such a thing I would opt for an enclosed track leading up a hill and away from home.

Anyhow - so we three riders walk our horses away from the assembled group of spectators and cameramen, reach the end of the field, prepare to turn around, and suddenly - bingo! The horses turn on their haunches and fly into a fast and extremely bouncy canter, swooping up and down like dolphins, if that makes sense. I am taken totally unawares. I can't stop Cyril, and am conscious that his bounciness is infecting the others. It feels as though I am charging back towards home, but dammit, I've gone the wrong way round the camera. So we have to do it again.

This time Tessa's horse does the most enormous leap into the air. She sits it well, and it feels as though mine wants to copy her. Oh no! "One more time!" cry the cameramen. The horses are beginning to go a bit bonkers now. They're not machines. Off we go, attempting to walk away but they're jogging. We try to turn them right instead of left, which is the direction they're used to, but no - off they bomb again.

"I'm bottling out," I announce, and go to stand next to Callum. Tom Parker the wonder-horse, continues to stand quietly, while the two more proficient riders have one more go at the canter.

At last it's time to ride the horses back to their boxes, and I heave a sigh of relief. Phew! That was a bit exciting! They don't behave like that out on the moor!

The Last Supper
10/05/2015

Supper with all my new friends is to be at the lovely Rugglestone Inn, just outside Widecombe - the pub of choice with the locals because of its good food, genuine rural atmosphere and friendly service. This is going to be the most wonderful finale to our adventure! And even better, Sashka has replied to the two devastated phone messages I've left her, explaining that she simply had to leave in order to do some work for her other clients! Phew, phew, phew.

"So why have you taken part in this programme?" Joan turns to me, over her shepherd's pie.

"Move the camera!" shouts the producer, before I have a chance to make up a reply.

And then Ivor gets going. With his back to me, and looking at the wall, he challenges me on my dog policy, and asks me why I run a B&B in the first place.

All these questions would be fine if my inquisitors looked me in the eye and questioned me in a smiley friendly way, but suddenly everything seems to have gone cold and aggressive.

I'm flustered, I go all defensive, I start banging on about private schools in a stupid way as nobody has attacked me on that front as yet.

And then I make my biggest gaff of all time.

"If you're so broke, why don't you open your smallest room for one night at a time?" somebody asks me, perfectly nicely and innocently.

"Oh because I can't be arsed," I reply nonchalantly.

Oh dear. There's a sudden atmosphere.

"Oh, quick, can you change that to 'because it's not efficient for me'?" I yell to the cameras, but no, of course they won't. Deary me. I've really buggered it up now.

I have been found out. I am arrogant. I am flippant. I don't take this business seriously. I look down on people who rely on it. I clearly don't need the money. I don't do it as my livelihood. I'm all platinum spoon after all. Oh dear.

I am deeply distressed. I have lost my new mates in one throw-away remark.

I am incredibly uncomfortable, and so massively, massively disappointed after what I had thought was going to be a thoroughly enjoyable evening.

And then, before anything has a chance to be resolved, or any of us has been allowed to have pudding, the crew is clearing up the cameras, ready for our LittleChats, which take part in various nooks and crannies of the pub, and/or outside in the freezing cold.

I tell the camera that I think Ivor has asked some useful, pertinent and fair questions, but that I am terribly upset by his body language.

When we get home I 'prep' breakfast - putting out all the pots, pans, bowls, utensils etc that last week I wrote down that I would be needing. Breakfast tomorrow will be the biggest challenge of the whole adventure - breakfast for six people, each of them asking for something different. Thank God I made that list well in advance. I am in such a state after that dinner that I can't really think straight.

Then I do what the TV crew do. I write up a Q&A crib sheet for myself.

"Why am I taking part in Four In A Bed?"

"Because I want to learn how to run my Bed and Breakfast better, from the most experienced and knowledgeable, and most critical judges I could possibly ever find," I lie merrily.

"What is your attitude to dogs?"

Well I have discovered that on the Home Page of my website, in the third paragraph I have written "sorry no dogs as they eat Twiglet and whine, and upset the other guests", and then further down in the fifth paragraph I've called Wydemeet a dog friendly B&B! Stupid me. So I immediately make up a new policy. I will take dogs in low season, but not at peak times. Hah! Sorted!

And finally ...

"I run the B&B because after the marital bust-up I lost my family - and I wasn't prepared to also lose the home that I know and love, that I bought for us all twenty years ago; or to take my children out of their schools, or sell my horses," I wrote down. "In the event, I did actually have to sell the car that I adored, replacing it with a Ford Focus I bought off eBay for eight hundred quid.

"My income was slashed, but I am hugely lucky enough to retain some, and the B&B is an attempt at enabling me to continue with my ridiculously grand lifestyle. Incidentally, I don't see any of you having to sleep on the sofa, or live without a bedroom when you have guests staying."

".... But I am massively busy looking after the children all on my own, and time is my enemy. So everything I do has to be highly efficient. It doesn't make sense for me to use the smallest room for B&B for a night at a time. I can make far more money, miles more quickly, by simply using the two big rooms, for a minimum of two nights each."

Well. Ivor has inadvertently forced me to address the real issue. He has taught me what it is that my oldest friends have failed to get through to me over the past 55 years. That I have a habit of getting carried away, in order to be provocative, to show off, to get attention, exaggerating, saying things that I don't entirely mean, in order to cause a reaction.

And sometimes, most especially with strangers from very different backgrounds, my audience doesn't get it, takes what I am saying at face value, and without even realising what I am doing, I cause massive, massive offence.

A fifth reason that I got involved with Four In A Bed was to find out how I come across. Well I have just found out. And I am shocked and shaken. And now I understand so much.

So, with my answers all written down and sorted in my head, I am ready to face the contributors and the cameras over breakfast tomorrow, and at the denouement on Friday. Now that I know what I am going to say, I am finally so relaxed that I oversleep on my big white sofa.

A Circus Act
10/05/2015

Faye, until today, had never heard of AbFab. Well now she has. She's watched eight old episodes and laughed her head off.

All starts calmly. Cooking breakfast for six on a two plate Aga is a challenge for anybody, but I've remembered to turn it up the previous night, and I'm heating all the water separately in an electric kettle, so that the Aga doesn't lose all its heat.

Initially I had said to the programme makers that I would just be offering a full English to the other contributors. But it turns out that this is against the rules - you have to offer them what you would normally offer to your guests.

Oh dear.

I habitually say - "You can have whatever you can think of for breakfast, except things that I don't like, such as kippers, haddock, black pudding and stuff. So here's a suggested menu, but you can try me with any other ideas, and I will have a go."

So that's what I am going to have to say. And I know Four In A Bed types - "A full English with no beans"; "A double full English with two sausages but only one egg," "Eggs Royale combined with Florentine", etc etc etc.

So I have had a wizard wheeze. I will cook eggs to order, but get Faye, aka Cinderella, to do silver service, or at least stainless steel service, with the rest.

I have decided that we will take the orders together, since this is Faye's first attempt at being a breakfast waitress, and under the cameras it appears to be so very difficult to get everything right, even though it looks a bit weird for us both to be standing there, pens and notepads poised.

"So, teas and coffees?" I query. Five English Breakfast Teas and one coffee are requested. Not too difficult, yet somehow even this simple order immediately flies out of my head.

Very soon all is ready, and I pour Joan a nice, big cafetiere full of coffee.

Oh no! There isn't enough hot water left in the poxy plastic electric kettle to fill three further teapots! I put enough in each one for a single cup of tea, and we take them through.

Dammit. Don lifts up his teapot, realizes it's very light, and looks inside.

"There's no water in here, Mary!" he laughs. There's not enough in Tessa's and Ivor's shared silver teapot for a cup of tea either. I can't believe it! How could I have been so stupid?! I pretend to shoot myself as I am filmed.

Once the hot beverages have been sorted, even lactose free warm milk for Joan's coffee, Faye and I go back again into the dining room, to take the dreaded cooked breakfast order, and I explain what's on offer.

Unlike the other contributors, I am cooking breakfast for six, not five, and then Joan goes and orders two breakfasts: a cheese omelette and a baked egg, so in the final analysis I am actually preparing seven breakfasts. Aaagghhh!

Meanwhile Faye reappears in the kitchen, interrupting my flow of intense concentration. "Joan says her bowl is dirty, and there aren't any more of the proper ones," she informs me. And calmly, in front of the cameras and everybody else, she gives Joan a little plastic baby bowl with a picture of Donald Duck's wife on it, with 'oops!' written on the bottom, left behind by the last people who rented Wydemeet.

Next, I reappear in the dining room with more pots of tea, porridge for Don, and we need a couple more mats to protect the rather nice polished mahogany table from all these hot utensils.

183

"Over there, Cinders!" I order Faye.

She opens a drawer.

"There's nothing but your old love letters in here," she says, and howls with laughter, tears streaming down her face.

I return to all my pans and quite quickly everything is ready in all its different dishes. I ask Faye to take through the sausages and (both back and streaky) dry cured bacon, all kept warm under silver foil, and put them on the new plate heater in the dining room. I stick the dish of tomatoes, sautéed potatoes and mushrooms on the side of the Aga while I complete the eggs.

Oh no! I've cooked fried instead of poached for Callum! Quickly I put more hot water on for the poached egg, and slide three fried eggs onto Ivor's plate - after all he did say, "As it comes."

I am about to send Ivor's eggs out with Faye to the table, when I notice a 'curly' stuck in one of them. I am shaking so much by now that I can't pick it off. I nearly have to ask Faye to do it.

Meanwhile - baked egg????!!!! I haven't done one of those since I was on the Cordon Bleu School of Cookery's Brides' Cookery Course which I did with a bloke when I was 17, and nearly got flung out for drinking the wine instead of putting it in the cooking.

I butter a little pot, break an egg into it and shove it into the top oven of the Aga for a few minutes.

Nigel the cameraman, who has been filming my activities in the kitchen, asks me to take it out and put it back in again. "NO!" I scream, aware that I am shaking so much by now that I will definitely drop it.

Faye takes the plates with their eggs on into the dining room, and together we provide our stainless steel service, moving to each contributor around the table, and then we leave them to it, to enjoy.

184

"How do you think it went?" queries Nigel, camera up close.

"God (by mistake I seem to prefix everything with 'God', which they can't use on a family TV show) - that was worse than a 2'9" cross country course," I exclaim. "But not as bad as a 3' one."

I go back in to clear the plates.

"That breakfast was absolutely divine!" exclaims Joan. I am touched to my core.

"My sausage was cold," says Ivor.

"I'm afraid my food was rather cold too," says lovely Callum.

Oh dear. Faye, not realising what it was for, had inadvertently taken the silver foil covering off the sausages and bacon.

Tessa has left both her specifically requested white toast (I actually gave her a 'Bit of Both' - slightly mouldy - all I had) and her rather runny scrambled egg. She will be hungry for the rest of the day because of me.

Aagghh!

"How did you all sleep?" I chirrup.

"We ran out of hot water in the shower," says Tessa.

"Ours went cold too," Callum says reluctantly.

Oh dear. My two absolute no-no's. Cold water and cold food. Oh well. I'm not 'In It To Win It' anyway - I have always said we would come last. These people are not my normal customer base. I do not normally cook for six or seven people all asking for different things at once. And I am targetting my real customers through the telly. It doesn't much matter what these six think - it is what the viewers think, and I am simply praying that the entire fiasco has looked like tremendous fun and very appealing.

185

Anyone with any intelligence will be able to see that cold food here is an anomaly (I hope!) Faye and I have been trying out a new system and it hasn't quite worked. But it will another time. And putting everything out at once did mean that anybody could change their mind about what they wanted at the last minute, if they wanted to.

The couples are taken away for their LittleChats and I go and sit outside in the sun, which has suddenly come out – hurray! A sheep and her lamb have appeared on the lawn, another favourite cameraman, Bob, is taking lovely pictures of the house, and all is looking gorgeous.

Faye and Twiglet bounce over. "That was SO FUN!!!" exclaims Faye, as Twiglet jumps six foot straight up in the air to retrieve a proffered dog treat. Faye is, without doubt, Television Gold.

But, I, on the other hand, am finding it very, very difficult to calm down. I have been so very outside my comfort zone.

"Sort yourself out, girl," I scold myself. "It went well! It was funny! And it was also perfectly clear that you can cook a really good breakfast under normal conditions too!"

The next stage is the goodbyes, each of which has to be shot from several different angles several times. Poor Ivor has to lug an enormous suitcase up and down my steps over and over again. Never mind. He's a strong, fit man. He was selected to play prop for the English rugby team, but then had a mining accident, and now has two metal plates in his back. A story that, if prompted, will make him break down and cry when repeated.

I am dying of curiosity to know whether Wydemeet is what my new friends expected. In a quick private moment, Tessa whispers to me off-air: "Judging by how you present yourself, I thought it was going to be immaculate!" and Joan says so too. I am chuffed to bits. Clearly they are both of the opinion that I have been looking chic and smart, in my three new, identical, black woollen jumpers. So they didn't notice my shellac manicure beginning to chip after disposing of mole hills, the fact that my socks are different lengths, and that under normal circumstances, I have flat greasy hair and am covered in straw.

I wave them all off, and now it is reading the Feedback Forms time. The most emotionally demanding part of this entire experience. I am absolutely scared stiff of what is about to be revealed.

No, No, Yes!
10/05/2015

"It's as though it's alive; pulsating and evil!" I exclaim to the camera, as I eye the Four In A Bed blue book in front of me, not allowed to open the front page until I'm told 'go'.

"How good was your hostess?" is the first question, and I've scored a 9. There's a smiley face, but also a sad one. This form has clearly been completed by Tessa.

Shame. I've always thought my best thing is my hostessing. The sad face is about their confusion as to who I am, and what exactly I am trying to say and do.

The rest of the marks, considering Wydemeet is the sort of place that they would never, ever choose to stay in, I think are relatively generous. Clever Tessa has spotted that my curtains haven't been cleaned for years. They hate the feeling that they're in 'my' room, they had cold water, but they like the spaciousness and the 'accessories'.

It's a 'no' to coming back again. No surprises there.

The next form is from Joan and Thomas. They've given me a relatively poor eight for my hostessing skills. "Welcoming, but lacked the one-to-one service that we would normally expect from a B&B," they write.

"What's that about?" I wonder to myself.

I move down to facilities. They've given me a 4. No wardrobe, marks on the wall, room too small for two, unfinished light fitting, knobs loose on bedhead - on and on it goes.

Damn. They've lifted up the dead sheep on the floor, and discovered the hole in the carpet where the old basin used to be. Bellever was a wash room complete with showers and loos when we bought the house, as Wydemeet used to be an adventure centre, accommodating 36 children at a time!

It's another 'no' as far as coming back is concerned. Again not a surprise. Joan has been clear that she doesn't like the look of Dartmoor. "Bleak, featureless and thin ponies" is how she describes it, compared with her beloved Shropshire.

This is all becoming a farce. I am beginning to laugh about the whole thing. Then I turn to the last page.

Hostessing skills: "TEN!!!!!!!!!!!!!! FANTASTIC!!!!!!!!!!!!! A giggle a minute!!!!!!" have written The Boys. Cleanliness: 10, Spotless! Sleep quality: 10.

Facilities: "very upset that the hat didn't fit" they comment - as they have been trying on the skiing clothes stored in the bottom two drawers of the large chest.

Would you come back? The biggest roundest YES ever - circled again and again until the pen has gone through the paper. "Can't wait for the next performance!" they add.

"That was absolutely great!" enthuses the camera crew. The producer is all smiley and helpful. "I can't believe we didn't have to go back over anything. Really, really good!"

I preen. Perhaps I will be able to get some regular part on the telly after all?

We move through to where Bob has moved things around in my sitting room, making it look much nicer than it normally does, for the final LittleChat of the day.

I explain to the camera that according to the competition criteria I can't possibly win this competition as it stands. I charge more than I think the room would otherwise be worth because of Wydemeet's unique location, and because I offer a 24/7 service with no rules, opening up my home to my guests as I would to family and friends, and waiting on them accordingly.

And my guests are really paying for 'probably the most remote B&B in southern England, with footpaths and bridleways stretching in every direction from the garden gate.'

"You can't say that - you'll just make the others cross," I am advised. "Their B&Bs are all unique in their different ways too, and anyway - yours is worth what you charge as a stand-alone B&B, as it is."

I am chuffed by this. Of all people, the producers of Four In A Bed must know!

The Denouement
10/05/2015

I oversleep again. This has been my first really good night's sleep of a fortnight!

It's all over now. I can hardly even be bothered to wash my hair for the nth time, and I put on an old pair of tights with snags in them.

I make myself realise that we are still being featured on global TV, with an audience of ten million, and begin to panic as it's clear that I'm about to be late for the 8am sharp start time requested, at the same rather bland hotel in Tavistock where last September I celebrated my birthday so happily with the school Mums.

I drive at 70mph across the moor - at a sharp bend, overtaking what looks to be the camera crew. As I might have predicted, when I finally get to the hotel, all is not ready and I am not needed for over an hour. It feels very, very odd being in this familiar lobby, surrounded by television cameras and these unlikely new friends of mine.

189

A school Mum I've known slightly for the past ten years suddenly appears - we first met at Faye's toddlers' tap dance class - and we settle down to discuss stollen dough, until the crew is finally ready.

The contributors are rounded up, and we all troop in to the meeting room and sit in our allotted places, round an enormous table. As ever they have put me nearest the cameras, making me feel as though the whole thing is revolving around me and my general hilarity. How I love that feeling. How much will I live to regret it?

We go through the feedback forms starting with Callum and Don. There is an endless argument between Joan and Callum about whose fault it was that the boys' new coffee percolator fell to pieces in Thomas's hands. In fact, the list of things that seem to have broken in Joan and Thomas's room at the boys' place is so long that the whole thing begins to sound farcical. Thomas went through a wicker chair in the courtyard. Their shower flooded. On and on it goes. I feel like banging my head on the table with boredom.

Then it's Tessa's and Ivor's turn. Wormgate. I have butterflies and am nearly shaking. Due to all the cloak and daggers, the subject has not been raised now for eight days! Festering! The others aren't even aware that it happened! I don't want to talk about it any further, as, for Tessa's and Ivor's sakes, I don't want the disastrous story to be given even more airtime.

Oh F***. It turns out that what has happened is that my hysteria, wailing "Oh Tessa, this is a PR disaster for you, I am so, so sorry!" has, of course, proved self-fulfilling. My extreme reaction has inadvertently served to inflame the situation, making things much worse for Tessa and Ivor than they need have been. What a total and entire F*** Up. Agghh! And, of course, because they don't know me properly, they assume that my histrionics are all part of some sort of sophisticated rich-bitch game, and I have played the situation up on purpose. They don't trust me, because they think I'm one of the posh, shallow, horse-racing-types that typically frequent their B&B.

They are totally confused because they can also see that I appear to have no interest in winning this competition. They absolutely cannot, cannot, cannot get their heads around why I have given them a 9 for cleanliness, and paid them the full asking price for their room.

"Because the worm thing has never happened before, will never happen again, and the room was pristine," I explain slowly and clearly, over and over again.

"I paid you the full amount because that is what I feel the room is worth."

Time for another LittleChat in the chilly hotel garden, and a spot of lunch, and we're back in 'the room' again.

It's Joan and Thomas's turn for a roasting.

Callum and Don have been quite nice about Joan's B&B until it comes to cleanliness. The boys found a huge matted ball of fluff on their bedroom floor. And then the bath, after I had used it, was full of my hair, and I'd left a dirty tide mark around it. I immediately hold my hand up as the culprit on this one.

Things are getting a bit twitchy.

"I paid Joan and Thomas full whack, despite the unremitting smell of dog, because at £27.50 each, if there were two of me, it's cheaper to move into their place than to live at home," I explain. "So for the right person, it's priced appropriately. But for me, well I would prefer to pay more for a bit of additional luxury, and not be surrounded by everybody's dogs all the time."

Again, the other contributors just don't seem to 'get' my approach, although it seems so straightforward to me.

By now, we are all, including the crew, extremely tired, hot, and on edge.

Finally it's my turn. I am under Ivor's spotlight, and I repeat the lines in answer to his questions that I taught myself the night before last. My drivel seems to go on endlessly. I am asked to start again, this time using short, sharp answers. I have no idea how much I have managed to explain on camera, but at least I have, at last, had an opportunity to discuss where I am coming from with Ivor and Tessa, whether they understand me yet, or not.

Going through Callum and Don's comments sheet is easy. "You can't possibly give me a ten for cleanliness!" I exclaim. "Didn't you look under the bed? It's disgusting!"

Everybody is most surprised by this outburst. But I know that under the bed there are bits of felt and canvas hanging down, from the 100 year old box sprung mattress which I have deliberately chosen to retain because it's so comfortable. Tessa would have had a fit if she'd seen it!

In the end, Callum and Don have docked me a fiver because of their cold hot water. Ivor and Tessa have given me £100 for my £130 room because of the water issue, the cold breakfast, undercooked scrambled egg, no wardrobe, dirty curtains, dirty drawers under the lining paper, feeling of invading someone's home, being in the middle of nowhere with nothing to do except walk/ride/fish/cycle/explore/rock-climb/relax etc.

And then we come to Joan and Thomas. I query my apparent lack of hostessing skills, and discover that I've been docked two marks because they have been made to feel like 'the poor relations' - being put in the smallest room, and because I didn't come up to check how they were getting on.

"I put everybody in rooms according to what they charge, so that the most expensive B&B got my most expensive room, and so on," I explain. "It seemed to me to be the fairest way of allocating them."
I find Joan so utterly predictable, and I can't help being rather fond of her as a result. In some ways she reminds me of Faye when she was six. I open the envelope and discover just what I was expecting, as I had predicted to the camera in the last LittleChat. Joan has paid me what she charges. £55. How hilarious! I can't even work out quickly how much the underpayment is, but it's a lot. And I don't care in the least, because, to the appropriate audience watching on TV, I think Wydemeet has come out

looking utterly beautiful and compelling.

Meanwhile Thomas mumbles that actually he would have liked to have come back, and Joan admits that she now thinks the part of Dartmoor she has travelled through this morning on the way to the hotel is nicer than the rough part around Wydemeet.

I think that Joan has probably inadvertently made herself look rather mean and a bit idiotic, whereas I hope and pray that, however mad, I have come out looking like a nice, decent person who is being given an unnecessarily hard time and is responding with good humour and grace.

Later, upon further reflection, though, I think that for the pair of them to pay me basically half of my asking price, equating my offering with theirs, and knowing how this will affect the final outcome of 'the game', is actually quite rude, unjustified, and not very funny really. I have only once, out of hundreds of Four In A Bed episodes, seen anybody underpay by such an enormous margin. And in that case I think it was probably justified.

Time for a coffee break and at last we are allowed to talk openly to each other.

"I haven't been able to tell you until now, but, unlike you guys, I never got involved with this in order to market my B&B - it was, from the start, in order to find a boyfriend!" I reveal to them all. At last!

"If your hysteria wasn't put on in order to win, I will feel quite bad," comments Tessa. I am so very disappointed that she and Ivor didn't trust me, just because I am posh. Wormgate has actually turned out to have rather ruined this whole experience for me, as I had anticipated it might.

"Why haven't you pushed the fact that Wydemeet is for walkers?" enquires Tessa.

"Because I was advised not to - I was told it would make you cross," I reply.

"Why on earth should it? Of course you should emphasise that!" she says firmly.

Bloody hell. I've got one last LittleChat to go - five minutes left of two weeks filming, in which to properly and clearly push my B&B, in the right way, to the right people, in words of one syllable. In fact, simply to repeat the first two sentences of my website, which have taken me a couple of years to perfect.

"My market is affluent walkers and fishermen (thank you Bob for reminding me about the fishermen). I believe Wydemeet is possibly the most remote B&B in southern England," I manage to squeeze into my final interview, this time with my favourite cameraman, Nigel.

But afterwards I am still kicking myself, because I think that I have forgotten to add: "We have footpaths and bridleways stretching in every direction, north, south, east and west, from right outside our garden gate; yet we are only 20 minutes from the A38 highway between Exeter and Plymouth."

Never mind.

And I've got one last little job that I think I must perform. I am sharing a beautifully presented, three-tiered, afternoon tea of titchy little sandwiches and cakes, with Joan and Thomas.

"Joan," I start (there are no cameras now). "Might you do a little something for me? Do you think that when your guests arrive, instead of shutting Thomas in the kitchen, you could push him forward and announce proudly:

'This is my husband Thomas. He is my rock, and without him, I couldn't do any of this.' "

There. I've said it. I do hope she thinks about that. So at least I've learned something from my divorce.

And I've thought of something else too. Here I have been, all on my own,

Billy No-Mates, surrounded by these lovey-dovey couples for two whole weeks. Tessa and Ivor, and Callum and Don, have been together for over 25 years! But who is actually the luckiest of us all? It turns out that Tessa and Ivor, and Joan and Thomas all wanted children, but never managed to have any.

I am the only contributor here who is lucky enough to have a beautiful brace of them.

And now it's time for the winners' announcement.

I am not surprised that they choose me to do the job. Apparently, the final B&B to be visited generally has a useful sitting room, that the crew can use, and the person selected to read out the results is the owner of that B&B, so perhaps this is pure coincidence. Whatever - I am absolutely delighted to be doing it! I am so enjoying all this showing off.

The top envelope says 'Fourth'.

"Last!" I cry. I open the envelope up. It is quite clear whose name is going to be on the card.

"ME!!" I shout grinning. "Well what a surprise!!!!!"

I slowly open the 'Third' envelope, keeping everybody waiting for the announcement, like they do on X-Factor. No surprises again. Dog Heaven for poor people.

So then I turn to the envelope saying 'First' and wave it around a lot, keeping everybody in suspenders. I have been told that the percentage difference in payment between the top two B&Bs is very close.

Slowly I open up the envelope, and even more slowly, I reveal the contents.

"The Boys!" I cry jubilantly, and rush over and hug them both.

Would I Do It Again?
10/05/2015

It's 9pm, and filming is finally over. I am free to collect Faye from her school on my way home from the hotel, where we have now been under the spotlight for thirteen hours. The others have still got nearly 200 miles to drive tonight.

While my head is bursting with all that has gone on over the past couple of weeks, Faye blithely fills me in on her school day as we drive home, and, as if I haven't had enough of it all by now, she insists on watching an episode of Four In A Bed for a laugh before going to bed.

I'm surprised that I'm feeling rather down.

Is it because I am exhausted?

This morning I still feel down. I have been going over and over everything that has happened without stopping, trying to work out what the problem is.

It was all such fun to begin with. I was singing excitedly as I drove along. I had new friends. I was on holiday. I was getting masses of attention and believing that I was being really funny. It was great!

And then, when everybody descended on my house, the stress and negativity kicked in.

I hope and believe that I have succeeded in remaining genial throughout the entire experience, and I am very proud of myself for that. I have found the last few days both slightly depressing, and very tiring, yet I have continued to smile.

I have been anticipating coming last of the four B&Bs in the competition, but I think perhaps it is beginning to grate that beautiful, successful, much-loved Wydemeet B&B, after all our care, excitement and hard work, has been publicly voted 'least good value' B&B. Especially by such a very enormous margin, however ridiculous the reasons behind the outcome, and however stunningly my home eventually comes across on the programme itself.

During the last two weeks I have achieved almost all of what I set out to do. For one thing, I now have a much better idea of how I come across to other people.

I have learned what it is that I do that makes people so very cross, that I never understood before.

And I have had it objectively reaffirmed that there is 'something about me' that could possibly be turned into 'Television Gold'.

How the programme makers choose to edit me, after all that, is anybody's guess.

But however they choose to portray me, there will always be at least 54 genuinely objective five-blob reviews on TripAdvisor, united in their agreement about the wonderful Wydemeet experience.

So, in the meantime, I might just write to the programme-makers, Studio Lambert, asking for a job.

Would I do it again? Yes. But it will take a day or two for this sense of 'down-ness' to dissipate. By the time the programme is actually aired, I don't suppose I will care what's in it all that much. But I hope that I can launch my book at the same time, and that it will lead to even more extraordinary adventures!

She Loved It!
20/05/2015

"We both had so much fun and just LOVED the experience and wish we could do it all again!"

This is what the other Dartmoor B&B (who also used the Rugglestone Inn at Widecombe for their Four, well actually Three, In A Bed dinner) thought of being on the programme.

"All in all it really was one of - if not THE - best experience of our lives," continued delightful Margaret.

I had emailed her to find out how she had felt about the whole thing, and to discover what had happened once it was transmitted. No hate mail and, interestingly, no booking requests, she commented, and that's despite her coming across as extraordinarily charming, and her B&B, although simple, appeared to be utterly beautiful.

And then came the best bit of all. Apparently one chap had contacted her to say that he thought that her step-daughter was 'a cracking bit of stuff' and could he marry her?!

7 Four In A Bed – What They Broadcast

Four In A Bed in September
13/08/2015

They rang.

It's going to be broadcast in September!

That wasn't the plan. They said it wouldn't be on until next January. I will still care about how everything comes across if they show it so soon!

Also my book's not ready, because with the children home for the holidays I spend minimal time away from them on the computer, and have done nothing with it for weeks. I'll just have to get it published on Kindle, double-quick.

So I've decided.

Instead of telling all my 3000 contacts when our episodes are going to be shown, I'm not going to tell anybody at all. As the whole thing could prove to be a complete disaster.

I shall watch the broadcast on my own, with a bottle of Cava and a packet of salt and vinegar Hula Hoops at my side, and see what they've done with me.

And record it for Faye to watch when she comes home from her new boarding school at the weekend.

Monday, September 21st
09/09/2015

.... is the date when I will discover what I am really like.

Because I have no idea how other people see me, and I am dying to know.

I think models must spend many hours in front of mirrors making faces, and shifting their bodies around in order to work out how to make themselves look their thinnest.

Victoria Beckham usually appears as though she's holding her legs together trying not to wet herself - and she must have tried smiling at least once in a mirror, to catch what it looks like, and decided against.

My feminine friends always sit with their legs either together or crossed, but to the side.

I am quite capable of sitting leaning forward, with my legs apart, elbows on knees.

Perhaps on Monday, September 21st, I will find out whether, after nearly 56 years, I'm going to have to put an end to this, and other, unattractive habits.

And also I'll discover whether it is absolutely imperative for my own sense of dignity that I lose weight. To date, as far as I am aware, over the past six years no one could give a monkey's whether I should be a couple of stone lighter. Except for my children, and their views on this subject don't count. They already think that I might have been born in Victorian times, so I don't mind too much if they think I am a fat Victorian.....

Because at 5pm, Monday, September 21st, Episode One, Series 8, of Four In A Bed will be aired on the telly. To ten million viewers around the world.

And guess what. At 5pm on Tuesday, September 22nd, Episode Two:

"Wormgate" goes live. As I celebrate my 56th birthday. On my own. Cava by my side. Fag in hand.

Crazy September
13/09/2015

The Countdown has begun.

My friend Polly has seen a trailer previewing Four In A Bed, while her children were watching something else on Channel 4.

I have arranged a boozy tea, rather than a boozy lunch, with Miriam and Nicola on Wednesday week, so that we can all watch the Shropshire episode together at 5pm - the one which was filmed at the mad Dog Lady's house.

I have pre-warned Miriam to have a large box of tissues handy for me to cry into, with grief at making such a fool of myself to so wide an audience.

I still plan to watch the first episode on my own, so that I am appropriately braced to face my family's and friends' derision after they have seen it.

Callum, one of the boys from the first B&B, called up yesterday for a chat. He told me about a preview of the Series in the TV Times which says: "and Callum needed a drink."

"What's that about?" he asked worriedly.

"Oh - that's just the driving the 4x4 bit," I reassured him. "The producer called me and implied they are going to be making a lot of that - she says it's really funny."

I spent a long time right into the early hours last night, feverishly attempting to track down this preview, but in the end I could only find a verbal description. "And Mary causes upset when she finds a worm wriggling in her toilet," it says. So now I've had another thought. Are they going to make it look as though I planted the worm? God I hope not! I would be sent hate mail for that!

It's Tonight!!!
21/09/2015

I am in suspenders with excitement about what else this programme might result in.

Faye and I would so like to be on Gogglebox, for instance.

Last week the Gogglebox people were made to watch a new drama called 'Dr Foster'. It's about a betrayed wife. Everybody's talking about it. "It's just the enormity of the betrayal that is so devasting and so gripping," they say.

Huh. What she went through is a walk in the park compared with my experience. And what I've been through is a walk in the park compared with what happened to my mate up the road.

Oh no. Four In A Bed tonight. I can't stop thinking about it. I am looking forward to watching it all on my own with some chocolate cake by my side. 5pm will be too early for Cava. And then I shall be poised ready to receive numerous phone calls from fans.

Tonight will be the most boring episode, when I refuse to get excited about tying knots and steering a yacht. And when, in real life, the programme makers took me aside and said I was being too dull to be included.

Anyhow. So now I have just seen myself for the first time in real life (sort of) on telly, I can see how mad, wrinkly and fat I can appear. I can definitely understand how I would not be to everybody's taste. And it is going to have to be an entirely black wardrobe for the future, summer or winter.

Otherwise. Well. Phew. Breathe. My - how the butterflies were building as I tried to concentrate on the previous programme "Somewhere Nice in the Sun", or something, about an elderly couple buying a shoebox on the Costa del Sol for £75,000.

And suddenly - here I am! I start off the entire Series 8 of Four In A Bed with the immortal words, as I turn to my lovely gay friend Callum: "So what would you have thought, aged 17, about to embark on your degree and everything, if you'd known that at 50 you would be cleaning lavatories?"

And off it all went - extremely jolly and uplifting. It felt so odd, re-living those fun experiences, and being reminded of all the things that I'd said. I hadn't realised quite how awful I look from the side, and how very weird my intonation can be, but some of the front shots are lovely. There was one close up which made me look about 80.

The programme makers have clearly bought into the Mad Mary thing. They didn't include anything I said that was thoughtful. I wonder whether there's any of that to come, or whether I just end up looking completely bonkers? So what anyway.

And my friends have called and emailed in droves saying that I am lovely, lovely, lovely! They have made me smile in a warm, squidgy sort of a way.

I'm not sure that the next four programmes will make quite such comfortable viewing.

Harshest Critic
22/09/2015

I am too bossy and there's too much about lavatories.

This is from the harshest critic of them all - my Mum.

What she means is that she thinks that I'm being arrogant, yacking on about "I like to do it my way and I don't care what anyone else thinks," and cleaning out loos.

She's right as usual, of course.

Mum has been the matriarch of our family for a while now, and she is the one who has instilled into all her progeny (except me) a sense of moderation, decorum, and taste.

Because actually, despite everything, I am quite pleased with the whole thing (so far). But that is because I suffer from Middle Child Syndrome, and I crave attention, good or bad.

I watched today's episode, "Wormgate", with Faye. Earlier this evening she had jumped some huge things on Mad Vegas in preparation for a terrifying Event coming up this Sunday. Throughout the hour-long session she was grinning from ear to ear and looking most determined, confident, and ambitious. At the end she got off her sweating beast and fell into my arms, crying.

"I am so tired and have such a tummy ache, can I come home?" she sobbed.

"Great! It's my birthday and I can take you home and we can watch my next TV demise together as soon as we get there!" I thought. "What a treat!"

And we did. And how we laughed. What a relief! I don't think either of my children is holding his/her head in shame as a result of my 2 1/2hrs of fame - not yet, at any rate.

Of course nobody except my best mate Anne understood that I couldn't give much of a shit (if that's the correct expression) about finding a worm in my loo. I was hysterical with grief for the owners of the B&B whose vast investment into this programme is more or less for nought as a result of Wormgate. I felt so terrible for them because I liked them so much.

Well now I've gone off them because they think I was deliberately hamming it up, to make their whole situation worse and to 'play the game'. Chippy idiots. This class thing is a pain in the arse.

Anyhow, so far I think the programme has been fair.

Tomorrow we approach murkier waters.

Bitch
28/09/2015

They bleeped out the offending word. You can't use the B-word on family TV.

I got the giggles describing the incident during my LittleChat afterwards. I am beginning to think that Joan might suffer mildly from Aspergers. Faye thinks she definitely does. I am convinced that she has no concept of the implications of what she is saying and doing.

I've driven over to Miriam's house to watch today's episode with her and Nicola, over a rather large amount of pink Cava considering it's only teatime. I think I'm looking quite good on the TV today, but still a little too mad for my liking, with lots of googly eyes and weird facial expressions, and an odd over-enunciated way of speaking.

"Oh no, you're much madder than that in real life," Miriam reassures me.

Faye is still with us too - all most jolly over Miriam's home-made lasagne, after admiring her new hot tub which has been delivered all the way from the States.

Over supper on the telly, I make my first gaff in front of the dog lovers.

"Well I'm pet unfriendly," I quip - attention-seeking as ever. It's not even particularly true!

Joan and Ivor turn to me, appalled. Ooops.

The programme overall I feel has been quite kind to Joan and to Thomas. They don't show the ball of fluff that landed on Callum's head, the padlocks on the cupboards of Ivor and Tessa's bedroom that makes it look like a bank vault; or mention a couple of the worst things that happened to me: the bloody cockerel cockadoodledoing just outside my window

205

from four in the morning, nor the fact that my nearest mirror was in the shared lavatory so I had to keep running hither and thither to blow-dry my fringe. Joan's fried eggs look quite nice, and we don't see her getting stressed and stroppy when breakfast has to be served up late.

I drive Faye back to school, feeling quite smug.

Tomorrow - Wydemeet Day! EEEK!

Wydemeet Day
28/09/2015

Ivor and Tessa are sitting side by side, Ivor with his bum stuck in the bidet, and Tessa on the loo, both admiring the view out of my Hexworthy Room's window.

The boys meanwhile are trying on Faye's ski clothes that they have found stored in one of the drawers in the Dartmeet Room. They pull out some weird sort of little-skirt thing - even I don't know what it is! They are then filmed together leaning out of the window, gazing at the view.

Joan is lying in the Bellever Room's bath, saying that she prefers the bathroom to the bedroom. They have the most extraordinary amount of luggage piled up to the ceiling and taking up most of the floorspace. Thomas has hardly said a word throughout the entire series so far, and silent he remains. Needless to say, the hole in the carpet is shown, and they comment on how small the bedroom is, but the chandelier falling off the ceiling, the broken window sash, the marks on the wall, the loose bedknob - all have been edited out. I think both bedroom and bathroom look beautifully lit and very inviting. Everybody is busy using the word 'cosy' as a euphemism for 'good for having loads of rampant sex in'.

Meanwhile Sashka, watching it all, sitting on the sofa beside me, has gone uncharacteristically quiet.

Now it turns out that every couple has found a couple of 'curlies' in their bedlinen.

This is after Sashka cleaned each room in preparation for The Visit, her mother, and then two friends, inspected each one in microscopic detail, and they were pristine.

Now Tessa has discovered a clump of dust in the dressing room table drawer under its new liner, that most certainly wasn't there when Sashka hoovered it out. Yet, amongst numerous other things, the stained curtains that haven't ever been cleaned in over ten years, have been omitted.

Ho hum.

And now I am shaking. It's time for our 'Activity'. Am I really going to look like the lady on the front cover of Jilly Cooper's 'Riders'???

NO!!! I just look fat! Not sexy in the least! And you can hardly even see my long whip!

Oh what a relief! Oh how disappointing!

The filming meanwhile has moved on to the grooming of the Clydesdales, and Joan is telling us all how qualified she is, and how I'm doing everything wrong.

And then - oh no! Straight on to supper! No pics of us all riding! What a swizz!

"I only do the B&B at all in order to pay the school fees. I couldn't be bothered to do it otherwise. I mean I'm just flat out all the time. Horses, swimming, lunches........."

Six horrified faces are filmed slowly, one by one.

I hate myself.

What have I done?

Next comes 'Breakfast The Circus Act'. Oh what a shame! Faye is only included in a couple of frames. Sashka is on the cutting room floor.

They've shown me, with mad hair, standing next to my daughter with my arm around her proudly, and Faye looking tall, slim, beautiful, graceful and smiley.

They miss out the 'no tea in the teapots'. They miss out the Love Letters, and the Silly Bowl. They make Tessa's too runny scrambled egg look delicious, and don't show that her 'white toast' is light brown and mouldy. They don't show me shaking, or picking the hair off one of Ivor's three fried eggs. They film Ivor and Tessa making ridiculous criticisms of my rather cold, but otherwise excellent breakfast. What a disappointment. Not AbFab at all. Certainly not the beginnings of a global stellar TV career for Faye.

And finally it's the Feedback Forms. They cut out my dramatic comments about the book looking as though it's alive and evil, and off I go, reading out everybody's comments to the camera. My best performance of the entire two weeks! Or is it? Bugger. I look completely mental throughout. All goggle eyes and mad gestures. Deeply, deeply unattractive. I really can't let a potential suitor see this.

"Oh." Sashka and I say together, struggling slowly up from the sofa, as the credits roll, over pictures of our log basket and Ex's silver horse which lives on the dining room table.

Definitely time to down a large bottle of Cava.

The Denouement
28/09/2015

"Today perhaps we will find out who the real Mary is," the programme starts with Ivor's LittleChat. So far, every expression he has worn when I have opened my mouth has been one of menace.

Meanwhile Tessa has hardly said anything, which is a pity, because she's really funny. I think it's because she couldn't see without her glasses on, and they have the most enormous FCUK branding along each arm, so they're not allowed to be shown.

I am watching this, the fifth and final episode, all alone in my five bedroom home in the middle of nowhere in central Dartmoor. This is the one that counts, and I really want to be able to concentrate hard on every word and every nuance. I am not even distracted by a cup of tea, piece of cake, or glass of Cava.

Callum's and Joan's argument about the broken coffee maker is now raging on and on, backwards and forwards. I mean - who cares whose fault it is if a stupid spring came off the pot? The camera homes in on me grinning wryly to myself.

The boys are effusively grateful to me for my over-payment of £15. They deserve it though - so why not?

So. To Wormgate.

"May I start by making the most serious, major and heartfelt apology," I begin.

"And now I don't want to speak about it anymore," I go on, in a vain attempt to put the story to bed, and prevent Ivor and Tessa from getting themselves into any deeper water.

"Well I do!" cries Tessa loudly and firmly, thumping the table.

'Oh no - you just don't get it, do you?' I groan inwardly to myself. Oh well. Their funeral.

So - the millionth shot of this little wriggly little thing in the bog, looking remarkably like an earthworm - which it most certainly wasn't - and me going hysterical, apparently about something of so little consequence. No one would ever have guessed what I was really upset about, except for Anne, and as it turns out, Miriam got it too.

"So you've overpaid us by a shilling," pronounces Ivor.

"You're showing your age," I quip back at him, quick as a flash. "I couldn't be bothered to count out £4.95 so I gave you £5 instead."

Oh no. That little phrase. "I can't be bothered". In real life it would be, "I can't be arsed," but I had no idea that I used either phrase quite so often.

Ivor and Tessa look at each other, both terribly pleased with my payment, and then a flash of recognition and understanding crosses their faces. I hope they are feeling really, really, bad about all that they have done and said.

I've written on Joan and Thomas's feedback form: "You could be a little more sensitive during lighthearted banter," in the box about hosting.

"Did you want all the men on top of you, when you were interrupting my talk on dog shiatsu, just to get attention as usual?" says Joan.

"That's what I mean," I explain gently. "Saying things like that to people you don't know very well - well it's just a bit risque, and could cause considerable offence."

Joan is clearly a bit surprised that I've paid her the full asking price, and then it's my turn.

The loose bedknob is not included in what's shown, and no explanations supplied for the two shocking underpayments, other than, "It wasn't for me," which doesn't begin to explain or justify them. Nothing bad is shown. No cold water. No dirty curtains. Nothing, really, except for the mysterious curlies.

"If I was Mary I would have hit her for that underpayment," exclaims Ivor later, during his LittleChat. "I think Mary let her get away very lightly."

They just don't get it. None of these couples does. We are playing to a global television audience. This room is a microcosm of a few B&Bers whose views are of no consequence.

I am daring to begin to feel jubilant. I am daring to believe that I am a proper, dyed-in-the-wool PR Pro after all. I am daring to believe that I might have pulled it off, got it right, and that the effort of staying nice, careful and controlled might have been worth all that pain and exhaustion.

The Outcome
28/09/2015

Sashka has been crying now for two days, and got well pissed on Friday night to drown her sorrows.

It's hard being a perfectionist and putting your all into everything you do for other people.

Wydemeet looked absolutely beautiful throughout the programme. Especially in the shots used of it during the denouement. I am sad that it proved impossible for Sashka to get due credit for the indispensable part she plays in the wonderful, award-winning service and quality we offer, and the incredible work that she put into making Wydemeet pristine for the programme - which it was.

Meanwhile I have been receiving a stream of phone calls and emails congratulating me - from friends; and advising me not to be too upset about the comments and behaviour of the mad dog-lady - from strangers.

A northern bloke named Jack called me to tell me that he had rung her up and bollocked her for bullying me. I told him to call her back and apologise. "She has no idea of the implications of what she is doing or saying," I explained to him. And then I emailed her myself to relay this conversation back to her, as I am worried about her.

On the other hand, I am very angry indeed, and hurt, by Ivor and Tessa. I think that they have been thoroughly chippy, two-faced, and unkind. Ivor took against me and refused to trust me or enjoy me on any front, simply because I'm posh. Well I can't help that, any more than he can help his background. And he's a Thatcherite too! Unlike Joan, Ivor and Tessa were perfectly conscious of what they were doing, and had numerous opportunities to put things right, which they didn't take. I will never forgive them.

I have spoken at length, twice, to Callum, and the boys have asked me to a small party next week to celebrate Don's 50th birthday.

And now, the tangible results:

Suiters' enquiries - one (but I don't fancy him)

B&B Bookings - none

B&B Booking enquiries - none

Rental enquiries - none

Book sales - Surviving Solo currently ranks 41,302 in Amazon's Best Sellers list

Would I do it again? Would I recommend that other people should do it? Was it fair? Am I happy with how I came across?

I don't think I would take part in another reality TV competition, eg Come Dine With Me, The Dating Game (or whatever its called), Big Brother, I'm a Celebrity etc for its own sake, now I know what the experience is like and how I appear to strangers and on the telly screen, unless I had another very clear and tangible end objective in mind.

I would recommend to others that they do it, provided they were capable of staying nice, nice, nice throughout the filming. The programme makers offer you endless nooses in which to hang yourself, and you must always resist. I have now realised why I pay through the nose for a good all round education for my children. I think for some reason, somehow, and I can't explain why, that it is education which helps prevent you from falling naively into the traps they set.

I'm not convinced that the programme was fair. I think they biased it a bit in favour of me, actually.

I am incredibly smug about how I came across as such a decent person, with my integrity utterly intact.

I thought from a distance I looked rather attractive (although I walk a bit funny), but now I understand why I don't have admirers queuing up at my door, and never have had.

It's because I look quite, quite, batty.

Jilly Cooper
28/09/2015

Studio Lambert has left a message for me to call them.

Eeek!

They must have found out about my book, and I'm going to get told off about it!

I return the call of somebody named Helen. I can hear my heart going thumperty thumperty thump really loud, and my voice is cracking. I hope she can't hear.

Helen is predictably perfectly pleasant and I find myself chatting away with nervous excitement, even though I'm sure she's in a hurry to hang up. She tells me that Joan is tearful, and Ivor and Tessa think they, and I, have come across well. Blimey! Everyone who has been in touch with me thinks they are dreadful! In fact the word my posh friends use more often than any other is 'ghastly'.

I ask Helen to say to Joan that I am fine about everything. Neither of us is surprised that Joan hasn't returned my kind email.

Then I admit to the existence of the book - I thought I'd better just bring it to their attention up front. I say I hope it will help make more people watch and take part in the programme, and to let me know if there's anything in it that they'd like me to change, as it's so easy to, on Amazon Kindle, and I would be delighted to do so. Helen was also unaware that I'd mentioned Four In A Bed in the Telegraph article.

I did say that I felt they had biased the programme a little in my favour, that they'd edited out a lot of the bad bits of everybody's B&Bs, but that they had offered nooses to the contributors and allowed them to hang themselves.

"You just need to stay true to yourself," she said. What a cliche. "I wasn't," I said. "I normally have rants and say fuck a lot. If you're naturally horrid, how does staying true to yourself help?"

I told her that I think Faye and I would be every bit as good as anyone else currently on Gogglebox, and that we'd quite like a job, so she's going to text me the twitter-thing that Studio Lambert advertises their casting through, and Faye will show me how to work it and respond.

But I've had a thought now of what I'd really like to be.

The next Jilly Cooper. She's posh, wrinkly, funny, attractive, and a tiny bit bonkers.

Gogglebox Kids Christmas Special
07/10/2015

Someone called Katy rang this afternoon, inviting Faye to audition for a one-off called "Gogglebox Kids Christmas Special," to be screened on Christmas Day.

What would you do about that if it were your daughter?

Almost speechless with excitement and glee, leaping up and down so that she nearly dropped the phone, Faye called from boarding school just now, interrupting the final episode of 'Dr Foster'.

So - thanks to Dr Foster, just as the horrors of the past six years are rushing up on me all over again - Ex and I need to make a decision about Gogglebox Kids, which could affect the rest of our daughter's life.

I think it is absolutely wonderful that we have been presented with a relatively cosy opportunity for her to find out what real fame is like. It's a pity the programme will be screened on Christmas day, in front of an audience of millions and millions. At least in Four In A Bed, I was tucked away on obscure daytime TV.

The upside is that she will not be committed to anything afterwards, and her appearance will be ancient history after a few months.

My instinct is, that's where it should stay. How many happy child-stars have you come across?

If we go ahead, immediately after Christmas there will be people wanting to be Faye's best friend, just because she is famous. Everyone in the school will know who she is, and will point at her. There will be trolls on Twitter saying how ghastly to be so posh and she's too fat, or too idiotic, and there'll be some sicko weird stuff because she's so pretty. But then it will all be over. Probably, hopefully, for ever.

What an opportunity. To be able to think "I know what five minutes of fame is like, and in preference I opted for a normal life and a crack at being a vet."

So here I am, all alone in the middle of the moor, wondering about all of this, with no one to talk to but Twiglet.

This invitation has come about because of my communications with the Four In A Bed people. This will be the second member of my family I've made famous. And Will could do well with his sax on Britain's Got Talent, too, if he wanted to. But he doesn't. Thank goodness for that!

Famous!
19/10/2015

"Gosh, I did like her," I commented to Will, as we drove off, having filled up with diesel from the Tesco's garage just outside his school, 100 miles from Wydemeet.

A couple of month's later and I'm back again, and it's the same lady behind the til. She's blonde and very pretty and smiley. Her name's Sally. I know this because of the badge pinned to her front.

"Don't I recognise you from somewhere?" she says.

"Hmmmm," I reply. "Maybe, perhaps, Four In A Bed?"

"That's right!" she exclaims. "You were the nice one! Hey, Trudy! Come over here! This lady was on Four In A Bed! She was the nice one!" She ushers over her friend, and they ask for my autograph.

Just a few days later, I am at Bristol airport, climbing aboard a Ryanair plane on my way to Gerona. Last time I did this trip my family ended up on the front page of various national newspapers after a near-death experience. This time I'm with my great mate Judith, who is entertaining most of the back half of the aeroplane regaling them at the top of her voice, post Sauvignon Blanc, about how her friend over there has just been on Four In A Bed. I bury my head in the in-flight magazine which informs me that a meal deal of lasagne, titchy bottle of wine and some Pringles will cost me thirteen euros.

"Oh I know her. She was the nice one!" exclaims the dazzling young Mum of an Oxbridge student, sitting in the row second from back. "Don't you worry about that horrid dog woman, pet," she leans forward and, between the seats, pats me on the shoulder.

Funny how many people see that programme, yet what a complete non-event really, it has turned out to be.

Film Goddess
19/10/2015

Last year when I stayed at Lindsey's Spanish home, she introduced me to a Mega Movie Star who, back in the early '90s, just so happened to have spent quite a lot of time living in the shack in the field at the end of the lane that goes past Wydemeet.

Well Mrs Film Goddess has invited our small Exeter Alumni contingent to join her for tea in her little hideaway, half way up a mountain, fifteen minutes from Lindsey's house. She's even made us a strange sort of apple/walnut teacake-thing!

While the rest of the party potters around the vertiginous slopes of her car-free hilltop village, I divest myself of my four inch heels and plonk myself on her sofa in order to discuss the subject of the moment: Being On Reality TV.

My experiences are a bit mere compared with hers. She was stuck in the Celebrity Big Brother House for nearly a month, as she was one of the last to be voted out. Prior to participating in the programme, she had asked an SAS trooper how you should behave if you are ever to find yourself in a hostage situation.

"Look after the underdog, and laugh when things go wrong," he had advised her. How she enjoyed her month!

She knows absolutely every iconic superstar in the whole world that you have ever heard of.

She's even friends with my muse, Jilly Cooper.

'What a life of contrasts,' I think to myself, as we meander our way back to the car, and Mega Hollywood SuperStar returns to gluing up the broken leg of her kitchen table.

Repeat
15/12/2015

"You're a very special lady. John" the computerised voice-text bleeps down my phone.

A few minutes later and I take a phone call from someone called Jade in Leicestershire, who eulogises with similar sentiments.

Then about six emails suddenly splurge into my in-box. One says: "Just watched Four In a Bed and I can honestly say if we were planning a trip to the UK we would be far more likely to stay in your B&B than any of the other three. Last! What nonsense."

Another - a bloke called Andrew who divides his time between New Zealand and Holland Park - is already halfway through the kindle edition of my book, flying at 33,000 feet over the Indian Ocean, sipping mojitos. "Some chuckles but mainly admiration for your honesty and gumption," he says. Well by golly wow!

So! It would seem that the telly has already repeated our Four In A Bed programmes. This time on something I've never heard of called 'More 4'. What a surprise! And who are these people who watch this obscure channel in the middle of the day?

Well, oddly enough, it turns out that two of my most respected friends caught it quite by chance! What is the likelihood of that? One is a household name writer, who was preparing her spare-room for her elderly Mum to watch telly in. She has already read my book and has been kind enough to go through it with a tooth-comb, providing me with a list of things I need to do to make it professional rather than 'raw'. Amazingly kind of her considering I don't know her all that well, whereas neither of my own children has even bothered to read it yet! So now I have nowhere to hide. She knows every last ounce of me!

But the best news is that Highly Revered Son, Will, just happens to be sitting with me in the kitchen as these accolades start flooding in. The evidence is indisputable. Not everybody thinks his Mum has made a total arse of herself, after all that.

8 MOVING ON

The Big Secret
10/11/2014

Now that I've taken my blog off-air and private, I can give you the Big Reveal. I have been thinking seriously of selling Wydemeet. After *all that*!

The main reason why I'm thinking of selling is because I am worried about my beloved Faye becoming socially marginalised by the people of the moor, rather as I have felt over the past twenty years.

A secondary reason is that I appear to have set up this B&B business in order to have people paying to use rooms that I wouldn't otherwise need, and can't afford. Basically the house is too big for just Faye and me, so we won't need B&Bers if we move to something smaller.

You have heard me moaning about being a Pariah before.

Well it all came to a head last Friday, Hallowe'en. Faye had had a disastrous day at the show-jumping competition, getting eliminated for three refusals at the second jump, having waited five hours for her turn to go. Driving back she was desperate to attend the Pony Club Hallowe'en Party - thirty miles in the opposite direction, for which we would arrive 1 1/2hrs late, exhausted.

"I've only been to three Hallowe'ens in my whole life, because of where we live!" she cried.

We hadn't yet come across anyone else planning to attend the party, because the three 13 year old girls who live within a three mile radius of our house were already having a party of their own and hadn't invited my darling Faye; the girls at the show-jumping competition already had something going on; as did Faye's normal group of friends from the Pony Club who mostly live 15 miles west of us, within a couple of miles of each other, they all go to the same school, and all have matey Dads as well as matey Mums.

So when we finally reached the Pony Club Hallowe'en party we were dismayed to find just five people there, knocking around in the cavernous village hall.

Faye went bravely in, while I sat in the local hotel until the dot of 9pm, when I whizzed back to collect her, and found her looking distinctly disconsolate by the entrance. No friends, and the boy whom she thought liked her having walked straight past as if she wasn't there.

We returned home to find Will almost comatose with his endless post-parties exhaustion, and therefore not in a very charming mood.

"Why do we live here anyway?" he queried. "Why can't we live near Granny in the middle of Dorset where all our friends are? What's the point of driving all the way out here all the time?"

Well. Maybe he's right. I have been hanging on to Wydemeet in order to give the children stability and continuity. So if they now don't want to live here, I guess it's time to go.

As a family of four: Mum, Dad and the two children, Wydemeet comprised the most utterly wonderful home. We were our own nucleus within the local community - which has varied from idyllic to dysfunctional and back again over the past couple of decades. We had a natural 'fit' with the other local families. We didn't feel weird throwing large parties for everybody in the hamlet, whereas on my own, it does, a bit. We gave, and were invited to Sunday lunches and dinner parties with other families from the posh school, who are dotted in a circle, of which we were at the centre, all around the edge of the moor.

But as a single parent the entire structure collapses. Mum and the children are left bereft.

My mood of gloom and despondency intensified. On Saturday nobody was interested in watching the X-Factor except me, and both children complained that I made supper late and it was horrible leftovers as usual.

And then, worst of all, on Sunday I smacked my nose so hard on Vegas The Mad Mare's neck that I think I have broken it. Anyway, I went all funny and giddy and morose, and cried when nobody was looking, between making everyone 'Breanner' - a cross between breakfast, lunch, tea and dinner, before Will went back to school. I could hardly stand up, but got reprimanded for providing turkey. Apparently they only like chicken. Agh!

So now I look as though I have been the victim of physical domestic abuse. A huge dark blue swollen bruise has appeared nowhere near the source of the pain - slipping halfway down my cheek to join the wrinkles.

Thanks a bunch, gravity. And no amount of Clarins Honeycomb Foundation (Medium) can hide it. Everyone keeps commenting. Grrrrrr.

So. There we have it. An unusually horrid, thought-provoking weekend.

We've got to move.

Shattered Dreams
10/11/2014

"It's not the location, it's the social life, isn't it," commented Ex.

It's so annoying he buggered off with my ex-friend, Her - five or more years ago now. I always felt that he and I were much better matched than most married couples. And now everything else has fallen over like dominoes.

In order not to get arrested, I had pulled into a lay-bye and was on my mobile, fully appraising Ex of my moving plans. I didn't hold back - letting him know that I thought a lot of the decision to move was because it has proved untenable, or un-sensible, or simply stupid, attempting to remain in the middle of nowhere all on my own, when it had been so do-able as a family unit.

Our shared dream had been to create a home for our two children for life.

So that when they were asked where they came from, they would always straight away say, "Dartmoor." The family home would always be here, and they would know that they could drop into the local pub anytime and bump into old mates they'd known since they were born.

Accordingly we sent them to the local babies' group, two local toddlers' groups, local pre-school, and local primary school. I would often take them to pre-school myself, rather than leaving it to the nanny, and I put myself on its committee. Initially nobody even turned around when we entered the hall where the classes were held, and no one ever started a conversation with 'blow-in' me.

My children were regularly left out of the others' social activities, and I had never felt so invisible. Over the years, though, gradually the locals have grown to understand that we weren't about to move back to London, and the committee proved to be one of the most effective groups of people I have ever worked with; and the most fun!

Disappointingly, our immediate neighbours, despite having children the same gender and almost the same age as ours, have never embraced us as family friends. Tears used to drip, plop, plop, plop from my eyes onto the concrete, as I mucked out the horses, their lack of interest almost palpably flooding down towards me in waves across the river. I dare write this, because they would never dream of reading this far in a book by boring old me!

I simply couldn't think of any way to change things. I felt that the next door Mum and I should have been living in each other's houses, sipping endless cups of coffee together like sisters, we have so much in common - but it was not to be.

When Ex went off, it seemed very few people gave much thought as to what it might be like for me, being a fifty year old Mum left alone in a large house in the middle of nowhere with two young children and not much cash. The other Mums continued driving past my gate to visit Neighbour, but seldom, if ever, dropped in to check that I was managing

OK on my own.

Over the years things have improved, but Hallowe'en demonstrated that our social situation isn't acceptable. I have invested two decades of my life into living here in the middle of Dartmoor. It was a very happy place to be as a nuclear family. But face it, Mary. Being here alone is just not really working. I am too busy, and have too many friends elsewhere to feel lonely. But I feel marginalised by the surrounding happy families. I've struggled and railed against it. And now I give up. My dream is well and truly over. I have failed.

So I think we should move towards Faye's new school in Tiverton. Where we can both get properly, instead of marginally, involved with the horsey set, through the school, the pony club, and the hunt. I will join the David Lloyd Health Club in Exeter, where I am already friendly with several members, and the men are hunky; and should all else fail, I could even get involved with my old university again - Exeter. The wheel turning full circle, 30 years on!

Oh - and maybe I could join a rock'n'roll club! How exciting it all might turn out to be!

Wood!
10/11/2014

Yesterday I ran the whole 'moving' thing past Malcolm's girlfriend, as we rode out together. She thinks it's an excellent plan.

Then I called my sister. I always do what she says without question.

"Before you go on any more," she said, "I think it's a great idea." Well that was fairly straightforward and rather quick. Bloody Hell. I'm going ahead. Yikes!!!!!!!!!!

So now I've got to sell this house and buy another.

How?

Well marketing is my thing, so I thought I'd have a go at doing it myself! I wonder whether I will manage to?

As you know, it's my belief that these days just absolutely everything sells through Google. Ads in the paper and those expensive property brochures could be a waste of money. Meanwhile, with my B&B marketing experience, I ought to be able to get Wydemeet to come up first for anyone googling: "Houses for Sale Dartmoor". And if I fail, well, it won't really have cost anything. I would really, really get a buzz from getting myself better SEO'd than the professional estate agents! Watch this space! We will see!

I have a problem though. It is this. There is a sea of wood reaching to the sky, right outside my garden gate.

My neighbour has invested in a sawmill and his farm is on the other side of a narrow bridge. So literally hundreds of tree trunks have been dumped outside my gate where they stay, year after year, and every year the piles get higher, deeper and longer until my home feels as though it is drowning behind them.

I don't like making trouble, but if someone is going to fall in love with Wydemeet, something will have to be done about those logs. I am going to have to have a meeting with the neighbours to discuss them. Oo-er.

"Whatever you do, don't start upsetting the neighbours," warned Malcolm's girlfriend. She advised me that there's now a clause in property contracts about neighbourly relations, so to make them cross would be really stupid. And anyway, she argued, the sort of people who would make a fuss about the wood are the sort of people who would never buy my property in the first place.

So instead I have emailed my neighbours advising them that they are the first to know of my plans, and please could they possibly keep the wood and mess to a minimum, and be nice to anyone making enquiries. (And please would they buy Wydemeet so I don't have to work any harder to sell it) was the undercurrent of my missive, but perhaps they don't have £1 million handy right now.

Meanwhile I have been looking at what I might buy. A clapped out house to improve, in a smallholding outside Exeter - with easy access to both children's schools, my Mum, old friends, new friends, Dartmoor, the sea, equestrian centres, the health club, the university, cinemas, shops, garages and a Rock'n'Roll club. They exist on Zoopla. Now I must go and find one ...

How exciting!

Selling On Line
23/11/2014

This website-making thing.

It's taken ages and ages and ages and ages and ages. And it's given me a headache.

But now it's done!

You can find Wydemeet for sale under "house-for-sale-dartmoor.com".

I've had quite a lot of fun doing this, actually, copying my friend's house-selling brochure, combined with my own brand of humour/observations.

For the immediate future, I am giving AdWords another go. So if you google something such as 'properties for sale dartmoor', up I will pop as an ad. Each click on it will cost me 40p, eating into the daily budget of £3 that I have awarded myself.

So far 73 people have clicked the ad, which has set me back £29.78. I expect they're all estate agents checking out what's on offer, as nobody has contacted me about my unique Dartmoor offering as yet.

The ad goes: *"Dartmoor House for Sale. house-for-sale-dartmoor.com. Freehold, Remote, Walkers' Dream. Hexworthy. 5+ Beds. Guide: £995,000".*

I have spent several hours dreaming up words and phrases which will ensure that my ad pops up a lot, for people looking for property on Dartmoor. The AdWords analysis advises me that the most effective phrases they've tried are 'houses for sale dartmoor' (11); 'for sale dartmoor' (12) and 'houses for sale in dartmoor' (10). So it's hardly rocket science and I really enjoy trying to second guess what people are going to go for.

I have already reduced the price - from £1 million 'offers', down to £995,000 'guide price', because I thought it sounded better. I can't see any other properties being sold privately if I do a Google search. It's as unlikely as coming across people representing themselves in the law courts. Everybody seems to automatically pay so-called experts to do these things that they could manage perfectly well themselves. Maybe there's a reason why nobody else appears to be doing what I'm up to, which I will discover after three months of no enquiries, and I'll go grovelling cap in hand to Knight Frank or whoever.

I keep checking whether the google 'spiders' have done their work so that Wydemeet pops up on its own, without the assistance of AdWords, but no joy as yet.

I have also contacted Zoopla, who haven't replied. I think they're probably only interested in representing proper estate agents, but I will call them again tomorrow and find out.

And I've been in touch with the property search people my sister recently used to find her mansion next door to Downton Abbey. These people are completely in touch with what is going on property-wise in their area so, for a commission, are able to offer properties to rich people before they come onto the open market. We'll see if they're prepared to work alongside someone like me, who isn't represented by an agent. If it worked, they wouldn't charge me anything for selling my house. That would be a mega-bonus! Fingers crossed! Watch this space!

Eighth Most Expensive Thing on eBay?
25/11/2014

Oh dear. Give me an unexpected hour to spare, and I do something stupid.

Mad Vegas has lost a shoe so I can't ride today. It's foul weather out there anyway - cold, grey and rainy. Typical Dartmoor November.

So instead I'm sitting here and I've put Wydemeet on eBay. I wonder what will happen. It's the eighth most expensive thing on the site. The most expensive of all is a house in Knightsbridge, on at £4,500,000. We come just under a beautiful looking place in Cornwall which has its own riverside quay.

eBay charged £35 to list Wydemeet, so it would be good if it sold this way.

Although rather surprising!

My next wizard wheeze is to phone up The Week and suggest they list it as 'Property of the Week'. They can only say 'non'.

How Rich Are the Booking Agents?
25/11/2014

I have bitten the bullet and re-signed up with Booking.com, now that they have, finally, finally, got back to me.

We're still Number 4 on TripAdvisor, and Top of the Pops if you google 'Luxury B&B Dartmoor" - above all the proper official companies and agents and everything! Annoyingly, however, it would appear that all this is still not enough - I can't manage without wretched Booking.com!

I've had lots of lazy lie-ins, with no customers to speak of, but recently I've been becoming a little frustrated.

And rather poor.

I think that the agents can afford to behave so unprofessionally because they are raking it in, while all they have to do is sit on their bums.

Do the maths. Say they've got half a million properties on their books...

And they take 15% + VAT on all bookings, every single night, even if the booking lasts a year!

They are BY FAR my biggest expense! That's why I hate them so much!

Say somebody booked for 7 nights, my second biggest expense after the agent, would probably be the laundry. If I bothered to change the sheets, and replaced the towels once mid-week, that would cost £26. Unlike the staff at Booking.com, though, my mates at Tavistock Laundrette are highly efficient and work jolly hard for their living!

Meanwhile I would be paying out around £140 in agency fees and tax! Crazy! And that would be just for one room!

If the booking agent has half a million properties, each with, say, five bedrooms occupied every night, at an average of, say, £100 a night, well how much does that come to, at 15%? It's gone off the scale on my Neanderthal calculator which is just showing me an 'e'.

I'll do it a different way. £37.5 million!!!! Every 24hrs!! For operating a website and an accounts department from an office in Holland! Have I made a mistake somewhere?

And a lot of their staff can't even speak English properly! And I don't think any of them ever actually set foot in most of the properties on their books.

I find the whole thing absolutely extraordinary. Fascinating. Appalling.

And rather worthy of respect! Clever old them to have captured the market and got us accommodation providers by the short and curlies!

Success on eBay
03/12/2014

Well it took 24 hours.

I received an enquiry from an eBay customer about my house. Hah hah! Beet you weren't expecting that! I certainly wasn't!

It turned out to be from a land agent-type selling company who said they would put Wydemeet on their books and market it, and get it onto Zoopla. And this wouldn't cost me anything as it is their buyers who pay their fees.

Whoop di doo! What's to lose?!

So now I'm on Zoopla even though they only list estate agents' properties!

That's the good bit.

The bad bit is that I've now only got 19 days and 22 hrs left on eBay, and, while 507 people have 'viewed' Wydemeet, I've had no other bites.

Meanwhile, the Google 'spiders' haven't worked their magic yet, so if you put 'house for sale dartmoor' in the search engine, Wydemeet doesn't appear. Instead you could have bought 'wreck of the week' which is a Duchy ruin for sale a couple of years ago.

So I will have to continue paying for AdWords - a bill of £59 for 164 'clicks' so far, but no enquiries, boo hoo.

Talking to friends about my decision to sell, 95% think it's a good idea for me to do so.

"You've given it five years since Ex went off, you haven't been pushed out, you've taken this decision on your own terms, after finding out that living on your own in a large property in the middle of nowhere isn't really for you. Do it," advised Malcolm.

"Don't do it! The children will soon realise that a Dartmoor address is the coolest place to live in the world!" exclaimed another friend who was born on Dartmoor. It's alright for her though - she's not having to be entirely self-reliant all on her own in the middle of nowhere - she's got a husband.

The idea of my children ever thinking Dartmoor is cool is laughable. I'm not sure that either of them has ever ventured out of the garden gate on their own!

With my current selling system I can change my mind and decide to stay if I want to. I'm definitely not ready to sign up with an estate agent yet. But a decisive factor came yesterday.

Vegas With The Mad Rolling Eye had lost a shoe after a 30 mile ride across the wildest, bleakest, boggiest part of South West Dartmoor, and my dear farrier did a 50 mile round trip to get it put back on in time for yesterday's riding lesson, fifty miles away.

Riding the wretched creature is scary enough; loading her into the trailer is a total nightmare.

I summoned up my courage and called Neighbour to ask if somebody might possibly pop down and help. They called back to say that they were too busy completing VAT forms.

So that is really the reason that I am going. Having them living up there, complete with children of the same gender and age as mine, all of them being so unfriendly, is more lonely than if they weren't there at all!

Come on and do your work, Zoopla!

Ground to a Halt
03/12/2014

I was getting a bit annoyed by a potential B&Ber who appeared incapable of booking herself in online through my website for the first two nights of 2015. She kept on bothering me with unnecessary emails and phone calls. I mean really, how incompetent could she be?

Eventually, in exasperation, I went into my Booking Online page myself, put her dates in, and discovered that the system was, for some reason, telling all prospective customers that the whole place was completely booked out, forever!! No wonder business has ground to a total halt!

I whisked off a furious email to Freetobook Customer Relations, and then rang them up.

As I ranted they checked my details and told me that I had neglected to put in any prices for any rooms beyond the end of November 2014.

Ooops.

The customer services lady was extremely patient, and very professional, as I grovelled, and metaphorically washed her feet with my hair.

How stupid can I be.

So I am welcoming with enormous gratitude, the couple who were so determined to come and stay at Wydemeet that they took the trouble to call me, and am hoping that their stay might even exceed their wildest expectations!

I Hate (other people's) Dogs (reprise)
03/12/2014

I think your own children and pets are always nicer than other people's.

I am pleased with my new 'no dogs' B&B policy, even though I have just discovered that I have paid AdWords £5.86 for the key phrase 'dog friendly accommodation' to stay in. I must put that right straight away!

Whereas my mate Fi's utterly wonderful Prince Hall Hotel, up the road welcomes all dogs, allows them in the bedrooms, gives them dog treats on arrival, etc etc.

The other evening I was lucky enough to be taken out to dinner there. After exquisite amuse bouches, followed by sea bass and raspberry parfait, my friend and I withdrew to the bar area for coffee, where there was a cute little ball of fluffy 14 week old border collie pup.

Its owners politely asked if it was OK if they let it off its lead. Half-an-hour later, bleeding, and with a hole in my expensive, sheer, stomach-pulling-in tights, I regretted our acquiescence.

Somehow, with dogs everywhere you look, the hotel doesn't smell, there are no hairs, no mud, and no barking. I don't know how she does it. But I am certainly not going to try.

And I still believe that there will be an overall greater demand for my B&B as a result of my 'no dogs', rather than 'masses of dogs' decree. We will see. At the moment there is absolutely no demand at all for Wydemeet, so perhaps I have got this wrong! But it means that Faye and I are having a rest, and I am getting rather fat.

Hiccups
15/12/2014

Ooops.

I really do seem to have gone too far with pruning down my internet marketing costs.

Having said a temporary goodbye to the booking agents; a permanent goodbye to lovely Sawdays, and totally ballsed up the booking system on my own site, I've had no punters for weeks now, and no more are due to stay until January 2nd!

Phew! Or I would have gone mad, or collapsed with exhaustion, or had a stroke or something. Lucky I don't completely rely on my B&B business for my livelihood. But nevertheless, I'm feeling a bit poor! And massively insulted by my unpopularity!

Also not a single enquiry about my house for sale on eBay. Nor via the land agent people who have it on Zoopla.

Except. For.

A rather cross email from some bloke who has somehow stumbled across my public blog and seen a copyrighted picture of his being used on the B&B and land agents' sales websites.

Uh oh. I really hate upsetting people, when everything is supposed to be so jolly. I've emailed him in a hopefully pacifying manner, and am currently wondering which pic he's referring to! I've used loads after googling 'Swincombe Images' - I hoped they were all so low res that they were fair game. I've already been fined once by Image Bank; I wonder what's going to happen this time!

And another little online social event. A previous owner of Wydemeet has contacted me, very sweetly offering me two pics of the house to buy. We are having lovely reminiscences - her son (now 45) is delighted and relieved to know that what they called the 'chalet', and we call the 'Bothy', has reverted back to its original use: as teenage boys den, complete with its lava lamps.

Well. So I am having grudgingly to come to the conclusion, that perhaps I am not such an oh so brilliant marketeer after all.

My B&B - the truth!
19/12/2014

"God I don't care about the B&B!" I exclaimed to TreeHugger, when he suggested that I might get upset if somebody criticised some aspect of my fledgling business on Four In a Bed, the telly programme that I have now agreed to participate in.

"I will just do absolutely anything for my normal guests, to make sure they really love their time here - like drive three sides of a square to collect them if they overdo it on a walk, or collect something they need from the chemist ten miles away, or make the tea or coffee hotter or colder or however weirdly they want it, graciously with a smile - or let them cook stuff in the kitchen, or play the piano badly all day.. but if they find a 'curly' between the mattress and the mattress cover well, that's just life."

But this momentary lull, actually weeks now, of no guests, has proved most relaxing. If things go wrong in the house these days - well who really cares?

In the current hurricane, the new motor on the gate has proved so robust that the gate has ripped down the granite wall that it's attached to, and the motor is still humming. The 5 bar gate is at a wonky angle, struggling limply away, up and down, for odd periods of time, like a dying animal, in the torrential downpour. Lovely farmer down the road says he'll fix it for me. Thank God for that. And meanwhile I needn't freak about how guests are going to get in and out.

Last week I had no water for four days. That was because my wonderful new plumber, Gary, had mended the tap in Dartmeet that didn't work, and fixed the leaking radiator that caused a smell of mildew, but hadn't realised that if you turn the water off, you have to press a small button on the side of a box in the tack-room to turn it back on again.

He has come back and found the button, so we've got water at last, he's mended the central heating in the sunroom, and taken up the floor in the cloakroom to unearth what's causing the smell there - is it really dead mouse, or a leaking waste pipe from the loo?

Oh no! A total mouse warren! Nest after cosy nest made up in the lagging surrounding the central heating pipes under the floor!

So it's the smell of their poo and wee, rather than necessarily dead bodies, that keeps wafting up through the floor boards! Right under Twiglet's bed!! What to do? I have no idea. We have put down lots of rat poison, so presumably shortly the smell will get even worse as the entire colony quietly perishes under our stockinged feet.

During the summer we had two much more serious incidents going on that I couldn't write about at the time on a website advertising Wydemeet as a B&B.

Last Spring I turned on the tap in Hexworthy and the bath filled with black bits. "Just a rotten washer," I was cheerfully advised by my plumber. A few months later and the same thing happened in Bellever. But Bellever's is a new tap. Not a very good one, but it's new.

Shortly after that a man insisted on coming from the council to check my water supply. I already have it checked once a year by a lady who arrives in the kitchen with lots of gear. I was so rude to him that Will made me apologise and offer him a biscuit. After the visit he sent me a thirty page document repeating everything that I had already told him. There didn't appear to be anything major to worry about, so I breathed a sigh of relief.

Some weeks after that, I was cleaning my teeth and I thought the water smelt funny. I summoned over my children, and then my plumber, they all sniffed, and nobody agreed with me. But nevertheless I started putting out bottled water in my guests' rooms.

Fast forward, I was washing my face in Bellever's basin, looked in the mirror, to find that it was covered in small black furry bits.

"EEEEEEEEEEEEEK!" I summoned a plumber urgently from Ashburton. He said he couldn't do anything about it.

Finally I tracked down Gary. He turned on the tap and out came bits of tiny bone and feathery stuff. "Aaggh! I've got people coming to stay on Friday! Please, please, please check those water tanks that I have been asking and asking various people to cover for me, for the last year and a half!"

So up went Gary into the roof, in pitch darkness, took a breath, and plunged his hand down deep into the nearest water tank. Bingo! Quick grab, a splosh and a plop of something into the washing up bowl he'd taken up with him. Half a dead bat. I've drunk the other half.

We flushed out the system as best we could, and I bought two water tank lids off eBay...

A month later the water-checking Lady was back with her specialist equipment. I had butterflies for the next few days until her report arrived. CLEAR! Phew!!!!!!

But that's not all! Your life is shortened by the stress of being a B&B Proprietor.

It's a lovely hot sunny day, after a long gorgeous warm spell, and I have my record of seven guests staying, as well as Ex and the children. Very full house.

Ugh. What's that smell wafting about, as I'm trying to sunbathe in the garden? Cow? No - it smells more like human. Poo. "Pleeeeeeeese don't try sunbathing or using the hot tub right now!" I am silently begging my guests in my head. I ring the number I've been given in case of crises with the cesspit, which had been emptied relatively recently. It was originally built to deal with a village, when the house was used as an Adventure Centre. It is a huge double green concrete and plastic thing, which you can only get to by chopping your way through a forest of bamboo - the only plant that thrives up here.

Well, £350 later, the bloke told me that there must be another pit somewhere, which should drain into the green plastic thing, and sure enough, a bit more bamboo hacking later, and he has found a mire of black stinky sludge. An overflowing cesspit that hasn't been emptied for twenty years!

Thank God my guests went riding instead of sunbathing, and we could deal with it quietly while they were out.

They don't write about such things in B&B guides. So I've written about it for you here instead.

Oh, and did I tell you about the night when I was coming upstairs at about midnight, to find Hexworthy door open and my guests jumping up and down on the bed in their pyjamas?

That time it was a bat flying round and round their room.

I got a double sheet and threw it over the stupid thing and we were sorted. But I think that was the one and only time that I received just four TripAdvisor blobs.

There must be a bat colony hanging from the eaves outside Hexworthy's window. Since then, I have advised guests to only open the bottom half during the summer.

Going For A Million Quid
08/01/2015

"Guys, saw the house featured for sale online and wondered what your current position is? To establish a little credibility and indicate that I'm not a "tyre kicker," I sold my business back in 2012 for a lot of money and could complete a deal very quickly, with no need for external funding or any downward chain. Modesty prevents me from saying much more, but you can check my credentials online, if you haven't nodded off already!

"On the back of that, price isn't the biggest driver here, but property style and position absolutely is and from what I've seen, your place has the latter two in spades. So, do please let me know if you're still looking for a buyer and even if not, my compliments on your guest house website, it really made me chuckle (in a good way!)"

Well guess who's chuckling now!

I've looked him up and he sold his business back in 2012 for £283 million.

And on top of that it's clear that he is a very nice, solid, family man, who likes horses.

How weird is my life.

He's coming to see Wydemeet tomorrow, and will also be discussing publishing my book.

Ha ha! How rich am I going to be this time tomorrow night?

Life-Changing Day
11/01/2015

I slept OK.

Rather well actually.

I've put myself back in my original bedroom, Hexworthy, the posh one which faces South East and South West so it gets all the best light until mid-afternoon which is when I get up for preference, and yesterday for once I almost slept solidly through the entire night. Surprising in the circumstances. I think it's the highly efficient black-out blinds which help. And probably all the interrupted nights of the past year are a 50 yr old woman's hormonal thing.

Because anyway. Today is a massive day. It could prove life-changing! Sashka gets the house and garden ready for the £1 million inspection while I faff around getting in her way making myself breakfast.

Bang on 11.30am, Twiglet is leaping 6' in the air by the stairs window, which means someone has arrived.

And here he is. Bald, as anticipated from Google, but tall and slim, and slightly aloof and scary.

I boast that, being the ultimate B&B, he can have any tea he likes, but when he asks for Darjeeling the best I can do is Assam teabags. After lots of kitchen chit-chat I finally say, "Well.. first impressions are everything. Would you still like to see around the house? Would that be a good use of your time?"

He says yes, so we inspect Wydemeet, and then go for a little walk to where you can see the nearest set of stepping stones. He has no cover for his bald head and is wearing black shiny leather shoes. There is a hurricane blowing based from somewhere in Scotland, and it is raining and wild. I shout over the wind that there are bridleways there, and there, and there, and there, gesturing frantically.

He leaves on time, and I feel a little frazzled. He is not warm and cosy but quite reserved, a stance which as ever has me prattling banal bollocks.

He wants the house as an investment, let out most of the time at £3-4,500 per week. It will need a lot of renovation to command that. He says he'll do the sums and will get back to me by the end of the weekend.

Devils Spawn
12/01/2015

That's how my multi-millionaire refers to estate agents.

Well I liked the chap who came from Savills. He knew all my huntin/fishin/shootin mates from around here, and we had a good gossip. He also made some quite interesting observations about selling property.

Apparently Savills has more offices in London and around the world even than Knight Frank. He says I have a very small, but keen market, who will be London-based.

And that the first month of putting your house on the market is what really counts, so I must not put an unrealistically high price on it.

"Why do you think rich people are rich?" he queried.

He showed me an example of a lovely looking place near Gidleigh Park - the poshest end of the moor - which he says has a history even sadder than mine. The owner was originally advised by somebody else to price it at £1.2 million, and so the house languished. Savills have taken over and reduced it to £895,000, but in the meantime, the owner has probably lost some people who might otherwise have been interested in buying.

"So don't overdo things on Zoopla etc," he advised, "as they show how long the house has been on the market, and how many people have looked at, and rejected it, which is very off-putting to potential purchasers, and also gives them bargaining power."

He wants a 2% commission, not the 1% that I was expecting.

"But I have already written all the copy and done all the photos for you!" I protested.

He appears immovable.

I'll wait to hear from Millionaire-Man, and, assuming it's a 'non', I'll see what Knight Frank has to say.

'Non'
13/01/2015

His figures do not add up. How surprising is that? Not.

Wydemeet is about living the dream. It's never going to work as a business investment.

But Millionaire Man's email is delightful, and he's asked me to stay and get to know his family at their palace on a peninsula on the River Fal in Cornwall. I may well take him up. I would like to know more about him.

Also, I am not sure whether I have ever seen a 73' private room before - the size of his sitting room - except possibly at Buckingham Palace.

I am neither disappointed nor deterred by this decision.

Let's see what Knight Frank has to say for themselves.

And summon the courage to call Neighbour for an adult discussion about those logs.

Rock Bottom
17/01/2015

He has destroyed everything that we built up together over 15 years.

Everything.

When we met I could have gone almost as far as I liked in the PR world. I had my own house in London which I swapped for Wydemeet, and I drove a bright red Golf GTi.

In getting rid of me, he has lost his profile, which was the key to his freedom in the workplace.

The business we built up together is finished, the family is over, our Devon-based social life at an end, £1/2 million savings earmarked for things that mattered gone, and the imminent loss of Wydemeet signifies the final end of all our joint dreams.

During our time together I was more-or-less sole breadwinner, child-carer and nest-maker, business advisor and publicist, and what is there left to show for it? I am down to my last £3,000. That will last a month.

Why did this happen? Because I was 'controlling', he says.

So now he has a nice, pretty, intelligent girlfriend eleven years my junior. Huh! Bet she wouldn't have got him to the North Pole!

Meanwhile I am back well behind Square One, looking to downsize my home, my career over.

It's a fucker. Yes, of course I am angry and bitter. Mostly, because I am lying in bed prostrate with 'flu.

Chemicals
26/01/2015

"What does 'mellow' mean?" asks Faye. I have just told her I'm feeling it.

We are driving home from another 'Trec' competition, the one where you get butterflies from making your horse do the most mundane things. They make you walk very fast, canter very slowly, stand still, and go over a large blue plastic bag. Most of the other competitors are old ladies on carthorses.

Hah hah! I beat my twelve year old daughter! That was in the first competition. In the second competition, where I have pitted Faye against people who represent the country in the sport, she beat me soundly. Foot perfect, fluid, like poetry – she scored straight tens over six obstacles.

The whole thing was just so proud-making, and 'such fun', as Miranda's Mum might say.

But I think I'm still ill.

Which Estate Agent?
02/02/2015

Who would you choose?

They both seem almost exactly the same to me.

They both boast excellent reputations, are highly professional, extremely charming, and I suspect delightful to work with.

I have enjoyed long visits from each, and they both said the same sort of things.

They both have lots of offices in London and abroad, with extensive contact lists of rich people.

One has been marginally more efficient and accurate in their eventual proposal document. And have slightly more offices. But the other valued Wydemeet slightly higher.

I did like it that one is apparently a private company, whereas the other has to please its shareholders, if I understood what they were saying correctly.

Each advised that I should go public on the house when its garden and the moor are looking good, and that the first month of selling is critical.

Each said that it should be put on 'at a figure starting with 8' inviting offers above that, and to hope for a bidding war.

So the deal-breaker was when one offered me a 1.5% commission, compared with the other's 2%.

I was just about to sign the contract when I spoke to a Property Developer Internet Date, who advised me that he typically puts his properties on with both at the same time, for a 2% commission.

So I'm holding my horses, and finding out about that.

Wood You Credit It?
02/02/2015

"Is your husband there?" I asked my next door neighbour.

"No, he's out at the moment," she replied.

"Do you think he could call me, because we need to talk about all that wood," I said. "I can't sell my house when it's like that."

I put the phone down and collapsed into a chair, with a fag.

I've been putting off making that phone call for ten years.

"If I was Mary I would have him up in court," I have heard is the general local consensus, but I don't like making waves, and I certainly don't want to cause a neighbourly grudge. Those can cause ructions for generations around here!

And despite these generally-held sentiments, no one, to my knowledge, has ever dared publicly complain about how all this wood has been allowed to ruin one of the prettiest valleys on Dartmoor. People just mutter and moan into their scrumpy and look at the floor in a grim, gloomy, dour, Dartmoorish sort of way, and regularly inquire of me "What do you think about all that wood stacked up outside your house?"

So it was that last week, at 2.30pm, in the pouring rain, me half dead with flu, Neighbour and I put on our macs and strolled along the lane next to the wood, discussing what it was all for, and what was to be done.

I was genuinely interested to find out all about this eyesore that has been piling up for the last fifteen years outside my gate, getting higher and higher and higher and higher and higher and higher.

"Do you think you could move that 'don't climb on the logs' garish sign 90 degrees so it's not the first thing potential buyers will see as they turn the corner, after their blissful moorland drive, as they approach my house?" I queried.

I learned that each 'bay' of tree trunks (there are about ten bays) weighs around 6-7 tons and is worth around £6-700, comprising around ten tree trunks, which can be removed and sawn up in about a day.

"Yes, it all makes about £30,000 a year," he said.

"WHAT?????? All that wood and effort? And it's just thirty grand?! That's what I do!" I exclaimed, waving at my home, shocked at the investment, effort and hideousness, generating such a small profit.

"In only two days a week," he continued.

We walked on.

I had been under the impression that some of the logs at the bottom of the pile had been sitting rotting for a decade, but it turns out they're all moved on fairly regularly.

Neighbour told me that he has several clients (two of whom it turns out I was at school with) whose estate foresters chop down a whole load of trees and then ring Neighbour up and tell him to come and collect them, before they're turned into firewood, or left to rot in situ. So he's not really in control of when the wood comes, or how much of it at a time.

But he volunteered for himself that there is now too much, and the 'bays' will gradually disappear.

So we moved on to the matter of the biggest log you've ever seen - grown from one of the first redwood seeds imported into this country - and a large pile of gravel sitting next to it right outside my gate, both of which have been there for years and years.

The huge log, about 150 years old, has been paid for by a sculptor, Neighbour told me - about £6-700 again - who is now going to be told it absolutely has to be collected. Meanwhile any excess gravel delivered by the council will in future be taken over the narrow bridge and up to Neighbour's farm/sawmill the day after it arrives.

The logs on the left-hand side of the lane were not supposed to have been left there, and have since been removed and won't be replaced; and the huge sea of tree trunks abutting my garden wall will gradually be reduced, he added.

"Please call me the day before anybody is due to look at your house, and I'll do some tidying up," Neighbour reassured me. "In the meantime, it won't be immediate, but you'll see that the majority of the logs will gradually disappear over the next few months."

And that's how we left it.

I am SO proud of myself. I felt we parted with really quite a lot of mutual respect. How mature can I be when it really, really matters?!

Action!
06/02/2015

Just as I was beginning to feel particularly poor, bookings have kicked in. I've had two a day on some days!

Things are not entirely moribund after all!

Whether it all adds up to enough to cover fantastic, lovely Gary the Plumber's recent invoice is another story.

But I do genuinely find a real sense of achievement in working and earning.

Despite everything, though, once I've paid the school ski trip bill I will have zero left in my account.

I drafted a letter to Faye's new school about possibly attempting to claim a bursary, but then worked out what my income for the next year might be, not counting selling the family home nor cashing in my pension, and I thought they might laugh, so I didn't send it.

The small issue that I have overlooked, is that living the life of Lady Muck is expensive, as you've probably guessed, if you've stayed with me this far.

Hunting two horses, health club, holidays abroad, large house, 3 litre four wheel drive gold tank, private school for two children, Sashka doing all the horrid things...they'd split their sides!

So in order not to have to give up any of the above, I must continue to live off my wits, or start doing my own housework and cleaning my own tack. Ugh.

At the moment we have our second 'Returns' staying, who run their own very successful six-bedroom B&B in Cornwall, opposite St Michael's Mount. They are already booked up for the whole of July. Meanwhile I don't have a single July booking for either of my two rooms.

So I told them that they must be undercharging. But we agreed that it would be really horrid to have a guest to stay who was unhappy and felt that they'd been ripped off. It's a very delicate balance.

Anyway - this couple brought their best friends with them, and they all had dinner around the kitchen table last night, and then sat in the cosy sitting room in front of the log fire for cheese and port. I found it very difficult to tear myself away from them - I really do have such lovely guests, and when they've come back for a second time they turn into friends.

This morning I was talking so much that I forgot to lay any forks, or the butter.

They didn't seem to mind, and told me that mine is the only B&B that they have ever returned to. They also gave me a bottle of Prosecco and some narcissi.

Bring on The Sale!
07/02/2015

We've dealt with the smell of dead mice in the cloakroom by ripping up the floorboards.

We've dealt with the smell of wee wee in the downstairs loo by washing the rug.

We've hopefully dealt with the smell of mildew under the £3000 newish front door by kicking the door hard, after locking it shut, hopefully preventing the rain from coming in under it in the future.

We've dealt with the smell of sewage in the garden by emptying out the second cess-pit.

We haven't dealt with the smell of mildew in the sitting room caused by damp coming in through the gap between the window casing and the granite walls.

Nor have we dealt with the smell of death emerging from the tack-room, finding its way into the kitchen through the cupboards. At some stage I am going to have to clear the whole place out, to reveal a rat's rotting carcass covered in maggots. It's funny how, of all these smells, the smell of death stays with you.

Godfrey, who used to be Mr Fixit for a 12,000 ton frigate in the navy, after twelve hours at £15 per hour, has finally tracked down the problem with the fusing downstairs electric sockets. This turned out to be a 50 yr old fraying wire under the dining room floor.

Once he's sorted that, he'll have to deal, as usual, with re-priming the central heating because it still leaks from somewhere, despite our sorting out the radiator in Bellever bathroom.

Do you know what? I can't wait to sell this place! It's doing my head in!

Do other large Edwardian houses suffer from such things? I'm sure they probably all do. And are eminently deal-able-with, if you are a proper family, with a Dad around to keep an eye on things.

But in my case - bring on that tiny modern bungalow!

III
07/02/2015

I brought out the drinks tray.

On it were Night Nurse, Day Nurse, Beechams All in One, Beechams Cough Tincture for Children, and Lemsip All Day. And two little plastic measuring cups.

I offered my guest to take his pick, then returned to the sunroom where Faye and I helped ourselves too. Flavour of the month proved to be Night Nurse. Annoying because you can't get it delivered by Tesco.

The phone rang the following morning, after I had dropped Faye off at school, interrupting my preparation of the most complicated breakfast four guests could possibly dream up.

"It's your daughter, she's ill. She's got a temperature of 38," gasped matron.

"I thought she would be. She was ill yesterday. Can she just stay there do you think? I've got a load of things to do this morning," I replied. These included joining some girlfriends for coffee, followed by swimming at the health club.

Sashka, overhearing, was appalled.

"It would be different if she'd broken a leg," I muttered, and carried on with my Egg Florentine with the muffin but without the hollandaise.

I blame the cross country run. This year Faye did well, only coming fifth last, using her inhaler every second step and crying most of the way round as usual; sobbing into my arms at the end. All totally predictable.

She and I aren't built for long-distance running. Our bones are too heavy.

If she had another year left at the school I think she might mysteriously suddenly find herself having an extra flute lesson on Cross Country afternoon, as her un-sporty friend did this time.

So she was ill the next day, but we ignored that because it was the highlight of the year - Danny's Valentine Disco!

"Nobody's asked me to the disco," sighed Faye sadly.

"Has anyone else been asked?" I queried.

"Florence has been asked by six different people, but turned them all down," she said.

"Anyone else?"

"No."

In the event the funniest (but rather fat) boy in the school did ask Faye, but when he asked her to dance she said no.

I think that was most unkind, and when she's recovered a bit, I will ask her to apologise to him. What he did was unbelievably brave in my opinion.

It turned out that staying vertical for the disco was worth it for Faye, as she was the only person there who knew the routine not only to the Time Warp, but also to Macaracca.

And her reward now, is to be able to sit in her pyjamas on the sofa in the sunroom glued to Disney Channel for twelve straight hours, two days running.

Meanwhile, with no riding, due to the icy weather and ill or busy Faye and me, the horses are getting fatter and fatter, and for once have retained all their shoes between farrier appointments. Also their hair has grown back where their saddle sores were. I'm just a bit nervous of quite how bouncy they're going to be, once all the snow and ice finally disappear.

What's Flu?
13/02/2015

I sit down on an upturned piece of granite, feeling a bit dizzy and sick.

"It's worth a million quid," I scold myself. Heaving my reluctant body to its legs again, I lug the frozen molehill heavily into the waiting wheelbarrow, and stomp about on the many dips and mounds left by the wild Dartmoor ponies the last time they escaped onto my so-called 'lawn' (what a joke) just a few days ago.

My own horses are nibbling placidly at the spindly bits of grass forcing their way up between the patches of frozen snow in the field, stables are swept, leaves gone off the back steps, and the fallen lumps of moss hiding the bothy's asbestos roof cleared. Now I must quickly give the interior of the house a major face-lift before my potential purchasers arrive.

I make up and light the log fire in the sitting room, make sure the rug in the hall is covering those Twiglet carpet mud-stains, move one of the many pot pourri's in the cloakroom into the downstairs loo to cover up the smell of wee, squirt my secret stash of Woods of Windsor Mimosa Room Fragrance around in my bathroom, and pray that a fresh cafetiere of Douwe Egberts freshly ground will drown the smell of death now permeating its way into the kitchen from the tack-room.

Clip clop, clip clop, and here they are. I can't believe it - how could I have forgotten that they are riding over? Thank God I've cleaned up properly in the stables for once.

So. My first proper viewing. It's taken me two hours to get the place ready and I'm on my deathbed. "This is even more important than making the place look nice for my B&Bers," I keep up the mantra in my head, despite my temperature of five million degrees, and manage to maintain a facade of charm throughout their visit.

As they plod off, I help myself to some cold coffee dregs, sigh, and struggle up the stairs one at a time to my bed, and my waiting copy of 'Gone Girl', left open at page 132.

I'm not looking forward to going to all this trouble over and over again, assuming that in due course the estate agents arrange one viewing after another.

And, I wonder, what is the definition of flu? Forty years ago they said it was when you felt too ill to go out into a field to pick up a £50 note.

Since inflation I guess it would now be a £1 million note. So I guess I haven't quite got proper flu yet.

See What Sticks
17/02/2015

To sell my home I have now sorted out:

- eBay

- my own website, to be found through SEO

- my own website, to be found via AdWords

- potential joint estate agency with the top two estate agents in the world, or at least in the UK

Ebay is currently going rather well! The agent who picked up on my entry has indeed put me on Zoopla for free, and has just asked me for information to pass on to an interested party, about local private schools. I sent them practically a book, as you can imagine! I haven't heard back after all that though. Boo hoo.

My own website to be found through SEO is less successful. After three months, if you google 'house-for-sale-dartmoor' it still doesn't appear. My IT man has given me lots of tips as to how to improve things. Including attaching my new For Sale website to my B&B one. I'll have to think about that. But amazingly, AdWords has just produced a frantically exciting enquiry! A retired naval officer rang, who knows all my mates at the top of the navy, and whose wife keeps her Andalusian horse at my best friend Daisy's livery down the road.

They are very interested in buying the house and running it as a B&B, they have called to tell me, and obviously they already know what it looks like, where it is, and all about Neighbour's wood. In fact they have been to a talk given by Neighbour so they know what he's like too!

They can afford the asking price, they say, because they own 19 buy-to-let properties in Plymouth and are selling a further house in Henley. They're coming to see inside the house this Wednesday. All too good to be true. So it probably won't happen.

My professional agents are on 'hold' until we know where we are with the above. We're not planning to go properly public until March/April/May anyway, when the moor and garden are looking at their best. The joint agency approach is going to cost me 2.66% + VAT in commission, which comes to a staggering £32,000 if we manage between us to sell the place for £1 million. But Savills and Knight Frank ought jointly to reach all the richest people in the world, so I do reckon it's worth a bit of a blast, and hopefully a whole load of Russian Oligarchs will start bidding against each other to reach some ridiculously stratospheric final figure.

The Smell of Death
23/02/2015

Two frisbees - must go. A junior Grays tennis racquet, circa 1935 - to go. Metal detector - oops, I've just trodden on something; I appear to have broken it in half, but anyway - bin it.

I am gradually making my way towards the back of the tack-room, throwing behind me all the rubbish that the charity shop might want but we don't.

I'm beginning to feel a bit sick as gradually I work my way inch by inch, closer and closer to the maggot-infested source of the hideous smell which now permeates throughout the house, squashed and dead behind or under the final Tesco crate right at the back of the room.

Trying not to gag, I heave out the crate, and there is ....

Nothing.

All I can see, rather than the rotting corpse of a rat, badger, or possibly even a human head, are three holes in the floor, leading down to some drains. They're located just beneath the water tanks that are something to do with the borehole and its pump, which supplies us with water. There is the most unholy reek coming out of one of them. God knows what's at the bottom of it.

I stuff in a couple of old Tesco's bags, and replace the lid that used to cover up the open end of the pipe.

The smell subsides.

My insides go back to where they are supposed to be.

Bunch of Bananas
02/03/2015

I was talking to a fellow Dartmoor B&Ber on Friday who only markets herself via Airbnb. She has a lovely house but no en-suites and her rooms are much cheaper than mine. She is pleased with Airbnb but it turns out that I have turned over more than £1500 in the first two months of 2015, while she has only just received her first guests of the year this week.

But am I looking after my guests properly, with my mind on other things?

This morning the Tesco's man arrived, carrying a bunch of bananas up the drive. I quite crossly told him that I had added to my original order, which was critical for the running of my B&B, and what was I to do now, since their stupid computer hadn't clocked all the breakfast staples that I had gone to such trouble to order last night?

Whereas, now, thinking about it, I believe I forgot! That's £9 for a bunch of bananas, and no breakfast for my guests!

Two nights ago, as I was indulging in watching another episode of Four in a Bed on catchup at about 11pm, minding my own business, one of my guests, fully dressed, tapped on the door of the sunroom.

"There seems to be some alarm going off," he said.

"I can't hear anything," I replied, but we braved the freezing cold outside, and there was indeed a quiet eee-awe sort of a whining noise. It wasn't our cars, and it wasn't Neighbour across the river - it turned out to be the burglar alarm box, high up on the wall, right outside my guests' window!

Aaagghhh!

We went back into the kitchen and I attempted to turn it off from the control box. But it continued to ignore my button-pressing.

There was a Newton Abbot telephone number on a card stuck on the wall below the control box panel, so I called it, and guess what? A miracle! Someone replied! And they still 'do' burglar alarms! And were prepared to come around and sort it out at midnight in the freezing cold, including climbing up a ladder in the pitch black, while I went back to the telly.

And, when the man arrived - very soon after I put the phone down - he was wearing shorts!

I now await the bill with some trepidation.

No Bananas
7/03/2015

Last night Tesco didn't bring me my B&B delivery. This time it really was their fault and it's a total mystery as to what has happened. It meant that my guests didn't get strawberries in their fruit salad, nor any crème fraiche.

I called the store immediately it was possible - this morning at 10am and not before, because it's a Sunday. Anyway. Can you believe it. They said they couldn't get the order out today either. Well I went into a rant about how if I was the manager I would 'pick' the order myself, and bring it in my own car. Or get a friend or child to do it.

I would do anything to prevent anyone ever saying anything horrid about my business.

And now because of them, I will be getting a black mark in turn. Me! The best B&B on Dartmoor! "Bring back Terry Leahy!" I yelled. But I don't think the Scottish lady manning Customer Services on a Sunday had ever heard of him.

So. No strawberries or crème fraiche for breakfast tomorrow morning either.

House Sale Progress (Lack of)
09/03/2015

Wydemeet has now received 848 clicks on 'AdWords' costing me £353, with the most popular Google search being 'houses for sale in Dartmoor', clicked 173 times.

Shame this hasn't translated into 173 sales. Mind you, one would be enough.

But it has produced two enquiries.

The couple who keep their horses up the road have been back again. I couldn't quite cope with the idea of removing all the mole hills for a second time, nor with making every bedroom immaculate all over again, so I hope I haven't blown things through laziness. They still need to sell their house in Henley, but were unaware that you can exchange now, and not complete for a year or whenever.

That would suit me very nicely, as it would mean that finding the next place would be miles less stressful because I could then do the same. So they are looking into the delayed completion option, I hope. They pointed out that a million quid appears to be rather more than equivalent house prices in the area, of which they say there are eighteen. So I'd better look into that.

And then there's a lovely sounding lady from Guernsey. She appears to be already smitten, but is worried that her husband might think Wydemeet too remote. I emphasised that we are nearer Exeter and London than Tavistock or Horrabridge are, where they are also looking, and that the best prep school in the southwest is less than 25 minutes away, so her two young sons would no longer need to board, and the school is good enough to get them into Eton if they're brainy enough.

Her husband is coming to see the house this Monday - she is not allowed to attend first viewings, because she is too emotional about it all, she tells me. I hope I can persuade him that it doesn't take terribly long to fetch a pint of milk from a shop, and the drive to school is very beautiful.

Meanwhile the agent who has put me onto Zoopla tells me that someone drove all the way from London to see Wydemeet, with no appointment, and wondered whether he had gone to the wrong place because "it's in the middle of a timber yard." Hopefully he had indeed gone to the wrong place and ended up in Neighbour's farmyard, because Neighbour has already removed half the wood - the piles are nothing like as bad as they were! If, to the objective observer, we still look as though we're in a timber yard, then I'm a bit stuffed.

So I expect that after all, I will find myself launching the house sale properly, using the tried and tested method of Estate Agents, as soon as everywhere has started to turn green and flowery.

My horses have escaped into the garden again, so the 'lawn' is full of deep hoof prints in amongst the molehills, and the wind has meant the whole place is covered in branches, dead leaves and twigs. Euurrggh.

Buying and Selling Houses
17/03/2015

Which is more important: geography? Or local community?

I find myself in a dilemma.

I'm on various estate agents' lists to be told about new properties available, and one has just sent me details of a nice Georgian house on sale at £595,000, five miles nearer than Wydemeet is to the A38.

What is so attractive about this particular house is that it is within walking distance of two of my 'Thunderbirds' group - the South Hams Mums I meet up with every month. And both have individually told me what a lovely community theirs is. If I moved there, I would be nearer my friends and it's good riding country, but I'd be hardly any nearer to the David Lloyd Club, my children's schools, my Mum, London, England, The World, The Galaxy, or The Universe. So it wouldn't really help with building up a new social life, if that's what I really want to do. Do I?

Meanwhile my 'viewer' from Guernsey arrived 1 1/2hrs early yesterday. He caught me enjoying a light, rather smelly lunch of Weightwatchers Beef Hot Pot for one, accompanied by a sherry glass of Cava, at 4.45pm. At least I wasn't still in my pyjamas. Luckily Sashka had performed miracles in tidying up the house, but it was rather cold and I hadn't yet got round to lighting the fire, making the place smell of coffee, or creating some 'mood lighting'.

The man told me about some other places he had been looking at. I think Wydemeet is rather outclassed by them. Grimstone Manor, for instance, on at £1.25m, has an indoor pool. Rather out of our league. I emphasised how cosy and homely Wydemeet is, and how its rooms don't echo. I had a sudden thought that the man might like Her house, which I believe She is shortly to put on the market. Perhaps I should tell him about it? Maybe not.

And then I learned that my Georgian potential purchase has already been snapped up for just under the asking price. No decisions necessary after all that.

Love Nest
24/05/2015

"WOW!" breathed Faye. Four times. Trying not to, because she knew that was what I wanted her to say.

This was the fifth house today that she had been forced to look at.

Being 13, what impressed her most about it were some modern light fittings, and a sunken trampoline.

There aren't very many houses in the triangle where I would like to buy, just west of Exeter, so even fewer available for purchase at any one time, and we were doing well to find so many to look at, I thought - any one of which I would have been happy to live in.

But this little love nest - a Scandinavian wooden single storey chalet - has the 'wow' factor, as it looks across the entire Exe valley towards Ottery St Mary. It would be like buying a two-seater open-top sports car. A mid-life crisis, mad, impractical thing to do. I think all three of us - Faye, Will, and myself - would be intensely proud to bring friends back to it.

I have urgently invited the estate agent to ask the owner, a rock star who used to play for Tangerine Dream, whether he might accept an early exchange on a low percentage, and delayed completion, until I sell wonderful Wydemeet.

But it's Bank Holiday Monday and there's nobody around to speak to.

So all is in the lap of the Gods.

I am trembling with excitement and apprehension.

Oo-er
30/05/2015

"I loved the house and can see why you love it. It's very different and the views are awesome," wrote Charming Charles, one of my two potential estate agents.

"It's a unique property, but one that I think will always fetch more than expected for the right buyer."

The green light.

I email Mr Rockstar saying I want to buy his home for the asking price, exchanging straight away (I can cash in a pension I'd forgotten about, thanks to the government and to my being so old) with a delayed completion; and then I head off to my new health club, heart pounding.

"Twist and Shout!!" Faye and I are singing along to my iPhone plugged into the Golden Monster's stereo system on the way home.

"Could you just check my emails?" I shout at her, over The Beatles.

3G leaps into action. "Time is not an issue," reads Faye.

"WHAT???????????!!!!!!!!!!!!!!!!!!" I scream at her. "Read that again!"

"Time is not an issue," she repeats.

Blimey! Mr Rockstar is happy for a delayed completion! I don't have to wait until Wydemeet's sold, but can buy my new little Love Nest whenever I'm ready! I am so excited I can't think straight.

It's as if a great big old door is creaking slowly open. Goodbye Dartmoor. Goodbye remote, bleak, rainy, cold, windy, nothing-ever-works, everything's-always-damp-and-smelling, scrimping-a-living, miles-from-anywhere-and-anyone, lonely old Wydemeet.

Hurray! Hurray! Hurray!

Hello, Love Nest! A whole, bright, new world. People! Traffic! Shops! Buses! Time! Leisure! Cafes! Men! Normal life! It's all out there! Just waiting for me. Beckoning...

A whole new chapter about to begin. Wowee! Finally! Well who would have thought it? After all that! Tomorrow really is - Another Day!